To: Mike †

Happy Birthday
and warmest best
wishes — I hope you
enjoy this book —

Mike Lude

"In this book, Mike tells of his career and dares to deal with complexity thus refusing to pander to readers and to provide simplistic answers that do more harm than good. *Walking the Line* is the perfect book for those who have met and known Mike Lude. It is also a perfect book for those who just love sports and want an inside view into that world."

— **Don James,** Retired Head Football Coach University of Washington and Kent State University.

"Mike Lude's story is a fascinating one. Anybody who believes that sports can make a difference in people and in a country's culture should read this book. Beyond Mike's personal story, his insight into the workings-good and bad- of intercollegiate athletics as a coach and administrator is without equal. Read this book and your daily trip to the sports page and the ranting of the so-called TV gurus will take on more meaning and help you make an honest judgment of the sporting events of our time."

— **Joseph V. Paterno,** Head Football Coach Penn State.

"The last years of Chuck Niemi's life were anything but pleasant. Suffering from Lou Gehrig's disease, the Washington sports information director could only adjust as best he could to the life-sapping illness for which there is no cure. But by providing the things Niemi needed to continue in his job, including installation of an electric lift to his second-floor office, Mike helped make his employee's final months somewhat tolerable. Great leadership is not just about balancing budgets and building things."

— **Dick Rockne,** Retired Sports Writer Seattle Times and Husky Beat Writer.

"This book is a must for anyone interested in sports management. Not just football, but all intercollegiate sports. If you are going into 'the business' read this and you'll know exactly what you are getting into…the good, the bad and the ugly. Whether you go into sports management, sports marketing, sports administration or are just interested in humanity, read this book!"

— **Bobby Bowden,** Head Football Coach Florida State University.

"Mike Lude is hands down the best Athletics Director I have ever worked with. If he had been allowed to continue to use his tremendous administrative skills at Auburn, we (yes, he and I) would still be winning big there today."

— **Terry Bowden**, ABC Studio Analyst, 1993 National Coach of the Year.

"Mike Lude has tackled this much anticipated, revealing book with the same enthusiasm that has long been the hallmark of his career. I have known and respected Mike for many years, and everything he has ever done has been with high energy and great passion. Don't miss reading this behind-the-scenes book by one of the most respected individuals in intercollegiate athletics."

— **Vince Dooley**, Director of Intercollegiate Athletics
University of Georgia.

"Mike Lude became one of the most respected individuals in collegiate athletics through hard work, integrity and developed practical knowledge as an athlete, coach and athletic administrator. Mike and Bill Knight have chronicled an inspirational life, while at the same time teaching sound principles of leadership and motivation. Mike and the world of athletics remind me of the old and effective commercial about E.F. Hutton: When Mike Lude speaks, everyone listens."

— **Grant Teaff**, Executive Director American Football Coaches Association.

"As one whose own experiences as a coach, athletics director and conference leader mirrors that of Mike Lude's in time and substance, I applaud Mike's story. He has chronicled more than 50 years of intercollegiate life in real terms of personal experience; inviting readers to benefit and share the vagaries. Mike's candor is evident."

— **John Toner**, retired Athletics Director University of Connecticut
and former President of NCAA.

"Mike Lude is one of the most respected leaders in college athletics. His long career and his wonderful influence in our profession are appropriately punctuated with this splendid and inspiring book. His perspective on important issues and the integration of his life experiences make this a rich, compelling volume. This book should be read by everyone involved in college athletics."

— **Deborah A Yow**, Director of Athletics University of Maryland
and Past President of the National Association of Collegiate
Directors of Athletics.

"Mike Lude is a rarity in today's world. His tenacity, moral fiber and true grit attitude toward football and life in general are an inspiration to those who have had the good fortune to know him as a coach, an athletic director and as a friend. Mike's story is an honest, behind the scenes look at a man of character and his rise in collegiate football. Mike's story will serve as a role model to young players just learning the game. The book also will bring a reality check to those currently active in the realm of collegiate athletics as they learn the inside details of the era that spawned the loss of innocence and high dollar stakes in college football. To those on the sidelines, the career of Mike Lude will serve as a chronicle of a life well lived and a game well played. May his legacy live long and serve well all those who follow in the footsteps of this great coach, athletics director and most of all, great man."

– **John Cervini,** Vice President for Institutional Advancement
Hillsdale College.

"Mike Lude is, from the very start, a straight shooter and that contributed to his lifetime of success. He never turned away from a challenge and recorded an unbroken string of accomplishments. He's the most honest man I've ever known in my own lifetime of sports and a role model whose story is well worth the read."

– **Jack Moss,** Retired Sports Editor/Columnist
Kalamazoo Gazette, Michigan.

"No one has given college athletics more energy, longevity, and just plain good common sense than Mike Lude. Mike never minced a word in his life and doesn't now. His career takes us from the Wing-T at Delaware in the 1950's as an assistant coach to the cauldron that is Auburn football in the mid 1990's. Don't be afraid to pick his brain in this book for there is a lot to be learned. Should be mandatory reading for every college administrator."

– **Blaine Newnham,** Associate Editor and Sport Columnist Seattle Times.

"I'm reading a great new book- Mike Lude's *Walking the Line* and I'm enjoying it immensely. I know you will too if you have any interest at all in college athletics or a delightful personal success story very rarely heard these days. I know this book is a must for anyone with any semblance of interest in sports."

– **Wayne Duke,** Retired Commissioner Big Ten Conference.

"Mike Lude is one of the icons for Husky football success and rightfully so. He is a 'doer' as opposed to a 'talker'. It was only when I read excerpts from this book's early chapters that I realized that it was his humble background, from salt-of-the-earth folks, which gave him the foundation that led to his honesty and loyalty, traits which have made him one of the great college athletics directors of all time. Mike Lude is a symbol of what is great about America, about college football, and most certainly, Husky football."

— **John Thompson,** Retired General Manager Seattle Seahawks.

"Coach Mike Lude mixes an equal amount of wit and wisdom in telling of a humble beginning and a life filled with football, football and more football. And he tells it all. He loves to tell of the best of his storied career, but he's not afraid to examine a few warts and bumps as he explores the nation's real favorite pastime of college football. He is the country's premier athletics director who loves the game and loathes those who would bend and break the rules."

— **Paul Davis,** President of Davis Publications of Auburn and Columnist for the Opelika-Auburn News.

"Mike Lude is a special man. His book, *Walking the Line*, is a testament to the character that is a result of hard work, sound morals, basic ethics and dedication to one's country. This book gives a factual insight into the world of college athletics from the standpoint of an athlete, coach and athletics director. Mike's honesty and forthrightness in detailing some of the inner workings behind the decision-making of an athletic director will be as big a shock to the readers as it was to me. A must read!"

— **Lute Olson,** Head Men's Basketball Coach University of Arizona.

"Mike Lude's book and his legacy will last for generations and generations and perhaps forever because he influenced so many lives in such a positive way."

— **Fred Jacoby,** Commissioner Lone Star Conference.

"Mike Lude represents intercollegiate athletics greatest virtues in every aspect. Loyalty, integrity, reliability, discipline, hard work, visionary, counselor, leader, and commitment to excellence all describe the man Mike Lude. His book is an insightful and interesting glimpse inside the life of a self-made man who rose from poverty to become one of the outstanding athletic administrators in the nation. Anyone interested in intercollegiate athletics should read this outstanding book."

— **Gary A. Cunningham,** Director of Athletics University of California Santa Barbara.

"Auburn was in a period of transition and Mike's knowledge, integrity and his relentless drive guided us through some rough times. Mike accepted the challenges facing the athletic department and his steady and experienced hand provided the stability that we needed. Mike has been there and his book offers first hand insight into the pressures, personalities and the politics of college athletics."

   – **E. L. Spencer Jr.**, Chairman Auburn Bank.

"On rare occasions you hear said of someone 'she was born to be a doctor,' or 'he was born to teach' or 'he was born to play the piano.' The speaker intends the highest accolade and that is precisely what the hearer understands. Well Milo, 'Mike' Lude was born to be an athletic director.' Whatever measuring rod you use, he meets the standards of excellence. His book is certain to be interesting, entertaining and instructive."

   – **Jerome Farris,** Former University of Washington Board of Regent.

"If you want to know and read about the inside of intercollegiate athletics from the point of view of an individual with a balanced and accurate perspective, and you enjoy reading about individuals who overcome obstacles and achieve success, this is the book for you!"

   – **John D. Swofford,** Commissioner Atlantic Coast Conference.

"Mike is a rare breed, and I have patterned my career and goals after leaders like him. Collegiate athletics has shaped many lives. Mike's book *Walking the Line* should be required reading by all."

   – **Herman Frazier,** Director of Athletics University of Hawaii and
      Vice President, United States Olympic Committee.

"Mike has devoted his entire career to college sports as a player, coach and athletic director. Each of the colleges or universities he touched improved because of his efforts. His opinions are of value to anyone involved or interested in university athletics."

   – **Tracy King,** Retired Executive Director UW Alumni Association.

"Mike Lude's story is fascinating as he enjoys success as a Marine, athlete, coach and athletics director. Everyone from the casual sports fan to the most rabid will find his years as a coach and administrator fascinating. This book showcases Mike's adventures and his talents. You will be impressed!"

   – **Tom Hansen,** Commissioner Pacific 10 Conference.

"Infectious, enthusiasm—total giving—sincerity. That's the Mike Lude that was with our Dave Nelson staff at Delaware. He was a pleasure to work with and is a friend forever."

    **– Irv "Whiz" Wisniewski,** Professor Emeritus University of Delaware.

"Mike certainly has embarked upon a wonderful project that will be of great value to the world of amateur athletics. The story you have written reflects the ideals, strength of character and endless energy that you have displayed throughout your life."

    **– Harold Westerman,** Director Emeritus of Physical Education and
        Athletics, former Head Football Coach University of Maine.

"I have the greatest admiration for Mike Lude. He is a genuine person with great integrity and insight. He is a tremendous credit to intercollegiate athletics and higher education."

    **– William V. Muse,** Former President Auburn University.

"I've known Coach Mike Lude for over 40 years and to me he represents all that is good about collegiate athletics. He is classy, honest and a man of unquestionable integrity. Mike is someone I've looked up to my entire coaching and television career."

    **– Lee Corso,** Former Football Coach and now ESPN Game Day Host.

"In over 50 years of tracking college sports, never have I seen an athletic director overcome such tremendous challenges as Mike Lude. Because of Mike, Auburn athletics returned to where they once were."

    **– Bill Lumpkin,** Retired Sports Editor of the Birmingham Post-Herald,
        and Former President of the Football Writers Association of America.

"Mike Lude's story is both entertaining and inspirational. From a poor but loving background he combines a story with work ethic, discipline and a sense of humor to rise to the pinnacle of his profession. He pulls no punches in talking about his experiences with university presidents and coaches. Anyone aspiring to become an athletic administrator or manager will benefit greatly from reading this book."

    **– Jim Mora Sr.,** Former Head Coach New Orleans Saints and
        Indianapolis Colts, and University of Washington Assistant Coach.

"When I think of Mike Lude I think of a man who is highly intelligent, highly motivated, very organized, honest and caring. With high goals, a focused vision and relentless determination, Mike began the process of building the Husky program. It was under Mike's guidance in which the University of Washington was built into one of the best athletic departments in the nation."

– **Gary Pinkel,** Head Football Coach University of Missouri and Former University of Washington Assistant Coach.

"There have been several books written on so many great athletic individuals, and Mike's book will certainly be one of the greats. It is difficult for me to articulate in a few lines all that is great about Mike Lude, as it does not do justice for a man who has meant so much to so many."

– **Isaiah "Ike" Kelley Jr.,** Former Director Rocky Mountain Region for HUD, played football for Colorado State University and ran for Lt. Governor.

"Mike Lude is a true gentleman and one of the great administrators of our time. He has been a mentor and a roll model to so many of us younger athletics directors. I give my highest recommendation to Mike Lude's book, and I know that it will be beneficial to people from all walks of life."

– **Gene DeFilippo,** Athletics Director at Boston College and Past President of The National Association of Collegiate Directors of Athletics.

"I can think of no one better equipped to 'tell all' about big time intercollegiate athletics than Mike Lude. For to 'tell all' it very much helps to 'know all' and Mike Lude spent the better part of his lifetime gaining that knowledge. As a player, coach and administrator, he has not only witnessed the evolution of college sports, he's been an actual part of the process. That he was successful along the way is no surprise."

– **Bob Rondeau,** Voice of the Huskies, Washington Football and Basketball Play-by-Play Announcer.

"I have read parts of Mike's book and have found it accurate and to the point... it is great!"

– **Connie Kanakis,** Class of 59 Auburn University.

"Mike's life as a young farm boy to an outstanding athlete, to college coaching ranks, and later to become one of the top athletic administrators in the history of collegiate sports is a story necessary to tell. (A great example of the true American Dream). This energetic ex-marine, a true family man, a devoted husband to his lovely wife, Rena and a real friend is the trademark that identifies Mike Lude. Everyone who has had the good fortune to be associated with this dynamic person is a benefactor. Read this book!"

> **– Homer Rice,** Former Athletics Director Georgia Tech, Rice University and University of North Carolina; Head Football Coach University of Cincinnati, Rice University and the NFL Cincinnati Bengals.

"The wisdom of Mike has brought and will bring inspiration and direction to those who aspire knowledge of and/or involvement in intercollegiate athletics. He is a winner!!"

> **– Dick Young,** Former Athletics Director Florida International University, Washington State University, Oklahoma State University and Bowling Green State University.

"As a student, athlete, coach and athletic administrator, Mike Lude has made a successful venture through the ranks of college athletics and left an indelible mark of achievement at every stage of his career."

> **– Jack Lengyel,** Retired Athletics Director United States Naval Academy.

"Mike has done it all. In between solving crises, Mike found time to give to NACDA, serving as our president and on many committees. His peers recognized him for his excellence as the recipient of NACDA's James J. Corbett Award. Despite his retirement, Mike has continued to remain involved with NACDA."

> **– Mike Cleary,** Executive Director NACDA, National Association of Collegiate Directors of Athletics.

"All the superlatives are relevant—honesty, integrity, hard working dedicated, loyal. Nothing too lofty could ever be said about Mike Lude. But he is more than that, much more."

> **– Dr. Michael O'Brien,** former President of Auburn University Touchdown Club.

# WALKING
# THE LINE

◆ ◆ ◆

## Mike Lude
## and Bill Knight

CLASSIC DAY
PUBLISHING

Seattle, Washington
Portland, Oregon
Denver, Colorado
Vancouver, B.C.
Scottsdale, Arizona
Minneapolis, Minnesota

CLASSIC DAY
PUBLISHING

Classic Day Publishing
2100 Westlake Avenue North, Suite 106
Seattle, Washington 98109
800-328-4348
www.classicdaypublishing.com
Email: info@classicdaypublishing.com

# FOREWORD

◆ ◆ ◆

This Warning for following mankind was written May 18, 1751…"Very few in any age have been able to raise themselves to reputation by writing histories…."

The good ole boy who committed that wisdom to parchment was Samuel Johnson.

Does it jar ya a wee bit…that such a quote should loom from the foreword that promises a succession of stories that have to do with what the Literati might call "jockdom." But what do they know…half of 'em have died from final chapter rigor mortis already.

This is a book from Mike Lude. Now the name alone brings an image. Steely blue eyes, thick neck, fixation on values and a complete lack of understanding of the word…can't.

The year 2004 will be my 52nd season of broadcasting college football…some local, some regional and many national. Across those decades you can figure out who will tell you the truth…and who is spreading fog.

Mike Lude has a story to tell. It has depth and if he decides to do it he can surely strike water…not scam…but truth.

Enjoy!

– Keith Jackson
ABC Football Broadcaster

# DEDICATION

◆ ◆ ◆

To my wonderful wife and lifetime companion, Rena Pifer Lude, and my three daughters, Cynthia, Janann, and Jill; my best buddy, grandson Michael Nelson; to my deceased parents, John and Doris Lude; to the best in-laws a person could have had, Earl and Mabel Pifer; to my high school coach, Clayton F. Linton, and my college coach and an exceptional boss, David M. Nelson, and finally, to all those student-athletes I recruited and coached, and to those I served as their director of intercollegiate athletics.

*Mike Lude and his "best buddy," grandson Michael*

# ACKNOWLEDGEMENTS

◆ ◆ ◆

This project never would have been launched without the highly significant and big time help of Bill Knight and Mike Wilson, and, of course, their wives, Dorothy and Pat. They are great friends and superior teammates.

I also wish to thank:

Elliott Wolf, publisher of Classic Day Publishing, for the courage to believe in this plan; Anne Greenberg, a super editor; Kristen Morris, who put it all together; and ABC Sportscaster, friend and Washington State University alum Keith Jackson for writing the foreword.

All of the assistant coaches I worked with, the athletes, and their parents.

All of those terrific friends who so willingly endorsed this book: Larry Arnn, Bobby Bowden, Terry Bowden, Frank Broyles, Bill Byrne, Ruly Carpenter, Joe Castiglione, John Cervini, Mike Cleary, Elsa Kircher-Cole, Lee Corso, Paul Cressman Sr., Gary Cunningham, Paul Davis, Gene DeFilippo, Cedric Dempsey, John Denson, Don Devoe, Vince Dooley, Wayne Duke, Judge Jerome Farris, Herman Frazier, Tom Glasgow, Tom Hansen, Marv Harshman, Ken Hatfield, Jim Host, Fred Jacoby, Don James, Kyle Kallander, Connie Kanakis, Joe Kearney, Isaiah Kelley, Tracy King, Chuck Knox, Jack Lengyel, Marv Levy, Bill Lumpkin, Hugh Millen, Art Modell, Jim Mora, Jack Moss, Shirley Nelson, Blaine Newnham,

Michael O'Brien, Lute Olson, John Owen, Joe Paterno, Gary Pinkel, Jim Quirk, Homer Rice, Dick Rockne, Bob Rondeau, Judy Rose, Fred Rullo, Jim Shelton, Gene Smith, Ed Spencer, Bob Stull, Bill Swartz, John Swofford, Grant Teaff, Glenn Terrell, Earlie Thomas, John Thompson, John Toner, Dan Tripodi, Harold Westerman, Kevin White, Irv Wisniewski, Dick Young, Deborah Yow.

Dr. William (Bill) V. Muse, one of the best college presidents I ever worked for.

Judy Biondi, Bev White and Mike Wilson, who provided the motivation in getting me to put my thoughts in print.

Everyone who has coached or been a director of intercollegiate athletics.

The National Association of Collegiate Directors of Athletics (NACDA), its executive director, Michael Cleary, and staff members who assisted me in numerous ways, and all of the professional collegiate athletic administrators I have been associated with.

Several great conference commissioners I have had the privilege to work with.

Every marching and pep band director, especially the late Bill Bissell, and those enthusiastic student members of the bands.

All those special team players who worked for and with me, especially those unsung heroes/heroines who are part of the total team: maintenance people, grounds crews, custodians, laundry room and equipment room personnel, clerical staff and administrative personnel.

At the request of my wife, Rena, I am not going to list all my friends because I know I would leave someone out. They all know who they are and I am eternally grateful for their friendship.

– Mike Lude

# CONTENTS

◆ ◆ ◆

# 1

# OUTHOUSE TO ONE-ROOM
# SCHOOLHOUSE

◆ ◆ ◆

*A-B-C-D-E-F-G-H-I got a gal in Kalamazoo*
*Don't want to boast,*
*But I know she's the toast*
*Of Kalamazoo-zoo, zoo, zoo, zoo, zoo.*

Followers of contemporary pop music in the new millennium are unlikely to be familiar with this tune made popular by the legendary Glenn Miller more than a half-century ago. The lyrics, starting with a building, same-note spellout, tell of an unnamed woman in an obscure town in southwest Michigan, well off the beaten track for most Americans in that period.

For me, Kalamazoo was far from remote. I was born there, christened Milo Ralph Lude. For the first eighteen years of my life, I was convinced it was the ultimate definition of a big city and that most people who resided there were experiencing a life of luxury and elegance.

At least, that was how Kalamazoo looked from the vantage point of my youth. The town that Glenn Miller made famous was twenty-two miles away and a world apart from the small two-story farmhouse on a remote dirt road where I grew up.

We had no electricity, no central heating, no indoor plumbing.

A car was out of the question. So was a telephone. I remember my mother telling me she couldn't write a note to her mother because we couldn't afford three cents for a stamp.

The nearest village of Fulton didn't even have a stoplight. It had four corners and consisted of a general store, a creamery, a hardware store and a filling station. That was pretty much it—not exactly the bright lights of, say, Kalamazoo.

At the school I attended, a few skips longer than a mile down the dirt road, all eight grades were jammed into one room with one teacher. My wardrobe consisted of bib overalls and sturdy work shoes, standard for all of my classmates. The other thing we had in common was working hard and long on the farms where our families were trying to eke out a living.

We all were poor. We were like millions of other Americans attempting to survive as the country went tumbling into the abyss of the worst economic depression in United States history.

The route to the farm where I grew up starts on what is now Highway 131, the paved road south from Kalamazoo. When I was a kid the road turned to gravel as it bent east to Vicksburg, a town of roughly two thousand. Another half-dozen miles the road became dirt—dust or mud, depending on the season—and two miles farther you would reach our farm.

In June 1928 my dad loaded our meager possessions onto a wagon pulled by a pair of horses and moved the family down the road from Vicksburg, where he had worked as a railroad section hand and in the local paper mill. I was six and the only child at the time.

The farm consisted of 220 acres of rocks and hills. My father was considered a tenant farmer, or share cropper. He provided everything it took to farm the land: seed, equipment, animals, and, of course, labor. The proceeds of everything he sold, crops or animals, he split fifty-fifty with the owner of the land.

Our farm produced marginal amounts of wheat, oats, and corn, and a little bit of rye, barley, and clover. We milked by hand as many as ten cows, twice a day. We also raised hogs, sheep, and chickens. I remember when hogs sold for three cents a pound, so if one weighed two hundred pounds we'd get six dollars for him. Wheat normally brought less than one dollar a bushel.

The owner of the property and essentially my dad's partner was a tough, tough guy. He was an immigrant from Germany who moved to the United States when he was about fifteen. He went to Montana and became a cowboy, then moved to Michigan, acquired some farmland in Wakashama Township, and settled down.

The German immigrant-cowboy-farmer was my grandfather. More about him later.

As the only offspring, I became a significant part of the labor force at a young age. I was assigned just about every menial chore that could be turned over to a kid growing up on a farm— mucking out the stalls of the animals, milking cows, planting and digging potatoes, working the horses in the fields. The hours were long, and there was not a lot of time for daydreaming or playing baseball.

I was aware of the Depression and how poor we were on the farm, compared to relatives who lived in Kalamazoo, whom I looked at as being very wealthy people. One uncle worked in a fishing equipment plant, and his wife worked as a beauty operator. Another aunt was a secretary, and her husband sold auto parts. I always thought, man, they really have it made. And they don't have to milk cows or clean stables or dig potatoes. They really must be rich.

Yet I can't say I felt deprived. There was always plenty of food and an abundance of love—discipline *and* love—for me. We didn't have Nike sneakers or the latest fashion wear from Nordstrom. Mom sewed her own dresses; the material came from the sacks that had contained the feed supplement Dad bought for the cattle. The sacks were printed with flower designs similar to the bolts of cloth available in the general store but out of our price range.

So were tractors, something that appeared only in our dreams and the Sears, Roebuck catalog. When we worked the fields, the heavy muscle was provided by draft horses, and there was a pre-scribed routine. You would go down to the end of the field, make the turn, and return to the starting point. After doing a round, down and back, the horses would be allowed a brief rest.

While the horses rested, my father designated me to pick up stones—they came in all sizes—and throw them in piles at the ends of the rows. I would say to him, "Dad, what about Mike rest-ing?" The response was always the same. "Mike, those horses are important and we need those stones picked up."

As hard as he worked and as hard as he worked me, my father occasionally showed he had a sense of humor and, in his own way, attempted to motivate me. One of my jobs was cleaning out the sta-bles, and again there was a routine: as the cow dung piled up, I filled the wheelbarrow and hauled it out to the barnyard and dumped the contents on the manure pile. In the early spring we hauled the manure out on a manure spreader and fertilized the fields.

Cleaning the stables one morning, I discovered what appeared to be a sign hanging over the barn door. I put down my scoop and moved close to read the words: "You become what you do." My father's message was clear if slightly stinky.

Living on a farm developed a serious personal philosophy in me; I learned that hard work was not wrong, that hard work was not made up of two dirty, four-letter words. My dad was strong on discipline and gave no quarter when it came to truth and honesty.

I well remember the first time I tested his resolve. I was probably eight or nine. He told me to fetch the milk pails down by the hog pens. I told him, no, I didn't feel like doing it. That was a mistake. Dad came running after me with his strop, the piece of leather he used to sharpen his straight-edge razor. I knew when he caught me I'd get what for—my first lesson in the discipline of following orders.

To be very frank, I was frightened of my dad. I always referred to him as being very tough. I thought he was the toughest guy around, and I didn't want to cross him.

John E. Lude stood a half-inch under six feet. He was husky, about two hundred pounds, and very strong. He had sandy hair and bright blue eyes. He rarely made jokes. He was quite serious because of the times, the Depression and having to work seven days a week, every week of the year. He worked hard and he worked with his hands. Our neighbors and the people in Fulton he did business with would say, "John Lude is a damn good farmer. He works hard and takes good care of his animals and his farm machinery."

My dad's unbending insistence on honesty, truthfulness, and hard work left an indelible mark on his older son. He told me time and again, supported by my mother, that honesty was absolutely essential; a man's word was the most important thing, and it had to be a truthful word.

One of my boyhood heroes was a man named Charlie Davidson, a Spanish-American War veteran, who lived a quarter-mile down the road. Uncle Charlie would sit me on his knee and stir my imagination with story after story about the war. What a wonderful man.

Charlie also had a watermelon patch. One of the rare childhood transgressions my dad ever admitted to was sneaking into the gardens of neighboring farms and swiping watermelons, so I guess I thought it was OK for me to do the same thing. The day after my criminal venture into Uncle Charlie's garden, he told my father that some of his watermelons were missing and there were footprints leading up the hill to our place.

Confronted, I lied. Who me? I didn't do that. Privileges were taken away and punishment meted out with a stern tongue-lashing: Dad said it was important in our family to always tell the truth, regardless of what sort of anguish the truth might create. You'll always be punished when you don't tell the truth, and the punishment will be more severe if you lie and we find out later you were dishonest. Dishonesty is not tolerated in this family.

My dad absolutely believed in the old saying, that a handshake is a contract and your word is your bond. If he told a neighbor he would help take in crops or husk corn, he would arrive early and stay late. If he borrowed money from the bank and told the banker he would be back on such-and-such a date at such-and-such a time, my dad was early. Everybody in our area knew John Lude as an honest and extremely dependable man.

My dad was equally candid in expressing his opinions about a wide range of subjects, even those aimed at helping the country escape the Depression and helping farmers. When Franklin D. Roosevelt took office, my father felt some of the programs he put in were just not right. People were getting paid to do very little work or not work hard, and that went against all of his principles. He thought you should work hard for very little. He didn't like entitlements, such as the program called soil banks. He felt it was ridiculous to get paid if you didn't till a field, if you didn't raise anything in it. You should not be paid for doing nothing. He refused any involvement.

In contrast, my mom rarely expressed herself or asserted her opinions. Doris Henderson Lude had grown up in Vicksburg, Michigan, and finished high school, which made her a well-educated person for her generation. She was a strong believer in education and helped me with homework in reading, writing, history, and geography. Dad's strength was mathematics, a necessity in calculating the market value of farm products, even though he dropped out of eighth grade to work in the fields.

Mother was a very loving person who never said anything unkind about anyone. Her feelings were easily wounded. Yet her determination could be unbendable. She was not raised on a farm, but when she and my dad moved from her parents' home, she wanted to become a good farm wife, regardless of the hardships involved.

Grandpa Lude thought Dad had married a city girl who was weak and not tough enough to be a farmer's wife, and he was less than supportive of my mom. Her determination helped her reach her goal. She took a lot of pride in her cooking, and her somewhat chubby appearance was a testimonial to how much she appreciated the fruits of her rather crude kitchen equipment and difficult culinary conditions. She put on great dinners for the relatives from Kalamazoo, and invitations to the farm for a Sunday feast rarely were declined.

I have a strong memory of my mom when I was very young and I'd say, "Hey, Mom, tickle me," and she would get me down on the floor and chase me through the kitchen, dining room, and living room. I felt her love for me was unconditional. She always called me Milo, but I never determined which, if any, of the men in Vicksburg bearing that name she had in mind when the name on my birth certificate was put in black and white. Dad always called me Mike.

Since we didn't have a choice, living without most of the things taken for granted now by many Americans was more of an inconvenience than a hardship. By present standards (heating and air conditioning, indoor plumbing, electric lights) and the myriad of appliances (stoves, dishwashers, clothes washers and dryers, television sets and stereo equipment), life was extremely primitive.

From the back door of our house it was about three first downs, thirty yards, to the backyard privy. The toilet tissue was an out-of-date Sears, Roebuck catalog or any other kind of available paper. If you had a bathroom call at night we had what was called a slop jar inside the house.

Our drinking water came from a well powered by a windmill next to the house, which pumped water into a storage tank. An overflow pipe ran underground to a pair of open tanks, one inside and one outside the barn, where the animals could drink.

The house was heated by two wood-burning stoves, one in the dining area and one in the living room, and the cooking was done on a third wood stove in the kitchen. To conserve wood we didn't fire up the living room stove in the winter. All winter we cut wood and stacked it in a shed next to the house, a never-ending chore.

Something we always had was plenty of food. We never, ever went hungry. At times the menu lacked the variety of what we now find every day at the local supermarket. I can still go for months and not miss potatoes. We had potatoes boiled, mashed, fried, hash brown and scalloped. We rarely had baked potatoes because we lacked the proper means of baking them. We had so many potatoes, at every meal, that I didn't appreciate them.

We ate so much chicken, that I thought I was going to start clucking. Mother could fix it in a dozen different ways. We raised chickens, and I still remember my mild-mannered, self-effacing mother going out to the coop, grabbing a bird, taking a hatchet, and chopping its head off.

Mother canned everything—vegetables, fruit, beef, pork, chicken—and stashed it away in a dirt cellar down a rickety set of stairs. In the summer we grew vegetables and we picked berries, peaches, and cherries. My dad butchered one head of beef and one or two hogs every winter. We'd grind up the throwaway parts for sausage and to stuff the sausage, we'd use the hog intestines. The carcasses would hang frozen in the woodshed, and Dad would cut off meat in pieces until spring when it started to thaw. Then Mother would can what was left of the beef and pork.

I tasted possum at a neighbor's house, but I didn't like it. I was offered raccoon meat but said no thanks. When I was about nine, I got my first shotgun, a 410-gauge single barrel that I used to hunt pheasants, ducks, rabbits, and squirrel. I still own the gun.

About the only meat we didn't eat was lamb. My dad called it mutton and said flatly that mutton was not good to eat. That went for the entire family. When I was in the Marine Corps years later, an Italian girl I met invited me to a family dinner, and leg of lamb was the main course. It was great and to this day I love lamb chops, rack of lamb and leg of lamb.

One of the memorable occasions of my youth was the weekly bath. It was a family ritual. In the summer we used a washtub that held about ten gallons of water. Mother would fill the tub in the morning, and the sun would heat the water. When we returned from working in the fields, extremely dirty, we would take our turn with a washrag and a bar of soap, first me, then mother, and then dad. There was enough water so the third person didn't have to bathe in dirty water. As for privacy, we put the tub behind the big lilac bushes in the yard. But traffic was almost nonexistent on the dirt road.

Winter baths were in a large receptacle that held about five gallons of hot water, taken from the reservoir on the cook stove. We would huddle around the dining room heating stove and go through a similar routine with the tub, pressing close to the stove while toweling off. I was glad I was the first in the water.

Michigan had winters that were severely cold. Did we sleep in our socks? Didn't everybody? We also wore flannel nightgowns that reached the floor. Our sheets also were flannel; linen and cotton were much too cold. Before we went to bed Dad would throw pieces of wood in the stove; chunks with big knots had the best chance to burn until morning although I can't remember the fire ever lasting through the night unless Dad got up and threw on more wood.

Each night we would stand by the stove to warm our backsides, and then Mom and Dad would say, "OK, time to go to bed," and we would race up the stairs and jump in bed to try to stay warm. Then in the morning we had to build a fire before going out to the barn to milk the cows. During the winter, when we got up the windows would be frozen with ice, and the "slop jar" would be frozen too.

Cold and snow didn't keep me from walking a mile and a half each way to school, but when the spring thaw came and the ruts turned to mud the road was almost impossible to navigate. The rural mail carriers had a hard time getting through. When I was about eight years old, I got a pair of high-top shoes. They came up about three or four inches from the knee. I wore undersocks plus long wool socks, and the leather repelled the moisture.

The school, named for a Civil War officer, was about as primitive as our house: no running water, no electricity, no indoor plumbing. It had a big cast-iron stove for heating, but it was still cold inside. I would put my lunchbox on a shelf, and often my food would be frozen by lunchtime.

The teacher—there were two in the eight years I attended Holcome School—sat in a big chair at a desk in front. Immediately opposite and facing the teacher was the recitation bench. Because there were so many different grades, classes were called separately for individual sessions. For example, grade one might be called for reading or grade seven for history.

There were four rows of desks across. The smaller desks for the lower grades were in front, and the desks got larger toward the back. Each row was six deep for a capacity of twenty-four students in eight grades. In all the years I went to that school, I can't remember all the desks ever being occupied. We had a huge dictionary but not a lot of books.

My first teacher, Walter Nidy, had also been my father's teacher. He was a big man, a very stern man. Shortly after I started school, he was replaced by Ruth Harmon, who lived in Fulton with her husband, a stone mason. Mrs. Harmon was bright and diminutive, just over five feet tall. She cared about the students and worked extremely hard at an extremely difficult job. She was still around when my brother, Ron, who is thirteen years younger than I, attended the same school.

Mrs. Harmon was strict about discipline. She wasn't reluctant to take on those big eighth-graders if they did something wrong. I didn't dare go home and say I got in trouble. Here was a little lady teaching all subjects to eight grades. Sometimes there were only two students in a grade. I had great admiration and respect for her, and I thought I'd love to have a sweetheart like Mrs. Harmon.

Every year we had a Christmas program and sang Christmas carols. A couple of sheets served as a curtain, hung on a wire strung across the room behind the recitation bench. The teacher played an organ, one she pumped with her feet to provide the air. That was the extent of our music.

I liked history and geography, and I enjoyed reading a lot. I was an average student, but my parents made sure I paid attention. Their goal was for me to be a C-plus student and get a few Bs, and that would be OK. I certainly wasn't a nerd.

Unfortunately, it was a rarity for any of the kids at this school to continue past the eighth grade. From my class only two of us went on to high school, and I was the only one who went to college, as far as I know. There were few eager learners. Many students dropped out in the spring to work on the farm, and others were late returning to school because of farming. The girls seemed to be the smart ones, and the boys were more eager to get outside to play ball or just horse around.

We played baseball every day at recess, or when there was snow and ice on the ground, we would go sledding on a nearby hill. I was becoming increasingly hooked on baseball, as a player and a fan. I loved playing catch when we got together with Grandpa Loren Henderson, a left-hander who was an avid fan. He showed me how he threw his drop and curve ball.

When I was about ten, my dad brought home a radio. It had a big horn for a speaker and was powered by what looked like an automobile battery. The radio had several dials and it squeaked and squawked before you could tune in a station and finally hear something.

I remember listening to WSM from Nashville, which carried the Grand Ole Opry, and WLS from Chicago, which had all the crop prices and other information for farmers. Later on we listened to Tigers and Cubs baseball games, but usually we had to work in the fields. We also listened to *The Shadow* and *The Lone Ranger*, two of the most popular radio programs at the time.

As my interest in baseball grew, I painted a strike zone on the barn, and I got an old baseball and started throwing at it. I was no Bob Feller, but my pitches were banging up the boards on the barn and my dad made me stop.

At school we put together a team, both boys and girls, and played games against other country schools when we could find someone to provide the transportation. I grew to be fairly proficient, and when I got to the eighth grade I was asked to play with the Sunday team in Fulton, the nearby town. I was the first baseman and did quite well.

Getting permission from my dad to skip work on the farm was the hard part. I'd ask Dad, "May I play baseball on Sunday?" He would answer, "Well, if it rains you can." I said, "Dad, they don't play baseball if it rains." He said, "We don't farm if it rains."

But he did make some concessions, and I did get a chance to play. That was my first exposure to athletics. I liked it.

It didn't take being around Grandpa Chris Lude long to figure out where my dad got his toughness and his respect for discipline. I had a great relationship with Grandpa Lude but he scared me to death. I thought he was a tough, ornery son of a gun and a hard one to please.

For my eighth birthday he gave me a registered Holstein calf. He thought I could raise the calf, breed it to a registered bull, and start a strain of registered cattle. The calf was about a yearling when I went to a horse sale with my dad and saw this hackney pony, a small thoroughbred horse, and fell in love with it. Dad said he couldn't afford to buy it

Acquiring this pony by trade for a registered Holstein calf infuriated Grandpa Chris Lude, who gave Mike the calf

but suggested trading my yearling calf for the horse, which I wanted for riding to round up cattle.

When Grandpa heard about the deal he was furious; he thought the horse was ugly; it had been half-gelded and had a nasty disposition. To me, the pony was fast and good looking, and I soon became a good rider.

When we weren't busy on the farm (we worked most of the time) we tried to have fun (rarely). We usually went to the Centerville County Fair, a gathering place for farmers every August. Occasionally we made it to the fair in Hillsdale, a big, big, big event. But we had to sandwich our morning and evening chores around the fair visits, limiting the time spent on rides, throwing baseballs at milk bottles, and watching horse-pulling contests.

We socialized with the Harrison family who lived on a farm about a mile and a half away. We played card games, and we went to Fulton in the summertime on Saturday nights to watch free outdoor movies. Without a nearby library we swapped books with our neighbors. We went on picnics in the summer, and for a special treat we would go to the old ice house in Fulton to get enough ice for home-made ice cream. That was a big, big deal.

When I was thirteen, I had a chance to earn money at a real job with Fred Unrath's traveling threshing operation. I was a bundle pitcher and made a dollar a day, starting at 6 a.m. and wrapping up about 7 p.m. The first time I jumped up on the threshing machine an old timer offered some advice: "Hey, kid, when you're up here with all this dust you gotta chew tobacco." He gave me a plug and I put it in my mouth. I chewed it and got deathly sick. I upchucked and everybody had a good laugh, except me.

It was my first and last time chewing tobacco.

Despite our family's modest circumstances, I was happy most of the time in those early years. Helping my dad work the farm he didn't even own was limiting, especially when I wanted to play baseball. I had to work extremely hard. That went with the territory. I had a little bit of the dickens in me, but most of the time I did what I was told. With my father, I knew the alternative wouldn't be a happy one.

I finished eighth grade in May 1936 and attended a county-wide commencement exercise at Central High School auditorium in Kalamazoo. Until then my uniform, at school or working, was bib overalls. When Dad and I went to town we wore our "good" bib overalls, or newer ones. Now I had dress slacks, and I was getting ready to start high school in new surroundings.

And if I never lived on a farm again I somehow would be able to survive.

# 2
## WING TIPS AND A HIGH SCHOOL INSPIRATION

◆ ◆ ◆

I will never forget my first pair of good dress shoes. They were brown wing tips with crepe soles.

They came from Thom McCan, a chain retail store, and as I recall I got them when I was a sophomore attending high school in Vicksburg, Michigan. Considering the muddy, grubby work shoes I wore on the farm, those shoes meant just as much to me as a glass slipper ever meant to another high school-aged kid named Cinderella.

I can't remember how much the shoes cost, but my guess would be no more than two or three bucks, which was a lot of money for someone who spent his childhood in poverty on a farm in rural Michigan and attended a one-room grade school.

What made these shoes so important was that they were the same style and color worn by Clayton F. (Whitey) Linton. In a matter of weeks from the time I met Whitey Linton he had become the most important person in my life.

Because of Whitey Linton, who was my first football coach, I wanted to be a football coach. I wanted to emulate Whitey Linton. I wanted to look like him and talk like him and walk like him.

He was the first and probably the only person I ever idolized. He became the most important and significant person in my total personal development.

Certainly, my father was my role model for truth, honesty, hard work, determination, and love. He had raised me on our family farm, where we labored so hard and so long just to survive in the Great Depression. He taught me the values that have remained with me all my life.

But Whitey Linton was a role model in a different way. He was handsome; he was articulate; he was an excellent coach; he was a fun person to go pheasant hunting with; he could get me to do just about anything.

It was Whitey Linton who inspired me to make coaching football a lifetime career, a decision that I still take immense pride in more than six decades later. Coach Linton also had the tact to tell me plain and simple that I wasn't big enough, fast enough, or talented enough to play collegiate football at the Big 10 level and steered me to his alma mater, Hillsdale College. He delivered the message without crushing my less-than-fragile ego. It was a critical turning point in my life.

He also conspired with my father to get my attention about complacent study habits and undisciplined effort in the classroom. What they did came as a total shock but it worked, although I never learned all the details of their ploy until years later.

Vicksburg High School was only about nine miles from my family's farm. That's no more than a fifteen-minute drive on today's roads in modern automobiles. But when you can't afford a car and there's no school bus, distance complicates the pursuit of education.

That's why my parents, insistent that I stay in school and get my high school diploma, agreed to let me live with my mother's parents in Vicksburg through the week and return to the farm on weekends.

None of this would have been possible if it weren't for a determined, take-charge woman who was years ahead of her time. That would be my grandmother Minnie Henderson. Without Grandma Henderson and her 1928 Chevrolet, I would have faced huge obstacles even getting to high school, much less graduating and going on to college.

Every Sunday night my loving grandmother drove to the farm and picked me up in the Chevrolet and took me to the house where she lived with Grandpa Loren Henderson. Every Friday after school—sometimes it was after a football game or baseball game— she would drive me back to the farm and my family.

Grandma Minnie's influence on me was considerable. This five-feet-nine, big-boned woman was the boss of the family. She had everything organized. She was straitlaced and stern and didn't smile without a reason. Grandma was a big lady but not fat. She wore her hair very straight and used little makeup. Her appearance was very plain. Grandpa Loren was totally deferential to her; he was more like my mother, compliant and sensitive. My grandparents never had much money. Grandpa Loren worked at the local paper mill and was not well paid. When I lived in Vicksburg while going to high school he got laid off. The situation turned out to be permanent.

But Grandma Minnie made the most of what they had, and she had a great impact on me. She taught me to drive that Chevrolet when I was a mere twelve. She cooked to please my taste and insisted that I come home from school for lunch.

That was quite a culture shock, going from a one-room schoolhouse in the sticks to Vicksburg High. As high schools go, it was relatively small. The gymnasium was tiny, and a dozen or so classrooms housed about 250 students. That's still quite a contrast with my previous school: one teacher with two dozen kids from eight grade levels stuffed into one room. Looking back, I realize how fortunate I was to be one of two students from my eighth-grade class who had the opportunity to move on to high school. The others dropped out to work on the farms where they lived.

That's what had happened to my dad years before, and he was adamant that I go to high school. He realized how much he had missed, and although he didn't have much money he was a strong supporter of taxes for better schools. My mother had graduated from Vicksburg High and wanted her son to do the same.

My introduction to football came when I was barely settled with my grandparents in Vicksburg. My dad liked the idea of me playing football and encouraged me to turn out for the team. Reflecting back, I think he considered football a tough game; it had body contact. It was a game for men and you hit people.

Maybe he thought I might not be tough enough, that toughness and hardness were manly, and he wanted me to be a real man. I remember when I was in the fourth or fifth grade I got into a fight with a kid on the way home and didn't fare too well. When I told my dad about it that night he said, "Now, tomorrow you get in another fight with him and you win." And I did.

He thought if someone challenged you, you had to stand up and be counted. If there was a fight, you had to be there, whether you won or lost the fight. You couldn't be a softy. His younger brother, Bob, had played football in high school and dad thought it had been a good experience for him.

Nowadays one would probably say that dad just liked the violence of football—a simplification, perhaps, but violence is part of the game.

On the day after Labor Day I reported for early practice and had my introduction to football and, just as important, to Whitey Linton, who got his nickname from his light-colored hair. The game was a totally new experience. I had played baseball sporadically the previous year with a Sunday team in Fulton, but I had no football experience. Just putting on the shoulder pads was a challenge. The leather helmets didn't fit too well, and the other equipment took time to figure out.

I didn't say much, but I watched the other players and learned. I'm not sure I didn't go through a practice the first week or so wondering if maybe I had something on backward.

One of the other players suggested that I ask for a practice jersey that was used because it might fit better, even if it needed mending. Your mom can fix that, he said, and you'll be better off. It was a good tip.

The most serious problem was football shoes. We couldn't afford a pair of new shoes. So I sorted through a box of beat-up used cleated shoes, trying to find some that fit and would work. I found one pair that had suitable cleats, but the nails came through the insoles and when I ran they cut the bottoms of my feet.

As a freshman, I was playing end on both offense and defense. When one of the first string ends was banged up it looked as though I might get to see some action. But my feet were killing me. I told Coach Linton, and he said, "Go in and see if there aren't any other old shoes in that box." By the time I got back, he'd moved another player into my spot, and I spent most of that freshman season on the bench.

For a small, Class C school, Vicksburg had a strong football tradition and a top program. There were numerous Vicksburg families of Polish extraction, attracted there by jobs in the paper mill. Their kids were leading members of the football team, and several went on to play college football. One of them, Joe Gembis, competed at the University of Michigan and later was the head coach at Wayne State for many years.

By my sophomore season I had learned most of the basics of playing guard and tackle, offense and defense, and was one of Vicksburg's most enthusiastic but hardly  most talented players. The key to my success was what I later would preach as a coach: I played extremely hard, I hit hard, I was tough, and I would do whatever the coach taught me or asked me to do. I was willing to hustle and work hard, and I was extremely dedicated. I played even when I was dinged up. No one considered me a delicate eater, and I added weight through high school and was just shy of 175 pounds by my senior season.

Great talent? No. Size, speed? No and no. Other than an occasional fumble recovery, I rarely touched the ball. Like most linemen, I took the greatest satisfaction from the success of the team, which was substantial, words of praise from the coach ("Mike, you use your hands really well on defense out there"), and making a tackle in the other team's backfield.

Our two biggest rivals were Comstock and Constantine, and we had a loyal following, even though our home field lacked spectator seating. The fans, who usually included both my parents and Charlie Davidson, the Spanish-American War veteran who lived near our farm, walked the sidelines. The boosters expected us to win, and we rarely sent them home disappointed. Throughout my high school career our teams were consistently successful.

The basketball gymnasium was even worse than the football field. The gym was so small that other schools refused to play in Vicksburg. It was impossible to shoot the ball on an arc from any distance without hitting the ceiling, and the free-throw circles overlapped the center circle. If both teams used a zone defense the final score would likely end up 2-0. It's no wonder we didn't have a basketball team.

I played catcher on the baseball team in the spring, but I was certainly better at football. Baseball was fun, but our coaches had limited skills in teaching fundamentals, like hitting.

My dad respected Whitey Linton's tough, no-nonsense approach to football, and they became friends. Coach Linton would come out to the farm in the fall, and we would all go hunting. My dad had a great springer spaniel named Duke, who flushed and retrieved pheasants extremely well.

In addition to coaching football, Whitey Linton taught history, and I thought I was doing quite well in his class. I was only a so-so student, but I wanted to impress Linton so I worked especially hard. To my absolute shock, in one grading period he flunked me. I was humiliated and decided I needed to take my classroom work a lot more seriously. Only after I had graduated from college did my dad tell me that he and the coach had agreed that I needed to be more disciplined about my study habits and giving me a failing grade might be a way to get my attention. It worked.

When I returned to the farm for Christmas vacation during my first year in high school, I developed a terrible stomachache; I was in excruciating pain. My dad got the doctor to come the eight miles from Athens and he poked around my belly and said, "I'll tell you, John, he's got an appendicitis. We better take him to the hospital." They hauled me to a big house in Vicksburg that had been converted into a hospital and yanked out my appendix. My dad actually scrubbed up and observed the surgery. "Wanted to keep a watch so the doctor wouldn't take anything else out," he said seriously.

I was beginning to emerge socially. During my sophomore year I had my first girl friend. Her name was Pauline Klein, and she was a senior. Her sister, Cecelia, was in my class and my best pal, Bill Miller, fell in love with her. So we were dating the Klein sisters. The family owned a mint farm that was very successful. The girls always had a new Ford to drive to school, more than a fringe benefit in the romance. But we split after Pauline graduated. Cecelia later married Joe Semyczuk, who went from Vicksburg to play football for and graduate from Notre Dame.

One of our favorite places was the Crystal Palace at Paw Paw Lake, where many of the touring big bands came to play. I remember when Bill Miller and I hauled coal ashes in a trailer behind Grandma's Chevy to earn cash to take our girlfriends to the Crystal Palace. In my senior year I was quite smitten with a red-haired Irish girl named Molly McGuire from Kalamazoo Central. We corresponded for a couple of months after I went to Hillsdale College, but soon the college girls started looking a lot better.

I got involved in FFA (Future Farmers of America) in high school, and the agriculture teacher convinced me I should raise a registered Berkshire hog to show at fairs. My hog's name was Blossom, and I'd get that porker's hair shining before parading her in the ring for judging.

But the longer I lived away from the farm the more unlikely it was that my future would involve farming. There were too many problems, too much work, and you always had a seven-day-a-week job. That wasn't the way I wanted to lead my life.

When I went back to the farm for Christmas of my sophomore year, I was shoveling manure to clean out the stables, and the horses in the barnyard were getting frisky. I wasn't paying close attention as I wheeled a load of manure, and one of the horses blasted me in the side with his hind hooves. Reeling in pain, I went to the doctor in Athens again. This time the damage was a couple of broken ribs, and the doctor taped up my whole side.

Although I came from a tiny rural school, I never was what anyone would consider shy. When I got to high school I discovered the drama program and decided I wanted to get involved. In grade school I had taken part in the Christmas plays and found it rather easy to memorize the lines.

I told Miss Mabel Hudson, the drama coach, that I'd like to try out for one of the plays. She also was my English teacher, and I thought participating in drama might help me in class. Our makeshift stage was set up on sawhorses at one end of the tiny gymnasium, with a curtain rigged on a long wire. I enjoyed the theatrics, sometimes in a supporting role, occasionally as a lead. I guess I liked the attention that went with performing in front of a crowd.

Being in drama helped me to develop better verbal communication skills. Besides, the best-looking girls in the school were involved, and that was exciting too.

I don't think I had a crush on Miss Hudson, but I thought she was a special teacher. She was pretty, slender, overall very attractive. She was authoritarian in the classroom but cared about her students. During my senior year I asked her for help in improving my English skills. I was going to college but was inept at diagramming sentences. During spring semester I reported to her for extra work, and she worked hard with me. She was an excellent teacher, both in fundamental English and literature. I always thought it would be fun to see Miss Hudson in a bathing suit.

During my junior year I had a role in one of Miss Hudson's plays when Coach Linton invited me to attend a banquet honoring the undefeated football team at Hillsdale College. Miss Hudson and I had a strong disagreement over whether I could attend because the dinner conflicted with a play rehearsal. Finally, she changed the time of the rehearsal. I went to the banquet and it was sensational.

I was disappointed to learn that Coach Linton was leaving Vicksburg to become head coach at a larger school. His replacement for my senior season was another Hillsdale College product, Al Rizzardi, and the program remained in high gear. We lost just one game that season, and I played well enough to win all-star recognition on the *Kalamazoo Gazette's* All-Southwestern Michigan team.

By this time I had convinced myself I was ready to go play in the Big 10, one of the toughest conferences in America. I had read enough about Neal Kennick, an All-American at Iowa, to convince me that was where I wanted to play college football. Understand that my goal at this point was not to get an education but to play more football. Linton, Rizzardi, and Hubert Smith, a former college lineman who was the Vicksburg High principal, agreed I should go to college. But not at Iowa or any other Big 10 school.

Why not? The words were hard for me to swallow, but as I later found out, they were accurate: not big enough, fast enough, or good enough.

If three high school faculty members delivered that same message to a hopeful athlete now, chances are his parents would threaten a lawsuit and have the ACLU and others raising a fuss. Fortunately for me, the advice I got was great. I was somewhat suspicious because Linton, Smith, and Rizzardi had played at Hillsdale College. But they had already arranged for me to receive a work scholarship at Hillsdale.

My parents backed Coach Linton's plan, and the director of admissions and the registrar came to our farmhouse to set things up. For the first year's tuition I would sell the hog I raised in FFA.

With the help of an aunt in Kalamazoo, I was hired for a summer construction job at the princely wage of eighty-five cents an hour.

During my high school years we had become increasingly aware of the gathering storm of war in Europe. Frequently we would listen to the radio in history class, and there was a lot of talk about whether or not we would be involved. But the war seemed so distant, and we thought it was for other people, those overseas, and that President Roosevelt would never get us drawn in. Because of our age, we students talked about the possibility of being part of the military.

Was the war menacing? Yes, but in 1940 it still seemed so remote.

I was much more focused on the chance I would have to keep playing football. My parents were happy for another reason: I would become the first member of our family to attend college.

# 3
## AVOIDING AN
## ACADEMIC SACK

◆ ◆ ◆

Less than a month into my career as an intercollegiate athlete, my situation at Hillsdale College resembled a quarterback scrambling with no blockers and a couple of huge linemen bearing down for the tackle.

It didn't take me long to realize the difficulty of making the transition from a 250-student high school in Vicksburg, Michigan, to Hillsdale College, a highly respected liberal arts school. I only hoped nobody was paying much attention.

Wrong. One morning, as I strolled out of his medieval history class, Dr. Windsor H. Roberts called me aside. His message was blunt: "Mike, you're in trouble academically."

To avoid the sack I came clean. "Yes sir, Dr. Roberts. I know I'm having problems," I said. "But I don't know what to do about it."

He threw me a lifeline. "Mike, you've shown me that you're a hard worker and I know you work just as hard in your athletics. I think you're disciplined. You never miss class and you pay attention." He volunteered to be my tutor, not only in the history class but in other courses, such as freshman English, where I needed a lot of help.

Dr. Roberts spent many hours with me. He taught me the basics of scholastic survival—how to organize my thoughts, take lecture notes, practice effective time management, and other good-study skills.

I give Dr. Windsor H. Roberts credit for saving my academic life.

Thanks to him, I was able to stay in school and pursue my goal of being a football coach—an ambition that had started to slip further and further from reality with each botched classroom assignment.

Part of my problem was my background. I had attended a one-room country school. Because the vast majority of my classmates never even continued on to high school, the teacher focused almost totally on the simple basics of reading, writing, and arithmetic. There was no time for anything else. The small high school I attended also had a limited curriculum.

The other part of the problem was my approach. Studying didn't have a high priority for me. I was a happy kid who had a good relationship with the faculty at Vicksburg High School, a C-plus student who didn't have to work very hard to get by. I was more concerned with sports than academics. Going to college didn't become a goal or a possibility until I was in my senior year. I just didn't apply myself as I might have, and my lack of preparation came back to haunt me at Hillsdale—in a hurry.

Even with the help and guidance of Dr. Roberts, I had to work extremely hard, and my academic existence for the first two years was touch and go. I was disciplined but nothing came easy. I would go to the library and study but I might take three hours to finish something that another student would get done in a half-hour.

At that stage of my life I never in my wildest imagination thought that in my professional career as a coach and athletic director I would work closely with college presidents and other top officials at some of the largest universities in America.

I strongly doubt any of my professors or classmates from those college days would have suspected that many years later I would return to Hillsdale College to be a convocation speaker and have conferred on me an honorary doctoral degree.

Many times since, I have thought about Dr. Roberts and how he and some other patient and forgiving Hillsdale professors and staff members helped me survive as a student, and I am grateful.

The compelling reason I went to Hillsdale, the first in my family ever to step inside a college classroom, was to play football. My high school coaches and principal were products of Hillsdale, and they convinced their former coach, Dwight Harwood, that I would help bring glory to his program.

Hillsdale is located in southern Michigan about eighty miles west of Detroit and twice that distance from Chicago. It reminds me a lot of the Midwestern county seats where I would travel later in life, the hub of a surrounding world of agriculture. Hillsdale College is an important part of the community but does not dominate the town the way some institutions do in smaller communities. Growth of the school—its enrollment has tripled from the 450 or so students when I first attended—has been faster than that of the city, which currently has a population of about 8,000.

When I arrived at Hillsdale in September 1940, I had about four hundred dollars in my wallet, thanks to a summer job in construction and sale of the hog I had raised in a Future Farmers of America project. As an athlete, I had been promised a job in the college's building and grounds department, which would help me get through the first year.

Like the rest of the football players, I checked in early and went through freshman orientation, including wearing a blue and white beanie and enduring some minor hazing. The frosh football players stuck together, and that good relationship helped me overcome a bad case of homesickness. This was the first time I had been away from my family for any extended time, and if it hadn't been for the friendships I made those first few weeks I probably would have quit school and gone home. A half-dozen or more of us pledged the same fraternity, Alpha Tau Omega, and became immediate buddies.

We all were well aware of Coach Dwight Harwood, a short (five-feet-eight), stocky (two hundred pounds) man who ran the football program, and we always gave a little extra effort when we thought he might be watching. But our daily taskmaster was Gordy Piatt, who coached the freshmen while finishing up his four-year degree.

Our 1940 frosh team had a good season, winning three of four games. I was a starting lineman but hardly a star. Most of us played both offense and defense. I was getting used to the obscurity of playing in the line, but this experience was extremely rewarding—the friendships, the camaraderie, and the togetherness of being a team.

Dwight Harwood was a veteran coach who had the unenviable job of keeping the Hillsdale football program functioning. Unlike my high school coach, whom I tried so desperately to imitate in every detail of mannerism and dress, Harwood was not a role model; rather he was a decent coach and a decent person. He had a fine singing voice and directed the choir at Hillsdale Presbyterian Church, not something you'd expect for a football coach. He wasn't a great tactician on game day, but he got a lot out of the talent on hand.

Harwood's most celebrated victory probably had come a decade earlier, in 1931, when he led Hillsdale against the University of Chicago team coached by the legendary Amos Alonzo Stagg. Hillsdale won 7-0, rolling up fourteen first downs to two for the Maroons. The game came two seasons before the University of Chicago dropped football, ending Stagg's forty-one-year tenure as head coach.

Coach Harwood seemed to appreciate my approach to football as a classic overachiever. I knew I had to make up for lack of ability and bulk with hustle, enthusiasm, and a willingness to pay the price.

For a college lineman, my size—I played at 177 pounds—was marginal even then, long before 300-pound guards and tackles became commonplace. But I knew how to use my hands on defense, and I could block much bigger defenders effectively. I considered myself very coachable. Harwood told me many of the same things I had heard from my high school coaches: as long as I was aggressive and tough, put pressure on opposing passers, and blocked hard I'd have a place in his program.

Like most linemen I derived the most satisfaction from team success. I always believed—and this never changed when I became a coach and later athletic director—that the team comes first. I do remember one specific game against Kalamazoo College, partly because I was from Kalamazoo County. I was our team captain, and we blanked a good Kalamazoo team 20-0, and in the locker room after the game I was presented the game ball. But individual recognition for me was rare.

I looked on Coach Harwood as a nice guy, a good friend, and an adviser who was sensitive to all the nuances of the Hillsdale campus. Early in my Hillsdale years, he tried to help with my classroom problems. He sug-

*Taking a break from football practice as a sophomore lineman at Hillsdale College*

gested that I enroll in a French course. I said I didn't have much interest in French until he explained that Dr. Harold Davidson, the French professor, was coach of the tennis team and our faculty athletic representative. "I'll almost guarantee you will pass his class if you don't cut it," Harwood said.

So I registered for French, had perfect attendance, and although I wasn't a very good student, I passed (with a D as in dog).

Coach Harwood also had a big part in determining which campus jobs were assigned to athletes on work scholarships. I figured out early that the jobs got easier as you progressed in your career, but only if you had Harwood's recommendation.

I also realized that no job on the campus was as hard or demanding as working on the farm where I had grown up. I started out raking leaves and mowing lawns. Later I waited tables in the East Hall dining room. Then I got the job of ringing the huge bell on the fourth floor of Central Hall, which was tolled hourly to mark the change of classes. The main thing was to be on time. As a junior I filled the coal stokers to keep the heating system in the fieldhouse running through the night. Then I got the best job of all, making the rounds of three sorority houses each night to replenish the coal supply for their furnaces.

During the summer after my freshman year I had my first experience in travel by boat. I found a vacation job waiting tables in the upscale dining room on one of the big ferries that chugged across Lake Michigan, a six-hour crossing. I got seasick only once, but there were times when the water was far too bumpy for a kid who grew up on a farm.

In addition to football, I played catcher on the Hillsdale baseball team, using hustle and enthusiasm to make up for my inability to hit a curve ball. My best hitting, unfortunately, seemed to come when we worked out indoors before the season. I rarely hit for power. I liked baseball because, for one thing, it got me out of spring football practice.

When I wasn't playing sports or hitting the books, I was learning some of the social graces I hadn't been exposed to on the farm. At the fraternity we were required to wear a tie and jacket for dinner. We had to stand until the house mother was seated. I learned how to say grace before a meal and took my turn giving thanks with the other fraternity pledges.

I got a taste of fraternity hazing, like being blindfolded and dropped off out in the countryside with other pledges and having to find our way back to campus. Pledges were required to make a paddle for a fraternity "big brother," and if you didn't follow the proper procedure you had to be ready to grab your ankles while he took the paddle to your backside. Thanks to a tremendous big brother who didn't take the routine too seriously I thought it was all pretty good-natured fun.

To help pay for my room and board at the fraternity, I made a deal to supply potatoes we raised on the farm, sacks and sacks of potatoes. I'd haul a load to school in my dad's old beat-up jalopy each fall and bring a new supply when I came back from the Christmas break.

Despite some intimidating classroom experiences, I made steady progress. My big goal was simply to keep my head above water academically. The day-to-day responsibilities took priority over a lot of deep thinking about the future, but I still wanted to get a college diploma and a coaching job.

One of the courses I enjoyed and the one I got the best grade in was freshman biology. So I said, hey, I'll make biology my major, even though it didn't have anything to do with my goal of being a football coach. Two biology professors with the same last name but unrelated, Dr. Bertram Barber and Dr. Ruth Barber, gave me significant help in my major course of scholastic work.

One of the other professors who left a lasting impression was Dr. James Masterson of the English Department, undoubtedly the most severe critic of my writing efforts. A self-styled eccentric, he frequented the off-campus coffee shop where I worked part-time; he demanded that we save and reheat day-old coffee for his marathon consumption as he chain-smoked cigarettes. He had big circles under his eyes, looking as if he seldom slept.

When it came to the use of the written word he was a tyrant. The first paper I turned in for his class came back covered in red ink. I had used the word *unique*, and around it he had put a big circle and the comment: "You don't have a clue what *unique* means. Never use a word if you don't know what it means. When you call something unique it means there is nothing in the world like it; that's the only one." I'll say this, the impression he left with those words was unforgettable, almost unique.

When I arrived at Hillsdale I had no inkling about the school's fiercely independent approach to higher education, something that has continued to the present day. Politically, it was and still is conservative. From its beginning in 1844, Hillsdale would not accept financial assistance from federal or state governments, and as a result could express those conservative opinions. The school has long sponsored an enormously popular series of seminars featuring almost every conservative leader and spokesperson, not only on the campus but at settings across the country.

Historically, Hillsdale was a strong opponent of slavery and admitted black students prior to the Civil War. A large number of male students, estimated at about four hundred, enlisted in the ranks of the North in the Civil War, producing some imposing figures: four won the Congressional Medal of Honor, three became generals and sixty were killed in battle. The growing enrollment during the Civil War was due at least partially by the many women attracted to Hillsdale by its nondiscriminatory policies.

One of the school's best-known products was Charles V. Gridley, the commander of Admiral George Dewey's flagship in the Battle of Manila Bay during the Spanish-American war. Dewey's famous order that launched the U.S. attack on the Spanish fleet at dawn on May 1, 1898, is part of the proud history taught every American sailor: "You may fire when you are ready, Gridley."

Early in Hillsdale's athletic history, the school played the likes of Michigan, Purdue, Michigan Agricultural College (now Michigan State University), and national power Notre Dame. In 1892 Hillsdale beat the Fighting Irish 14-12, in one of three games between the schools in as many seasons. According to one report in the college archives, the Notre Dame hosts "gave the Hillsdale players fine accommodations, a big dinner, and cigars to smoke on the train ride home."

About the same time, Hillsdale oarsmen won four straight national amateur rowing championships, going unbeaten for three years before finally losing to a crew from the Thames Rowing Club in England. Unknowingly, I was endowed with this Hillsdale rowing heritage even before my career took me to the University of

Washington where both men's and women's rowing programs have established national reputations.

In the 1980s Hillsdale's lawyers went to the Supreme Court to avoid following federal restrictions because some students received aid from the government. The college raised private funds to replace the federal support and still rejects about $5 million annually in U.S. taxpayer cash. In the words of Dr. Larry Arnn, the school president, "Hillsdale is famous because it refused to count its students and its employees by the color of their skin." The college's monthly publication *Imprimis* has a huge circulation and has raised millions to support Hillsdale's audacious and gutsy independent reaction to government handouts.

The college survived other serious problems, including a devastating fire in 1874 and the threat of mortgage foreclosures during the Depression. The most recent trouble came with the unexpected departure of Dr. George Roche, Hillsdale's president for twenty-eight years. He left in late 1999 after rescuing the school from near bankruptcy and transforming it into a monument of the free enterprise system.

Dr. Roche left under the cloud of a tragedy, the death of his daughter-in-law and some unfortunate allegations, none of them confirmed. His resignation left a scar on the fantastic job he did at Hillsdale, being the right man at the right time. As president he championed the school's independence and put Hillsdale in the forefront of private colleges providing a liberal arts education. He wrote numerous books and raised millions of dollars.

Fortunately, Hillsdale has rebounded strongly under the leadership of Dr. Arnn, who has done a magnificent job of keeping the school on track. He has sustained the financial backing of the college's loyal supporters and the significant budget surpluses of recent years have remained steady.

College was a huge transition for me, getting away from the farm and reaffirming my resolve never to return to that lifestyle. I thought at the time that if I never saw a cow again it would be too soon and the same went for potatoes, no matter how they were prepared. I was finally getting used to indoor plumbing, electric lights, and central heating. I had no problem getting dates with coeds, and as my grades started to improve I became more and more confident. I had a lot of friends, and I was involved in campus activities. If you were to ask my colleagues at Hillsdale what I was like in those days I think the response would be something like this: "He was a very friendly person, an enthusiastic guy who had a lot of energy, who was a very average student and put a premium on liking people. His athletic career was very important to him."

The most imposing obstacle for all of us attending college at that time was the prospect of the United States getting involved in the war that had already thrown Europe into turmoil. We had moved from the shadow of the Great Depression to the menace of a global war. We thought about the impending conflict and the threat it posed to our future.

During my sophomore year in late 1941 I was attending a pancake supper at the Chi Omega sorority house when one of the women rushed into the room, talking about something horrible that had just happened. She said the Japanese had bombed our naval base at Pearl Harbor, in Hawaii. Everybody was in shock. Later we sat around and listened on the radio to President Franklin D. Roosevelt's famous declaration-of-war speech.

A few days later Coach Harwood called a meeting of the football team. He told us about a Marine Corps platoon leader training program that would keep us from being drafted into the military until after we finished college. He said we would be able to stick together as a team and graduate and then become Marine officers.

The proposal sounded great to me. Where do I sign, Coach? On March 4, 1942, a recruiting officer came to Hillsdale, and I enlisted in the Marines. So much for promises. We were not permitted to finish college. By May 1943, as action in the Pacific intensified, many of the men on campus received notices to report for induction. Soon those of us on the football team who had signed up for the Marines received orders to report for active duty in the V-12 program at Denison University in Granville, Ohio.

I remember many farewells at the bus station, coeds in tears as boyfriends left to report for active duty. Some never came back.

# 4

# "You Can't Fool Me, You Bleep, Bleep, Bleep"

◆ ◆ ◆

Having played football in high school and college, I was hardly a stranger to getting chewed out in words that covered a
broad range in the vernacular of profanity. I thought I had heard
it all.

That was before I was confronted by Lieutenant Colonel A. T.
Hunt, commanding officer of the U.S. Marines amphibious tractor
group, the military unit with which I was training prior to being
sent into battle in the Pacific theater during World War II.

The setting was Camp Pendleton, on the coast of Southern
California. The mood was edgy because we knew the job ahead
would be extremely dangerous. We were going island-hopping
through the South Pacific against well-entrenched Japanese
defenders. The names of these remote locations were to become
too familiar to most Americans and military historians because of
the heavy casualties incurred by Allied forces.

My amphibious landing unit was scheduled to move out in late
January 1945, but I still had not received the appropriate orders. As
the date neared, I was called into the office of Colonel Hunt, a
place I rarely visited. He proceeded to give me the chewing out of
a lifetime, shouting and screaming obscenities, a performance that
confused me as much as it intimidated me.

The gist of the blowup was that somehow, someone in high places—like Washington, D.C.—had used influence to prevent me from being sent into battle. Eyes blazing in contempt, Colonel Hunt said bluntly: "Obviously, your father is a politician or he has connections in Washington." He uttered a string of bleep words, describing me, my ancestors, and the bleeping shame of what had been done on my behalf.

When he caught his breath I tried to plead my innocence, explain that my

*Mike in Marine Corps Uniform*

dad was a sharecropper on a farm in rural Michigan who didn't have a high school education and didn't even know the township commissioner in Kalamazoo County.

Waving a finger in my face and pressing close, the Marine officer said: "Well you can't fool me, you bleep, bleep, bleep."

My bleeping orders apparently were lost somewhere between the Bureau of Personnel in Washington, D.C., and Camp Pendleton, so when my battalion shipped out I stayed behind.

Several months later, when I had been assigned to duty with an amphibious tractor battalion in Maui, whom did I run into by chance? The unforgettable Colonel Hunt, of course. Once again he unloaded on me. I thought I'd heard every four-letter word that first time, but he coined new words in our second meeting. I reminded him again of my total lack of influence with anyone but he was having none of it.

My original unit had just returned from taking part in the famous landing on Iwo Jima and had suffered heavy casualties. It was one of the deadliest battles of the Pacific war, widely remembered for the photograph of Marines raising the American flag at Mount Suribachi. Our units took part in the landing and the initial assault, and then brought in supplies once the beachhead was secure. By the time of that famous flag raising, our troops had the amphibious tractors back on the bigger ships and were ready to move out.

The fact that my orders were lost might have saved my life.

My career in the Marines started after I finished my junior year at Hillsdale College. When Pearl Harbor was bombed all of the men in college knew it would only be a matter of time before we were involved. Many of us had enlisted in the V-12 officers training program with the promise of being able to stay out of the war until we completed college. But as action intensified in the Pacific, we were abruptly summoned to active duty.

The day before I got on the train, Grandpa Chris Lude took me aside for a pep talk. This hard-nosed German immigrant told me, "Mike, there's no reason why you shouldn't end up being a general before you're through." It was his way of telling me he respected me and thought I would do well. Growing up, I wasn't around him that much, but we had a good relationship. It wasn't a buddy-buddy, friendly thing, more "I am the patriarch of this family and you better pay attention to what I say."

Grandpa was an extremely hard worker, and he was very, very tough. A bull almost killed him when he was in the pen of the state hospital's cattle barn, where he worked after giving up farming. When he got out of the hospital he went back into that pen and whipped the bull. If he had an ego it wasn't noticeable, other than making sure he was always neat and clean with a well-trimmed mustache. Grandpa was straightforward and honest. He was exceptionally tenacious, whatever he did. When I was a kid I was intimidated but I loved him, and his discipline, persistence, and willingness was a great example.

I reported for indoctrination training at Denison University in Granville, Ohio, in July 1943. We were issued uniforms and learned the basics of military rules and close-order drills. We lived in dormitories. Training was more like college than boot camp. For several months we took courses in physics, mathematics, mechanical drawing, map reading, military history, and psychology.

The next step was boot camp in Parris Island, South Carolina, my real introduction to the Marine Corps. The only way to reach the island was aboard a barge that reminded me of a garbage scow. In fact, it was a garbage scow. We unloaded from the bus that carried us to the waterfront, grabbed the sea bags that held all of our worldly possessions, and crowded onto the boat. At the time I felt as if I was going to prison, like Alcatraz. Only it was Parris Island and Marine boot camp.

We were welcomed by a drill instructor, a noncom who was a corporal but who talked to us as if he thought he was a four-star general. He told us bluntly, "You college guys aren't half as smart as you think you are," making no secret of the fact that the enlisted men didn't have much use for officers-to-be and would make boot training as difficult for us as they could.

Shock treatment was part of the psychology of the whole routine. I remember a drill instructor approaching me when we were marching in close-order drill, putting his face inches from my ear, and shouting: "Lude, square yourself away; you're bouncing; keep that head still. You look like a bubble on a pisspot."

The concepts of discipline—keeping focused on the objectives, physical and mental toughness, and leadership—were stressed in everything we did. I felt the camaraderie with my fellow trainees helped all of us over the rough spots; you could share frustrations and down feelings with your buddies and vice versa.

Every recruit was issued a bucket. It was your stool to sit on. It was where you washed your clothes. You used it when scrubbing the Quonset hut floors with brick and sand. I remember how we were warned to be ready to protect our bucket from someone who had lost his. I remember the old Marine response when somebody asked "Where's my bucket?" The response was "Bleep you Jack, I got mine." Most guys would shorten the answer to six letters, "FYJIGM."

To toughen us up they marched us through swamps and made us run for miles at a time. If we slowed down they'd make us drop and do push-ups. There were constant rifle inspections. You had to field strip your rifle and clean it, and it was never clean enough for the DI (drill instructor). It was commonplace for a lieutenant walking down the line to grab your rifle, pull it up, and say, "What's that?" and you said, "Sir, that's a front sight," and he said, "That's dust."

The next three months at Officer Candidate School in Quantico, Virginia, got considerably harder. The program was heavy on academic work, heavy on physical work, and heavy on field training. It was light on sleep. But the last thing you wanted to happen was to stumble on this final step to becoming an officer and be shipped immediately to a replacement unit in the Pacific as a private. During OCS and so many other times during my Marine career I reflected on how fortunate I was to have played football. I'd think, this is tough but it's not any tougher than two-a-day practices in the early fall when it's hot and humid. If I could handle that I can handle this. I was confident the training received at Quantico had absolutely prepared me—mentally, physically, and strategically—to be a Marine Corps leader. I was ready to go to war.

I felt that I was ready to live up to Grandpa Chris Lude's pep talk about ending up a general.

At the time I was at Quantico, there was a major distraction back home in Michigan. Lightning hit our silo and started a fire that swept through the barn. Flames destroyed the farm equipment and all of the buildings except the house. Unable to farm, my father found a job with the Kalamazoo County road commission. With most of the younger men in the military, he was offered a job as a truck driver. My parents moved closer to Vicksburg, and my mother used her cooking skills to get a job at an elementary school lunchroom. It was a far easier life than working the farm.

Of the 226 would-be officers who were in my OCS class at Quantico, 182 were commissioned second lieutenants at a brief ceremony on May 3, 1944. When I was ordered to report for training with the amphibious tractor battalion on the beach at Oceanside, California, it was pretty clear this war was not going to be any picnic. Simply, our job was leading the invasion of enemy-held islands, of which there were many in the South Pacific theater.

Our boats were called landing vehicle tractors; they were more like tanks that floated, and they were open on the top—at the same time having the traction to move on land once they hit the beach. They were launched from larger ships offshore, and each carried about thirty Marines. The goal was to get on the beach, often under heavy fire, open the big ramp of the vehicle, and turn the Marines loose.

A lot of people called the tractors seagoing tomato cans because they had a low profile in the water and little protection. The crew consisted of a boat driver, a gunner manning a 50-caliber machine gun on the top of the cab, and a lieutenant—that's me—in charge of several tractors. We made numerous practice runs in training on the California beaches. Later, back in our quarters, we speculated about our chances of surviving the action under fire.

But I never got that far after my orders were delayed. When my old battalion returned from the front, several of my former fellow officers told me in no uncertain terms how lucky I was. I don't recall any precise casualty numbers, but it was tough. I was very fortunate, indeed.

When my orders finally caught up with me, they were changed and I was shuffled to Mare Island in the San Francisco area, then to Pearl Harbor and finally to the Fifth Amphibious Tractor Battalion in Maui. When I arrived at that then-primitive Hawaiian outpost, I shared a tent with a survivor of amphibious landings at Saipan, Tinian, and Iwo Jima, each a costly victory for American forces in terms of casualties. Art Hass had played football at Coe College in Iowa and went on to become a successful football coach in Austin, Minnesota. We became lifelong friends; I was best man at his wedding, and Rena and I named our middle daughter, Janann, after his wife.

In the summer of 1945 the dropping of nuclear bombs on two Japanese cities heralded a quick surrender and the end of hostilities. My commanding officer, Major George Shead, wanted to start a sports program for his troops and, knowing about my athletic background, decided I should be involved. We formed a baseball team, with me as the catcher, and played teams from other military groups and civilian teams on Maui. About the same time I tore up an ankle sliding into third base, Major Shead called me in and appointed me coach of his football team, the Fifth Amphibious Tractor Battalion Bulldogs. It was my first role as a football coach, and we played eight games that season on Maui.

Major Shead wanted to give his troops a chance to have some fun in sports but this cocky, little (five-feet-eight, 155 pounds) career Marine wanted to keep their minds on something other than going home. The war was over, but we were still in uniform, still living a military existence, and still a long, long way from rejoining our families and friends. Shead was a good officer and a competent leader, and he had a sense of humor.

One night Art Hass and I were in our tent talking rather loudly and a faraway voice hollered, "Hey, knock it off." I figured it was just some wise guy mouthing off, so I yelled back, "Blow it out your rear end." The voice, as it turned out, had been that of Major Shead. Somehow I still managed to get good fitness reports and remained as coach of the football team.

Shead also assigned me the job of building an officers' club, a retreat where we could sip our regular liquor rations in peace overlooking the ocean. I consider it one of my most creative efforts. I didn't know anything about construction, but I knew the Seabees (Construction Battalion) had worked wonders under extremely adverse conditions during the war and there was a unit available at division headquarters.

First, I held a strategy session with a platoon sergeant who was a veteran at cutting through red tape. He said, "Lieutenant, here's what we've got to do. You get a truck. We have a bunch of obsolete tools down at the tractor maintenance barn. I'll load the tools into the back of the truck. You go around to all the officers and gather up as much liquor as you can from their monthly rations."

We gathered up about two and one-half cases of hard liquor and an assortment of tools and headed for division headquarters about three o'clock the next morning. The sergeant talked to a chief petty officer in the CB unit. The chief said it would be at least six weeks before his construction specialists could help us. Then the sergeant said, "Oh, Lieutenant Lude, don't we have something in the back of our truck that the Seabees might be able to use?" After looking at the load of tools, the chief said maybe they could do the job in two weeks.

Then my platoon sergeant said, "Mr. Lude, could you show the chief what you have in the cab of the truck?" The chief petty officer took one look at the booze and said, "We'll be there tomorrow morning."

They arrived about 6 a.m., and by the end of the day, using quick-hardening chemicals on the concrete, they had a nice building slapped together on a chunk of property overlooking the ocean. We opened and dedicated it that night. There was no air conditioning, but we had ocean breezes. We lacked food service; that had to come from the galley, which was a big tent. But there was a nice bar at one end of the room, which was about 30 by 70 feet. It had a thatched roof and window coverings on pulleys which could be closed in case of rain or severe wind.

The Seabees did wonders; they were terrific. So was that platoon sergeant who made it happen and made me look good.

We planned a party to dedicate the new club, and when Art Hass and I suggested we might even have a little female companionship at the affair, the other officers scoffed. Wagers were placed. Art and I had met a couple of local girls and were able to patch through a phone call to their home to get their parents' OK to come to the club. I didn't do much dancing because a badly sprained injured ankle had me on crutches. But Art and I each won fifty dollars when we showed up with the local girls.

I was also learning about the power politics of the military system. Not long after arriving in Hawaii, I was dispatched with a group of sixteen Marines to load 120 new amphibious tractors aboard LSTs and move them from Pearl Harbor to our base of operations in Maui. When we arrived at Pearl, the commanding admiral where I had been sent ordered me to send two of my Marines to kitchen duty as long as we were around.

I called the Pacific theater Marine headquarters and talked to the commanding general to complain, citing the pressing time schedule. He agreed, adding: "I outrank him." So the two-star general told the one-star admiral we would not be furnishing any mess cooks from my detail. We loaded the tractors on the LSTs and got them back to Maui. I never saw the admiral again, but I wasn't looking for him either.

More than six months after the Japanese surrender I arrived in San Diego and immediately requested two weeks' leave to visit my family in Michigan. I borrowed Grandpa Lude's 1941 DeSoto coupe and drove to Hillsdale to visit friends. At one of the hangouts near the campus entrance where students would gather between classes for snacks and socializing I spotted an incredibly attractive brunette coed. Her name was Rena Pifer, and I remembered meeting her when I was a sophomore. She was the sister of a fraternity brother, Bill Pifer, a guy I had run into earlier in Honolulu, where he worked with a naval repair unit. After dating Rena the next night I decided she was a very special lady, and that I should do everything I could to recruit her to my program.

In no time I fell in love with her, and it's been that way for a lifetime.

# 5
## HILLSDALE REVISITED: CALL ME COACH

◆ ◆ ◆

Dave Nelson, who won widespread fame and recognition as one of the most cerebral and creative college football coaches in history, was an untried rookie when I first met him at Hillsdale College.

Hillsdale was Nelson's first stop in a coaching career that was eminently successful and somewhat remarkable because none of the schools where he practiced his trade and made such innovative waves were big-time programs in huge media markets. They didn't compete in the Big 10, the Pac-10 or the Southeastern Conference.

I was the captain of Dave Nelson's first team as a head coach.

Then, for most of the next fifteen years at Hillsdale College, the University of Maine and the University of Delaware, I had the good fortune to serve as an assistant coach with Nelson; I was a trusted strategist and disciple of the man who created and taught the Winged-T offense. We spread the Winged-T gospel at hundreds of clinics and blackboard sessions in football war rooms in universities across the country.

But I'm getting ahead of myself here.

I had returned to Hillsdale from a three-year stint in the Marine Corps in World War II in 1946 to finish my senior year and, almost as important, my final season of college football.

When my former coach, Dwight Harwood, retired after a long career, Dave Nelson was lured to Hillsdale as his replacement. Nelson had played wingback at the University of Michigan for legendary coach Fritz Crisler during the careers of better-known teammates Tom Harmon, an All-American running back, and Forrest Evashevski, who became even more famous as a national championship coach at the University of Iowa. Nelson was named Hillsdale athletic director as well as head football coach.

Like most campuses after World War II, Hillsdale was crowded with returning military veterans. They were, of course, older, more confident, and more serious about doing whatever it took to collect a diploma and get on with their lives.

I was no exception. I wanted my bachelor of science degree, majoring in biology. The next step, I hoped, would be a coaching job, probably at the high school level.

There was another new person in my life, a college coed named Rena Pifer who, like me, would be a Hillsdale senior in the fall. That summer I worked on a Kalamazoo County road crew, driving a tractor and mowing the sides of county roads. I had saved enough money from the Marine Corps to buy a new car, and I put on a lot of mileage between Vicksburg and Hillsdale, where the lovely Rena lived with her family.

Dave Nelson's inaugural season as a head coach was successful. Our Hillsdale College team lost just one game, a 13-6 setback at the hands of Albion, one of the school's longtime rivals in the Michigan Intercollegiate Athletic Association. We were co-champions of the MIAA, and no one took more pride in that season than I did. Besides serving as team captain, I played almost every down at guard.

Nelson commanded our respect from the start of two-a-day practices going into the 1946 season. The team was a mix of returning veterans and an assortment of talent Nelson had recruited to play the same Michigan Single Wing formation he competed in as a prewar Wolverine. Nelson wasn't more than a few years older than those of us who had returned from World War II, so we developed a special rapport with our new coach. Yet he could be tough and demanding, a strong leader who never lost the reins of control.

We had two outstanding running backs, Tom Wood from Imlay City, Michigan, and Bill Young from the Detroit area. Other standouts on the team included Dick Pifer, a Hillsdale product and brother of Rena; center Alex Clelland from Detroit, and Carl Sweig, a transfer who had played at Albion before the war.

In the classroom, I was much improved. Good grades came a lot easier now that I had learned to study and prioritize my time. The biology department was proud of me. I was having a great year, with one exception. Rena Pifer, the love interest in my life, had received a scholarship to a preschool education specialty institution in Detroit, during spring semester. That was a downer, but the romance still thrived. Just a few days after our graduation ceremony we were married in Rena's Hillsdale Presbyterian Church, on June 5, 1947. After a short honeymoon in Chicago we

*Mike and bride Rena depart for honeymoon after wedding reception at Pi Beta Phi sorority in 1947*

headed for Port Huron, Michigan, where we had jobs in the city's summer recreation program. In September Rena would teach kindergarten and I would become a high school assistant football and head baseball coach.

Then Dave Nelson threw me a curveball.

He offered me a job.

Rena and I had returned to Hillsdale for a weekend in late August, when the football team was getting ready to start practice. We stopped by to visit Dave and his wife, Shirley. He didn't mince any words in our conversation. "I kept telling you that at some point I'd like to have you as an assistant football coach," he said. I remembered him saying that before, but I hadn't thought he was serious. Now he was offering me a job on his staff as line coach.

I told him, "Dave, if you're not kidding you may have just hired an assistant football coach." I had hoped by the time I was forty years old my alma mater might hire me as a coach.

There were a few obstacles, though, before I could join Nelson's staff. I had to talk to Harvey Turner, the Hillsdale president, who was concerned about the ethics of my breaking the contract I had in Port Huron. Turner's approval was contingent on getting a release from the superintendent of schools in Port Huron; the superintendent was very understanding, but Brick Fowler, his athletic director, was not. He ripped me every bit as effectively as I had been by some senior Marine officers. But finally he said, "Well, I can't stop you if the superintendent has given you the OK."

So, three months out of college I was on the Hillsdale payroll for the 1947-48 school year as offensive and defensive line coach, trainer, director of intramurals and physical education instructor. After

*The perks of an assistant coaching job at Hillsdale: an office and a desk plus a salary of $2,400 a year*

the end of football season Dave Nelson said being football coach and athletic director was taking all his time so he was appointing me head baseball coach. All these responsibilities for a salary of $2,400—that's for a year, not a month.

I had a hard time comprehending such an unbelievable, incredible, wonderful, astonishing thing could happen to me. If I looked just a little bit smug would you blame me?

We went through my first season as a coach undefeated, with two ties. I tried to make up in enthusiasm and dedication what I lacked in coaching experience and expertise. Coaching a bunch of linemen who just the year before were my side-by-side teammates wasn't always easy, but most of the time they at least pretended to listen. I thought I might miss the satisfaction of making a key tackle or throwing a block on a big play, but I was so fired up about getting a chance to coach that I didn't worry about being retired as a player.

Because I had played in Nelson's system—we used the Single Wing he had played in at Michigan—making the transition to coaching was relatively easy. But I soaked up everything I could from the head coach. He was the boss, and he was becoming a respected friend.

After my rookie season as an assistant coach, I came down with the mumps, and Dave came to visit during the Christmas break. I had been in agony when one of my testicles had swollen up about the size of a grapefruit. I couldn't even roll over in bed. Dave handed me a championship gold football and said, "Mike, I don't know what's going to happen to you, but I want you to have this gold ball because every man needs two."

After two successful seasons at Hillsdale, Dave Nelson was targeted by other, larger schools. That spring, while I was busy coaching the baseball team, Dave told me he was accepting the job of backfield coach at Harvard. President Turner brought in James (Gib) Holgate, another University of Michigan product, as our new coach. He asked Harold Westerman, the other assistant on Nelson's staff, and me to stay on. We had another good season, scoring 287 points and holding opponents to 67, but we missed a third straight MIAA championship with two losses and a tie.

Back to my career in baseball. I had played from the time I was the first baseman on the town team in Fulton when I was in high school, through college, and in the Marines in Maui. But I had never coached the game. I wasn't all that confident I understood the nuances of baseball. I got some advice from John Williams, a Hillsdale man who had played in the New York Yankee farm system. Another helpful source was a textbook on baseball written by former Duke coach Jack Coombs. That was my bible.

Surprisingly, we won the MIAA baseball championship that first season. My strategy moves, such as when to replace a struggling pitcher or when to use the hit and run, seemed to be working. One of our best players was shortstop Bill Young, who split time with the baseball team and the track squad, where he was an outstanding sprinter. A few other key players included Tommy McCarthy, who later signed with the Yankees; outfielder Terry Thomas, first baseman Rod Oberlin, and infielder Merv Holbeck. We repeated as conference champs in 1949, improving the team with several talented additions.

During those first two years coaching at Hillsdale, Rena and I lived in what had been her family's summer cottage at a nearby lake. Because no one had ever occupied the place in the winter, the sewer pipes and water pipes occasionally froze, and we would move into town with Rena's parents until it warmed up. Her dad, Earl Pifer, encouraged me to get my masters degree so I spent the summer of 1949 back in the classroom at Michigan State, working toward the advanced degree I received five years later.

Meanwhile, Dave Nelson was ready to make another move. After one year at Harvard he was offered the head coaching job at the University of Maine. When the athletic director, Elton (Tad) Wieman, picked Nelson, Dave called his former Hillsdale assistants, Harold Westerman and me. "I've got the job and I want you two guys to join me," he told us over the phone. "Can you come tomorrow?"

Harold wore just as many hats at Hillsdale as I did; he was the backfield coach in football, head basketball coach, and head track coach in the spring. But he slipped away during our spring break to help Nelson get settled in Maine, and I wasn't far behind as soon as the baseball season ended.

I was on the coaching carousel now, and I never knew when or where it might stop. I just knew I didn't want to get off.

# 6
# FLYING WITH THE WING-T

◆ ◆ ◆

The offensive formation called the Wing-T had a profound, widespread influence on the game of football at all levels. High-profile coaches at national college powers used this offensive system with enormous success. Many high school teams ran it and won state championships. Some high school programs still do.

During the peak of the Wing-T's popularity, the system—a hybrid mix of the quarterback snap and handoff of the T-formation and the blocking schemes of the Single Wing formation—was referred to as the Delaware Winged-T.

That's because the mastermind of the system, Dave Nelson, was head football coach at the University of Delaware, which was somewhat isolated from the well-known collegiate football powerhouses of that era (Notre Dame, USC, Michigan, Alabama, etc.).

What most of the fans and serious practitioners of the offense didn't know was that the "Delaware" Winged-T actually was launched at the University of Maine. I was there as a member of Dave Nelson's coaching staff when it all happened. The birth name of Nelson's innovation was Winged-T; as the popularity of his creation increased the name evolved and was simplified to Wing-T.

If Nelson was the father of the Winged-T, then Harold Westerman and I ought to be considered at least illegitimate sons.

Harold and I were on Nelson's coaching staff at Hillsdale and when Nelson was hired at Maine in 1949 he asked us to rejoin him there.

In that first season we ran the Michigan Single Wing offense, but our tailbacks were constantly getting hurt, including a serious shoulder injury to our star, Harold Marden. We finally decided to convert to the T-formation, with the quarterback taking a direct snap from the center on every play. We hoped this would prevent further injury to Marden, who later became an executive with one of the world's largest chemical firms.

Before the 1950 season Nelson sent Westerman, our backfield coach, to Notre Dame to pick the brain of Frank Leahy, the noted coach of the Fighting Irish and a T-formation master. Dave had conferred earlier with Rick Engel, then at Brown University, another pioneer in that offense.

Then Dave did his own innovating, working his red and blue pencils to stubs; those modifications produced the Winged-T. Our offense would feature a balanced line (equal number of players on each side of the center in the offensive line) with a wingback in the backfield. We tried to keep the blocking principles of the Single Wing. Simply, instead of just shoving a defending player away as most blocking is practiced now, our goal was to have the blocker stay welded to his opponent and sustain that move.

At 2 a.m. the night before the players were scheduled to report for the start of two-a-day practices we still hadn't made a final decision to make the change. Finally, Nelson said, "Let's not lose our guts; let's go with it. Let's go home and get a few hours sleep, and come back here and get ready to coach it tomorrow." And we did.

That was the beginning of the famous Winged-T offense. We used it successfully that season at the University of Maine. But the formation's popularity didn't take off until Nelson, accompanied by me as his line coach, moved to the University of Delaware the following season (1951).

Maine's new coaching brain trust took a season to get adjusted. We assumed that the four larger schools on our Yankee Conference schedule—the universities of Massachusetts, Rhode Island, New Hampshire and Connecticut—would be our biggest rivals. So we focused on those games and won the conference. We shrugged off the advice of the locals who kept telling us that success or failure at Maine was measured by games against traditional rivals we had never heard of—Bates, Bowdin and Colby—in what was called the State Series. We lost all three of those games in 1950. Former Yale coach Ducky Pond was at Bates; the coach at Bowdin was Adam Walsh, the center at Notre Dame when the legendary Four Horsemen played in the backfield. I can't recall who was at Colby. No matter. These guys taught us something about coaching.

*Ready for practice in hat and jacket as line coach of the University of Maine Black Bears*

We played only seven games, and I lobbied Dave to schedule eight or nine, as many other schools did. He was skeptical, pointing out that we didn't get paid any more for coaching eight or nine games, and if we lost, it would only put more pressure on what we were trying to accomplish.

Orono, the small town just north of Bangor where the Maine campus is located, had one thing in common with Hillsdale, Michigan: bitterly cold winters. Unable to find any other place that we could afford, Rena and I lived in student housing. The apartment units had been converted from World War II barracks. Our place had walls like cardboard and a space heater. We cooked on a kitchen range that had been converted from wood to oil. In those severe winters I remember walking 150 yards to an oil shack to get a refill for the heater. You'd take a breath, and your nostrils would stick together and immediately freeze.

When Dave Nelson was hiring me as his line coach at Maine he mentioned to Tad Wieman, the athletic director, that I had coached baseball at Hillsdale. Coincidentally, Maine's baseball coach had just left. The job was mine.

Most of our baseball practices that spring were held indoors. We had hitting cages for batting practice, and we ran bases and did other drills in a big fieldhouse. Occasionally, the snowplows would clear a parking lot, and I was able to take our players outside long enough to hit fly balls to the outfielders and infielders.

The solution, of course, would be a preseason trip to warmer climes. Many northern schools do that routinely to escape the snow and cold, but it was unheard-of for Maine baseball teams. I talked to Tad Wieman about it, but he said there was no money. I tried to raise some cash, with little success. Then I suggested staying at the Coast Guard Academy in New London, Connecticut, and playing some games in the Washington, D.C., area against schools like George Washington, Georgetown, and Hampden-Sydney, in Virginia.

One of our neighbors in student housing was Jed Brewster, the nephew of Maine senator Owen Brewster. Maybe the senator could use his influence to let my team stay at the academy in New London? He did precisely that and we used private automobiles to provide the transportation for Maine's first "southern" baseball trip.

We won the Yankee Conference championship that season, and I spent the summer coaching a team in a league sponsored by the Bangor newspaper and the Boston Braves. One of my star players was a young pitcher named Carlton Willey from Cherryfield, a town that still calls itself the blueberry capital of the world. Willey had an amazing fastball which caught the attention of the Braves. He played for them in Boston and Milwaukee, when the team moved there, then finished his major league career with the New York Mets.

A couple of important milestones came in 1950, one before and one after the first football season at Maine. Just before practices started in August, Cynthia Ruth Lude, our first daughter, was born in Bangor. We took her home to a modest rental house. It was small but it had a heat duct in the living room and a vent up in the master bedroom.

After the season, I attended my first American Football Coaches Association convention and the Coach of the Year dinner. Dave Nelson, Tad Wieman and I—plus our wives—drove to New York. I was dazzled. I had the chance to talk with Army coach Earl (Red) Blaik, who had six unbeaten seasons in seventeen years at the U.S. Military Academy; Bud Wilkinson of Oklahoma, Bobby Dodd of Georgia Tech, and many others. Those great coaches took time to share some of their expertise with newcomers like me. The Coach of the Year dinner was my first visit to the original Mama Leoni's restaurant. What a great time.

Fresh seafood, not too easy to find in Michigan, was readily available in Maine, and Rena and I enjoyed buying clams and lobsters straight from the sea. We would have picnics on the rocky shore. Most of the restaurants featured sandwiches they called lobster rolls. The bread resembled a hot dog bun, toasted on the outside, only it featured lobster instead of a frankfurter.

Meanwhile, I took graduate courses at Maine. One of my professors was Rome Rankin, the head basketball coach and a great storyteller. He helped me get involved in sports psychology. I created a test that measured the reaction times of football and baseball players and it proved to be a good coaching support. A few years later I finished my masters degree during the summer at Michigan State University.

One unforgettable character at Maine was the campus snowplow driver. The only name I knew him by was Sparky, but for some reason he got very attached to me. During a severe storm he called me aside. "Coach Lude, will you come with me to see my boss?" I asked what the problem was. He explained that he had worked completely around the clock in the snow and marked twenty-five hours on his time card. "But the boss wouldn't let me do that," he said. I asked, "Sparky, how did you figure those twenty-five hours in one day?" He explained patiently. "Well, I didn't stop for anything. I worked right through my lunch time and my dinner time, a half-hour for each, and that's an additional hour. It comes out to twenty-five hours." Sparky should have checked with the math department.

When Bill Murray took the head football coaching job at Duke, there was considerable speculation over whom Dr. John Perkins, the president at the University of Delaware, would hire as Murray's replacement. Perkins called the coach at his alma mater, Michigan, and Fritz Crisler recommended Dave Nelson. I was asked to go along as an assistant coach. Nelson also would serve as athletic director.

So in July 1951, Rena, Cynthia and I moved from Orono, Maine, to Newark, Delaware. We would end up spending eleven years there, using it as the stepping stone to what had become my ultimate goal: a head coaching job.

# 7

# THE DELAWARE YEARS—
# TRAVELING SALESMAN

◆ ◆ ◆

Forrest Evashevski, the Iowa coaching guru, wanted the Wing-T. Paul Dietzel of Louisiana State University couldn't wait to learn all of its intricacies. Ditto for Frank Broyles at Arkansas and Eddie Robinson at Grambling.

As the offensive system known as the Wing-T became a national phenomenon, my job as an assistant coach at the University of Delaware took me far beyond the campus in Newark, situated in northern Delaware near I-95, between Philadelphia and Baltimore.

Dave Nelson, my head coach, had created the Winged-T in 1950 at the University of Maine. The name was simplified to Wing-T as it became the offense of choice for many football teams across America. I taught the blocking schemes to our offensive linemen that first season and helped Dave perfect the system in future years after we moved to Delaware.

Evashevski played a major role in the wide recognition and acceptance of the Wing-T. One of the first coaches at a major school to employ the system, he gave it a huge boost by winning a national championship. Dave went to Iowa City and worked closely with his former University of Michigan teammate to teach the coaching staff and the Iowa players every detail of the offensive formation.

With Evashevski as co-author, Nelson produced a highly successful book, *Scoring Power with the Winged T Offense,* which became a bible for coaches at all levels who were switching to the new system. The book contained detailed diagrams and photographs to explain how the formation worked. I appreciate Coach Nelson's crediting me, along with his other assistant, Harold Westerman, as one who "helped originate the system."

As the offense became better known and more successful, I became one of the Wing-T offense's busiest advocates. I had the opportunity to speak at football clinics around the country, spreading the word among coaches, especially in the East and the South. I put on a clinic at the national convention of the American Football Coaches Association in Philadelphia. We had players in pads to demonstrate what we were teaching. I lectured at clinics in New York, Maryland, Tennessee, Kentucky, New Jersey, Louisiana, and Ohio.

I worked with Dietzel putting in the offense at LSU, spending hours with Carl Maddox, the LSU backfield coach, and Bill Peterson, the line coach. Peterson later became head coach at Florida State, and one of his assistants was Don James, later my head coach at Kent State and Washington. In Frank Broyles' first year as head coach at Arkansas, I helped him install the Wing-T, long before he became athletic director.

Peterson, who later was head coach of the Houston Oilers, called me when I was taking part in a clinic at Southern University in Baton Rouge. He wanted me to come to the LSU campus, in the same city, to help sort out the system's principles of line play and blocking. My schedule was tight, so I suggested he attend sessions that already were planned. He explained that because LSU had just been integrated it would not be appropriate for him to go to Southern U, an all-black school at the time.

I spent a few days helping the LSU staff install the Wing-T offense, and that job grew into a full-season exercise. Each week the offensive coaching staff would call me to go over their game plan and the defense they would be facing. After their scrimmage on Tuesday, I'd get a call Wednesday to advise them about any needed changes. On Thursday they'd put the game plan to bed.

Louisiana State went unbeaten that season and won the national championship. In his book, *The Wing-T and the Chinese Bandits*, Coach Paul Dietzel gave me credit in the forward for the success of the LSU offense.

Broyles, who became a lifetime friend as a coach and later athletic director, sounded frantic when he called Dave Nelson one spring day. He told Dave, "Look, my line coach, Dixie White, is ill. He has fluid on the lungs and can't coach at all in spring practice. Can I borrow Mike Lude for spring practice?" Dave said it was OK with him, if it was OK with me and as long as I had a good handle on my recruiting responsibilities.

So I said, "Fine. I'll be there before the week's out." That may be the only lend-lease deal in college football history.

I spent the next sixteen days in Fayetteville, Ark., and it was a great time. The center of that Arkansas team was Barry Switzer, who later coached Big Eight championship teams at Oklahoma. The coaching staff included Doug Dickey, later head coach at Florida and Tennessee and athletic director at Tennessee, as well as Jim McKenzie, who later coached at Oklahoma.

One of the genuine characters on the Arkansas staff was Wilson Matthews, a former drill instructor who had come through the prep ranks in Little Rock, Arkansas. We all worked well past midnight every night, installing the new offense. One night we had worked late and the coaches were getting weary of the long hours. Matthews got up and paced around the table.

Broyles spoke up. "Wilson, aren't you interested in what Mike is doing and what we'll be doing tomorrow in practice?" Matthews responded, "Yes sir, coach, I am. I know how important this is; I really do. But, Coach, my wife is fixing to have love made to her tonight and, if possible, I'd like to be there." After the laughs subsided, Broyles called it a night and sent us home.

Wilson was a colorful guy who loved the game. When a defender came through with a fierce hit he called it a slobberknocker. I borrowed the phrase and used it at Delaware and Colorado State University when I became head coach.

Dave Nelson was a brilliant, innovative football coach. He was able to take features of arguably the two most effective offensive systems of roughly a century of football—the Single Wing and the

T-formation—and create a hybrid, the Wing-T. With all the patience of an inventor, he tinkered and mixed different elements to improve the product. He took immense pride when the system produced successful teams.

At times Dave could be somewhat distant or seem preoccupied. He knew how critical

*Innovative Dave Nelson (right) credited Lude for helping him perfect the Wing-T offense as an assistant coach at Delaware*

recruiting was to the success of any college program, but it wasn't his favorite part of the job. Like most former running backs, he was more interested in the offensive side of the game than defense.

By contrast, I liked the recruiting experience, meeting athletes and their families and making the sale. I think I am a good salesman. And I loved defense, the total team aspect of that side of football. Perhaps that's why Dave and I were a good combination.

He could be demanding. He was patient but he wouldn't settle for an inferior performance. If you blundered you could expect to hear about it. Although I know how much he appreciated what every person on his staff did for the program, he rarely handed out praise.

Harold (Tubby) Raymond, who joined the Delaware staff in 1954, was one of our neighbors in the Brookside area of Newark, and we often carpooled to work. During those drives Tubby would ask me, "Mike, does Dave like me?" or "Does he like the job I'm doing?"

I always had the same response. "Well, Tubby, has Dave ever told you that he doesn't like you or doesn't like what you're doing?" He said no, that wasn't the case. I said, "I have worked for Dave since 1947, and he has never told me that he liked me or liked what I was doing. He told me I had enthusiasm and not to ever lose that enthusiasm." But Dave Nelson is one of those people who, if you did a great job for him, he would seldom give you a compliment. You would know, however, if you screwed up.

Obviously, he liked Tubby because when he retired from coaching Dave picked Tubby as his successor as head coach and Tubby lasted for thirty-six years.

Irv Wisniewski, another former Michigan player, joined the staff in 1952 as end coach, and he was a very positive contributor to the development of the Wing-T. So was Ed Maley. Both "Whiz" and Maley retired at Delaware.

While Nelson was a fierce competitor, he was not without mercy when an opponent was outclassed. I remember a game in 1959 against Temple when we were six or seven touchdowns ahead. I was upstairs in the press box when Dave got me on the phone and said, "Mike, what do you think about sending the manager over to their coach to ask if we could keep the clock running, with no timeouts for incomplete passes or out-of-bounds plays?" I agreed it would be a good idea. So he sent the manager to the visiting bench and he returned quickly. "What did he say?" I asked Dave. "The coach said please." And that's the way it ended.

High school coaches were joining the parade to the Wing-T. One day a short, plump man, a coach in Eunice, Louisiana, walked into my office, wanting to learn about the system. Faize Mahfouz became a close friend. I spoke at his clinics in Eunice and in New

Iberia when he moved there and at meetings of the Louisiana State Coaches Association.

Those contacts were helpful in one of my other responsibilities at Delaware, running our recruiting efforts. In those years I had the privilege of selling our football program to hundreds of players, and so many of them have kept in touch with me over the years.

My first Delaware recruit was Jimmy Flynn, a running back I went after when I was still at Maine. His coach at Central Catholic High School in Pittsburgh was Nick Skorich, a former professional player with the Steelers and a classmate of mine in graduate school at Michigan State University. When the Maine coaching staff departed for Delaware, Jimmy called me and said, "What happens to me?" I told him he was obligated to stay at Maine. He replied, "Well, Coach Skorich said that wherever Coach Lude goes, I go too." He got a release from Maine and became an outstanding tailback and a sprinter at Delaware.

My first quarterback recruit was Don Miller from Prospect Park (Pennsylvania) High School, who was a perfect fit for the system we used at Delaware. Besides being a talented passer, he was a standout ball handler whose deception in handing off the ball to his running backs perplexed rival defenses.

I learned about selling our program to parents as well as the athletes. Ronnie McCoy of Smyrna was a good prospect whose father was a state police captain. He took me goose hunting about 4:30 a.m. one day, and after bagging several geese we returned to the McCoy home for breakfast. The doorbell rang and it was a rival recruiter, Mike Cooley, an assistant coach at Lehigh. I went out to the door and grinned: "Coach, you just gotta get up early in the morning in this game. Ronnie has decided to become a Fightin' Blue Hen and be with us at Delaware."

That nickname often triggered snide comments from our opponents and snickers from outsiders who thought it lacked the tough, aggressive image normally associated with such labels. During the Revolutionary War, troops from the Delaware colony carried fighting cocks, and between battles they'd match the birds in deadly combat. The blue hen was considered the most ferocious strain of these cocks. That historical link led to the university's nickname.

In the early 1950s I was approached at a football clinic in Atlantic City by a young coach named Tommy Phillips at Struthers High School in Ohio. He asked if he could visit our spring practice. Tommy came back for about six years. He ended up staying at our house and babysat our kids. He developed a top quarterback named John Mackovic when he coached at Barberton. Phillips predicted that Mackovic one day would be an outstanding head football coach. I tried to recruit him but he picked Wake Forest. John went on to coach at his alma mater, then Illinois, University of Texas and more recently the University of Arizona. Phillips later was an assistant when I was AD at Kent State where he had a heart attack. He was concerned I wasn't going to keep him on staff. I told him that as long as I had a job, there would be a place for him at Kent State.

Delaware had become a comfortable situation, in my job and with my family. After a year, Rena and I bought our first home, three bedrooms with one bath and a carport, located in a tract of

*Mike and Rena with daughters (left to right) Cynthia, Jill and Janann and dog Ginger at Delaware in 1961*

new houses on the outskirts of Newark. The price was $9,900. Janann, our second daughter, was born November 5, 1953, followed by Jill, January 31, 1956. Three years later we moved into a two-story colonial in the Fairfield Crest area. Hard work and success were starting to pay dividends.

It took four days and overcoming the hazards of a fierce snowstorm before I made it to the hospital to see Janann for the first time. It started snowing the night she was born, and all the roads were impossible to navigate. I walked three miles to get to the office, and our weekend game was eventually called off because all the trains were shut down.

Those Delaware teams rarely lost, and I guess I can take the heat for one of those defeats, a 24-20 setback against West Chester in 1952. On the day of the game Dave Nelson was involved in a neighborhood automobile mishap. Dave was shaken by the incident, and I was delegated to be the acting head coach that night. Late in the game, with Delaware leading, 20-17, the West Chester tailback ran off tackle on fourth down. He fumbled the ball, and it went forward into the end zone, where an end recovered. It was an illegal forward fumble—I'm certain the play was designed that way by coach Glenn Killinger—but the officials didn't make the call. So we ended up losing.

In my recruiting responsibilities I worked with the college's director of admissions and served on the student personnel committee that looked at discipline situations. I was also involved in setting up a scholarship program for athletes that put me in touch with some of the Delaware supporters and members of the board of trustees. One of these was Bob Carpenter, son of a prominent and affluent family. As a summer job I tutored his son, Ruly (R. R. M. Carpenter III), on the fundamentals of football.

Ruly was a solid high school player and picked Yale for college. After his freshman year, Bob called me and said Ruly was disenchanted and wanted to quit Yale. It was during two-a-day practices. He didn't like the coaches and football wasn't fun. He was ready to transfer to Delaware. I told Ruly if he came to Delaware the coaches would be just as tough, just as demanding, and that he wouldn't like me, either. "Go back, suck it up, hang with it, and you'll be OK," was my message. Ruly went back, played four years, and graduated from Yale as the team captain. He later became a Delaware trustee.

Bob Carpenter gave me two jobs with the Philadelphia Phillies, the baseball team he owned at the time. One summer I scouted the Alabama-Florida League, bouncing between the six small towns of Panama City, Fort Walton Beach, Pensacola, Montgomery, Selma, and Dotham. Later I set up a group called Friends of the Phillies, which was basically made up of high school coaches. I organized a network of scouts in surrounding states—Delaware, New Jersey, New York, Pennsylvania, Ohio, Maryland, and Virginia—to single out baseball prospects in those areas.

When a head coach starts getting attention as Dave Nelson did at Delaware, his assistants normally become targets of athletic directors looking for would-be head coaches. It was an exhilarating experience.

At one point I was offered the Bucknell job, but Nelson pointed out that I'd be facing Delaware every year. I wasn't sure I wanted that. Dave said, be patient; other jobs would come along. Later he recommended me for the Colgate job, but they picked someone else. I was interviewed for the University of Massachusetts job, but the salary was less than I was making as an assistant. Tulane pushed hard to bring me in as an assistant, and New Orleans was an attractive lure. But I wanted my own team.

In the late 1950s, at the national coaches' convention in Cincinnati, Tad Wieman, the AD at Maine when I was there, wanted me to come to Denver University as his head coach. Let's talk some more tomorrow, he said. I was starting to get excited. That same night, the school president at Denver made the decision to drop football. That's how fast job offers can disappear.

After the 1961 football season, Colorado State fired Tuffy Mullison. In his search for Mullison's replacement, Bob Davis, the CSU athletic director, asked Wieman if he had any suggestions. Tad related the story of how he had offered me the job at Denver University before the president dropped the football program. Davis liked the idea of hiring me, and I was headed for Fort Collins and my first job as a head coach.

# 8
## FROM 0 AND 26
## TO RESPECTABILITY

◆ ◆ ◆

My head coaching career started off like a Boeing jetliner taxiing halfway to San Francisco before it finally got off the ground.

By the start of my second season I had achieved the distinction of coaching the college football team with the longest current losing streak in the country—twenty-six games without success. Yes, it was something I'd just as soon forget, and, no, it was not a situation I ever could have imagined when I became the head coach at Colorado State University.

The squad I inherited at Fort Collins in 1962 had been drubbed, thumped, and hammered for sixteen consecutive defeats before I arrived. I tacked ten more defeats onto the streak in my rookie head coaching season (1961) before we found a team we could beat.

Finally, on a warm September night in Stockton, California, I reached that milestone first victory as a head coach, when Colorado State defeated University of the Pacific, 20-0.

Losing was not something I found easy to tolerate. As a player and an assistant coach at three different universities all of the teams had been successful. Even back in high school in Vicksburg, Michigan, we won most of our games. Going out and getting beat up for ten consecutive Saturdays was difficult to stomach. For the first time I could identify with what other coaches who were mired in losing streaks—even two or three games—had felt when they said they didn't think they'd ever win again. In my case, since my record was 0-10 I kind of wondered if I'd ever win, period.

What perplexed me was how my team reacted when the losing streak ended. If there was any sort of a big celebration or emotional expression—even relief—it wasn't apparent in our locker room in Stockton. It wasn't what I had expected.

We had just put an end to football's most enduring period of disgrace, so where's the whooping and hollering?

I had not been back in my hotel room long when I got a call from one of the players. He said a teammate was ill and asked me to come downstairs to the lobby to help figure out what to do. One of our major boosters, Stan Williams, was there, and we speculated that there had been some celebrating and the "sick" player was not ill at all.

When I got off the elevator, I was surprised to see the whole team waiting, wearing big grins. They grabbed me and pitched me into the hotel swimming pool, clothes and all. It was the kind of wet celebration I preferred for my athletes. Yes, they *were* excited. Some had been involved from the start of that lengthy string of setbacks. They were overdue for something other than heartbreak and head hanging.

Our next-door neighbor in Fort Collins, Ralph Kotich, and several of his buddies were so encouraged by the victory they decided to sneak a flask of booze into the home games and take a swig every time Colorado State scored a touchdown. This tradition would begin the next week against the Air Force Academy.

Unfortunately, Air Force whipped us, 69-0. Ralph told me the next day: "We gave up on you and decided to take a drink every time Air Force scored. We were feeling no pain."

In that same game I found out what it feels like to have somebody run up the score. I lost a lot of respect for Ben Martin, the Air

Force coach. Dominating us all afternoon wasn't enough for the Falcons. They not only scored on the final play of the game, they elected to go for a two-point conversion after time had run out.

Homer Smith, one of their assistants, tried to explain to me later in the dressing room that Martin was under pressure and "we needed to do something to maybe help him save his job." I responded, "What about Mike Lude? What about his job?" In the emotion of the loss I told Homer, "Some day this will come back to you." And it did.

I had accepted the offer to be Colorado State's head coach in December 1961 after a superb apprenticeship with Dave Nelson at three schools. When I arrived in Fort Collins, a town of about 25,000 (it's about four times that size now) I was cautious but enthusiastic. In fact, it didn't take long for the Denver media to nickname me Mr. Enthusiasm.

The first challenge of taking over a football program where the previous coach was fired is finding the cause of the problem. That wasn't too difficult for me at CSU. Without demeaning the character or willingness of the talent of the squad, it was obvious too many of our players were lacking the ability to play at this level.

After getting a chance to assess the talent of the football players in spring practice, I had no doubts that we needed better athletes if we were going to turn the CSU program around. The recruiting done by my predecessors had fallen way down, and we needed a major overhaul. We had to upgrade the talent pool.

I asked two former Delaware players, quarterback Don Miller and linebacker Jim Garvin, to help us in spring drills, and they were so unimpressed they decided not to stick around. Miller later became a successful head coach at Trinity College. Garvin took one look at the players and decided to attend law school. He soon became a successful attorney in Newark, Delaware. My top assistants would be Lou Baker, who had worked as an assistant at Illinois, as offensive coach; Paul Lanham, the frosh coach at

Dayton, as the ends coach; and Bill Craver, a former Delaware line-man, as the line coach. I retained Joe Cribari from the former staff as freshman coach.

The year before I was hired at Colorado State the team had lost all ten games, scoring just 74 points and giving up 249 points. I couldn't imagine we could be any worse than that. Wrong. We also went 0-10, scored 66 points and gave up 269. We were shut out three times, and in only two games did we score more than a single touchdown.

In our next-to-last game against Oregon State we were big underdogs. The night before the game, Tommy Prothro, the OSU coach, stopped by our hotel with a rather unusual message. He said, "Mike, I've looked at the films and you have a [bleep] football team. We have a chance tomorrow of breaking a record with Terry Baker, our Heisman Trophy candidate, and his receiver, Vern Burke. So if I leave them in the game for a while longer than nor-mal you will understand we're not just trying to run up the score." I said I understood that the contract says the game goes sixty min-utes and it doesn't have anything to do with the score.

At halftime, we were leading, 14-13. Going up the ramp, Prothro put his arm around me and said, "You little rascal, you're after my butt, aren't you?" I said, "Well, it's just a football game, Tommy, sixty minutes." We couldn't hold on and lost, 25-14, but it was a good game and a good experience.

So we went into the final game of the season with a 0-9 record. No wonder the only fans who showed up in our ancient stadium were the parents of the players and a few students and friends. That venue held only about 14,000, but it still seemed empty. The com-petition was a University of Montana team that was about as bad as we were. Its coach was a former Colorado star, Ray Jenkins, whose pride was the kicking game.

We took a 7-0 lead, but just before halftime Montana scored and made a two-point conversion for the lead, 8-7. We scored again and elected to go for two, and we made it for a 15-8 edge.

Late in the game Montana punted out of bounds on our one-yard line and we took over. I instructed our quarterback, Billy Wrenn, a senior from Sherman, Texas, to go for a QB sneak, cover the ball so he wouldn't lose it, and set up a punt. As fate would have it, the ball popped loose and Montana recovered. They scored and went for a two-point conversion and a 16-15 victory. Our losing streak was unbroken.

The bitter residue of that loss lasted through the long, long off-season.

Nobody on our staff was idle that winter. The key to improving this team was to get better players, which meant a dramatic upgrade in recruiting. In some cases it meant going head-to-head with bigger, better-known schools. This task was less intimidating to me than it might be to many young coaches (I was thirty-nine when hired by Colorado State). I had developed a lot of contacts with high school coaches, first as the Delaware recruiting coordinator and also teaching our Wing-T offense at clinics around the country.

One of those contacts was a coach in Tennessee named Esau Lathon. Esau coached at an all-black high school. Later he became one of the first blacks to coach an integrated school in that state. He told me about a great running prospect named Oscar Reed and said he would help me recruit him for Colorado State.

In that era it was uncomfortable—sometimes dangerous—in many parts of the South for blacks to ride in the same car with whites. Anti-integration forces were on the loose, administering their own form of justice through threats, intimidation, and worse. When Esau picked me up at the airport, he told me, "You sit in the back because I've got to pretend I'm your driver." I protested but he insisted. "You just don't understand what's going on down here." The same sort of discrimination still took place in most restaurants, and when we stopped for lunch I'd go in and ask if they served black people. Usually, the answer was no. So we'd go to the black section of town and eat a great meal. Esau and I became good friends. His youngest son, Gerald, eventually enrolled at the University of Washington and graduated. I was proud to have been his mentor.

One of the traditions at Oscar Reed's high school was to allow unusually talented running backs to wear gold-colored football shoes. So Oscar's nickname was Golden Shoes Reed. When he rambled they twinkled.

There was plenty of competition to recruit Reed, and one of the coaches who made a strong pitch was Tommy Prothro. The Oregon State coach had played football at Duke but had grown up in Tennessee and still had connections there. Thanks to Esau Lathon's introduction, I convinced Oscar's mother that we would look out for her son's best interests at Colorado State. One of our boosters, Norman Cousins, helped Oscar get a summer job in Denver, paving the way for him to become one of our first great players.

Oscar Reed became a member of the CSU Hall of Fame after setting numerous school rushing records. Later he played in the Super Bowl with the Minnesota Vikings.

Our recruiting work was starting to pay off. By the third season we had become competitive with any of the teams on our schedule. For example, one year after that 69-0 whipping by Air Force, we gave them a close game, 14-6, in 1963.

The final game of that season was played in Hawaii, and we approached the trip as a special treat for our players. We won but only after getting a taste of the partisan officiating that had been inflicted on visiting teams for many years. Late in the game we had a one-touchdown lead. Deep in Hawaii territory, we ran a quarterback sneak into the end zone. But the ball popped loose, and Larry French, our offensive guard, recovered for an apparent touchdown.

The officials huddled and took the ball out to the twenty-yard line and pointed the other way: the referee signaled Hawaii's ball, no score. I called the referee over to the sideline. "We scored," I said. He said, "No, there was a fumble." I said, "There was a fumble, and the ball was loose in the end zone, yes or no?" He said yes.

I asked, "Who recovered it?" He answered with the number on Larry's jersey. I said, "That's our man, white jersey. He recovered the fumble in the end zone, and by rule that's a touchdown for Colorado State."

The referee looked at the other officials and stood there, mute. Finally, after a considerable delay, he stepped close to me, put a finger on my chest and said: "Coach, that may be, but that's not the way we play here in Honolulu." Despite that bad call we finally stopped them and wrapped up the victory.

One of the hardest things for me at CSU was firing an assistant coach. But after three seasons as Colorado State's head coach I decided Lou Baker, the backfield coach, wasn't the man for that job. Other staff members had to step in to handle some of his responsibilities and it distracted all of us. What concerned me was Baker's wife and children. I had a long chat about the situation with my minister, Bill Hagge. Then I went back to my office, called Baker over and told him he was out. He was bitter, which is understandable; in reorganizing I made Paul Lanham backfield coach, and things went a lot smoother.

One of the true free spirits ever to don a Colorado State uniform was an early recruit. He later became famous, but not as an athlete. John Amos had been recommended by Tommy Dean, a former Bucknell quarterback who was coaching in East Orange, New Jersey. He touted Amos as a fullback who was "a great physical specimen."

Amos had fun skirting most of the rules of our program and the university. One time he was walking across the intersection near the student center and a car pulled up close. John said, "You shouldn't be here," and put his fist through the side window.

Later he "borrowed" a chair from the student union and put it in his room. I had to intercede when he was threatened with serious disciplinary action. I said, "John, the police say you stole a chair." He said, "No, I did not steal a chair; I borrowed it from the student union and put it in another university building—in my dorm room."

During spring practice of John's senior year, I got a call from the Boulder police. "Coach Lude, I think we have one of your football players in jail. He's accused of stealing a motor scooter and riding it to Boulder to visit friends."

I asked who the player was. They said John Amos. I responded, "John who? I don't have a football player by that name. I guess he'll have to stay in jail."

This happy-go-lucky guy was a talented stand-up comedian. His fame has stretched far beyond college football. John Amos became a celebrated writer and actor. He was nominated for an Emmy in the role of Kunta Kinte in Alex Haley's *Roots* and has won plaudits for his work on the stage, in movies and in television.

One of his numerous movies featured a college coach with whom he had constant problems. He insisted the coach be called Milo. I felt honored.

With our football talent pool improving steadily, the program was on the rise. We no longer were getting outmanned and out-classed. It was the 1966 team that finished with the best record in my eight seasons at CSU. We were one win short of a bowl bid.

Led by the running of Oscar Reed, that team won seven games—including a major upset over tenth-ranked Wyoming. We had been saving a trick play for the Cowboys, something Paul Lanham had picked up from a high school coach in Texas. Here's how the play went: We would send a flanker wide left, dropping off two to three yards. The quarterback would throw the ball into the ground, bouncing it into the hands of the receiver. The rival defenders, thinking the play was an incomplete pass, relaxed. Meanwhile, our tight end would run a post pattern and become the target for the flanker-turned-passer. We called it the Wyoming Special.

Because the original pass was backward—and we made sure to tell the officials in advance what we were doing—the ball was live. The first time we tried the play our quarterback, Bobby Wolfe, threw way over the head of flanker Larry Jackson. I called the play again. This time it worked. As Wyoming's defenders were walking back to the line of scrimmage, Tom Pack took Jackson's looping pass and walked into the end zone, good for a 9-7 lead. We swapped field goals in the second half and held on for a 12-10 victory, Wyoming's only loss of the year.

The victory moved Colorado State into the top twenty of the weekly college football rankings.

Larry Berliffi, the Wyoming broadcaster and a writer for the paper in Cheyenne, called me unethical and a lot of other not-so-nice things. For us it was a satisfying win, and the bounce pass play has become part of CSU football legend. I still receive an occasional call from the media wanting me to recreate the details of that Wyoming Special bounce pass play.

As we stretched our 1966 winning streak to five, bowl game scouts started showing up and a post-season invitation was within reach. We were 6-2 with two games remaining, but I

*Walking the sidelines as head coach at Colorado State; The 1966 team climbed into the top 20 in national polls after beating Wyoming*

could sense a letdown. When we went on the road to play Wichita State, a team that was having a terrible season, there was no focus. No matter what I said, our players seemed much more interested in a group of young women who were still hanging around our hotel after attending a rock concert in the Wichita stadium a day or so earlier. My fears were justified. Wichita State took a big lead, and by the time our kids woke up it was too late and we lost 37-23. Our bowl hopes were shattered, despite a solid victory a week later over Iowa State, 34-10.

We stayed home during the bowl season, but I was appreciative when United Press International picked me as Colorado Sportsman of the Year.

The success we had in the 1966 season actually backfired on the football program. Jim Williams, who had become the third of four athletic directors I would work for at Colorado State, called me into his office and announced: "Now that you've got this program turned around, I'm going to move twelve scholarships from the football allotment and give six to men's gymnastics and six to men's swimming." He said he had discussed the move with the university's executive branch and school officials agreed.

I was stunned. "You can't sustain a program by diluting it," I protested. "You can destroy a program much faster than you can improve it."

It didn't take long for my words to come true. The program I thought we had moving in the right direction was taking a turn backward. Depth is critical to every college program and that's where the loss of those scholarships hurt. In 1967, '68 and '69 we had mediocre records because we didn't have the resources. My rebuilding effort started to crumble with the retirement of Dr. William Morgan as CSU president. Supported by VP for business and finance, Joe Whaley, Dr. Morgan pushed for new athletic facilities, first a basketball arena and then a football stadium, a 30,000-seat facility that opened in 1968. It helped the school get an invitation to join the Western Athletic Conference.

The athletic director who hired me, Bob Davis, died of cancer after I'd been there about three years. Next came an acting AD, former swimming coach Tommy Tompkins. In my opinion Tompkins didn't know if the football was stuffed or pumped, oblong or round. Yet he wanted to meet with me weekly to go over offensive and defensive game plans. My coaching staff teased me and laughed about those meetings to get his suggestions and final approval of the game plan. To them and to me it was a joke and a waste of time, but I listened, nodded, and then did just what we had planned.

Next came Williams, who had been the Colorado State basketball coach and a good one, but he left a lot to be desired as athletic director.

Perry Moore, who became AD in the summer of 1968, had been an assistant at a strong football school, the University of Florida. Had he replaced Bob Davis things might have been a lot different. Perry liked to stick a cigar in his mouth and give the impression of being important. He could be abrasive with some media people, and I can remember him getting into an argument with a sports writer from New Mexico that almost came to blows.

The spring before what would be my final football season was marked by the appointment of a new president, Dr. A. R. Chamberlain, Morgan's executive vice president. Chamberlain was described in newspaper stories as an avid sports booster and reportedly was seen often at practices and various sports events on campus. I never remember seeing him at one of our football workouts. I do remember a conversation I had when I pleaded for more resources for the football program.

He looked me in the eye and said bluntly: "Mike, let me tell you something. I would not go across the street to see an intercollegiate athletic contest if it were not for the fact it was politically expedient for me to do so." This guy was no friend of the football team or the athletic program.

With Oscar Reed gone we needed a superstar tailback in our offense, and we found the perfect replacement in Plainview, Texas. His name was Lawrence McCutcheon, but there was nothing plain about him. Paul Lanham, who had developed some good recruiting contacts in football-rich Texas, took me to visit the McCutcheon family and his high school.

Oklahoma and most of the other major Southwest football powers were anxious to get a commitment from McCutcheon. But Paul's close relationship with the school officials gave Colorado State the inside track. Still, the Sooners wouldn't give up until he was committed and on our campus. It didn't take him long to make an impact.

The first time he took a handoff for the Rams, McCutcheon dashed eighty yards for a touchdown. It was a great start of a great career. He smashed Reed's single-game rushing record in his second game, piling up 213 yards on 13 carries. That season he set a Western Athletic Conference record for most rushing yards by a sophomore (freshmen didn't play on the varsity in those days). He ran for 797 yards and ten touchdowns despite missing the final two games with a wrist and hand injury.

We had high hopes that Lawrence would play against a good Arizona State team in Tempe in our next-to-last game in 1969. He made the trip and his hand was much better. The team doctor asked Lawrence to do some fingertip pushups and asked if it hurt. Being an honest person, he said, "yes." The doctor said, "Sorry, he can't play."

With those words, team morale went from very good to very bad, and the result was a rout. It was a disaster, a record loss, 79-7.

McCutcheon was a superb running back and an outstanding young man, a tough runner and a great person to coach. Lawrence had a fine career at Colorado State and went on to stardom with the Los Angeles Rams of the National Football League. My only regret was having had only one season as his head coach. After McCutcheon's first varsity season my contract was not renewed.

In our final game against New Mexico State we had a 20-14 lead late in the game. But with 1:36 remaining, they scored and kicked the extra point for a 21-20 victory. It was our third loss that year in which we were beaten at the wire. We lost to Brigham Young 22-20 on a 54-yard field goal with fifteen seconds left. Texas-El Paso beat us in the last sixteen seconds, 17-16 on a 38-yard field goal.

An Associated Press story summed up my last CSU season: "Four points and 127 seconds meant the difference between Colorado State University's four-win, six-loss football record last season and what might have been seven and three." It would have been extremely hard to justify not giving me a new contract if we had gone 7-3, especially when we were picked to finish near the bottom of the conference going into the season.

During that final year my secretary, Mary Dalton, came into the staff room one morning, extremely upset. She had just received a phone call from someone saying he represented the Black Panthers and that they were going to bomb my house that night.

The Colorado State campus had been having racial unrest, and the Panthers had been active. They had staged several demonstrations, but I felt our football program had made considerable progress. We had numerous black athletes and a couple of black assistant coaches—Jim Hillyer, a former Lubbock, Texas, high school veteran, and Al Lavan, our former defensive back and place kicker, who moved on to coach at many big-school programs.

I told Mary not to worry, that most of these calls were harmless threats. I told my staff what was going on, though, and because I had a speaking engagement that night out of town, Hillyer volunteered to stay with my family. We notified the police and they put surveillance on our home, but nothing happened.

In those eight years in Fort Collins, I continued to be active in the Fellowship of Christian Athletes. I served on the group's board for ten years and got to know so many class individuals, including Bill Bradley, basketball star turned senator; Steve Spurrier, football coach; Homer Rice, coach and athletic director at several colleges and the Cincinnati Bengals; Don Moomaw, UCLA football great and minister; Tom Landry of the Dallas Cowboys; Dr. Louis Evans, minister of the popular Hollywood Presbyterian Church; Gary Demerest, a California-Berkeley baseball player and Presbyterian minister; and FCA staff leaders Leroy King and Bill Krisher and many others.

It didn't save my job, but a newspaper editorial about my departure from Colorado State made me feel a little better. The piece pointed out how I had inherited "one of the saddest messes in college football . . . a hapless team to play some nationally known competitors." Pointing a finger at school officials, the editorial said:

"But Colorado State officials never quite gave Mike Lude enough to work with. The university's desire to be big-time in athletics outstripped its budget. Embarrassment has been the result. As the symbol of CSU's football defeats, Coach Mike Lude is the natural scapegoat; but CSU is not without fault for needing a scapegoat. In essence, Lude is taking the rap for the State Board of Agriculture [board of trustees], the CSU administration and athletic director. Collectively, they made too many athletic financial misjudgments.

"Mike Lude took the CSU football program over one of the roughest stretches of its long road and many of us will remember him as a good coach and a fine person."

Nice words but I had a family to support. I helped my assistants find jobs—Clarence Daniel and Larry French at Houston, Bill Hickey at his alma mater, Notre Dame, Paul Lanham at Arkansas, Urban Bowman, Joe Cribgari and Jersey Jermier remained at CSU. Then I started thinking about my future.

One job option had come from Max Moore, a sponsor of my weekly television show and a Colorado State booster. He told me if I ever got tired of coaching I could go into real estate management with his Denver-area firm. The offer was still good, and it looked better than my coaching future. I passed the state exam after a crash course in real estate law, and the first month on the job I made more than I'd ever earned in two months of football (the CSU salary was $18,000 plus five grand more for the TV show).

Meanwhile, Lou Sabin, the Denver Broncos' head coach and general manager, offered me a temporary job scouting college spring practices and evaluating personnel.

During a scouting visit to the College of William and Mary in Virginia, Lou Holtz, a longtime friend and the head football coach, suggested I might be interested in becoming the athletic director at his alma mater, Kent State University in Ohio. The president is a friend, Lou said.

At Lou's suggestion I made the call. It led to a career change that took me far beyond the coaching lines.

# 9

# KENT STATE: REBUILDING IN THE AFTERMATH OF TRAGEDY

◆ ◆ ◆

I gawked at the TV screen in my motel room in Iowa City with an eerie feeling, wanting to make sure I had heard the name of the college correctly.

These were the turbulent times of 1970, perhaps more turbulent for me because for the first time in twenty-four years I didn't have a coaching job. That's why I took a temporary scouting assignment with the Denver Broncos and that's how I ended up in Iowa, having just had a glass of wine and an enjoyable dinner with University of Iowa football coach Ray Nagel.

Every television channel that night—May 4—was reporting in dramatic detail a tragic incident that had taken place on the campus of Kent State University in Kent, Ohio, about thirty miles southeast of Cleveland. A student demonstration protesting a recent speech by President Richard Nixon had been transformed into tragedy when National Guardsmen turned their guns on the protesters. Four students were dead and nine others were injured.

Did they really say Kent State? I squinted at the small screen, seeking more confirmation. You see, it was Kent State University where, earlier that spring, I had applied for the job of athletic director. I was still hoping to hear from school officials when the sound of gunshots echoed across the campus.

Viewing the television coverage of what would be remembered years later as the Kent State massacre totally flattened my enthusiasm for working there. My immediate thought: I have no idea if I'll ever hear again from Kent State University, but if I do I'll have an answer in two letters:

N-O.

When the question finally came, though, some five months later, the answer was:

Y-E-S.

Since losing my first—and last—head coaching job, at Colorado State University after the 1969 season, I had been selling real estate. I enjoyed the scouting job with Denver, but it was nothing permanent. During separate stops to visit with two confidantes and coaching colleagues, Lou Holtz and Steve Sebo, I became convinced I should look for work as an athletic director.

When I conversed with Holtz at William and Mary he mentioned the Kent State job. Better known later in his career as the coach at Arkansas, Minnesota, Notre Dame, and, more recently, South Carolina, Lou is a Kent State graduate and has close ties there. He offered to recommend me to the college's president.

Sebo, the athletic director at the University of Virginia, also urged me to apply. He thought Kent State would be a good place for me to start if I wanted to shift gears from coaching to the administration level.

Summer came. I was selling real estate. I finally got a response to my job application, a phone call in June from Dr. Tom Marshall, the Kent State faculty representative and an English professor. He asked if I'd be interested in coming to Kent for an interview, adding: "We've had a few problems here, as you may know."

I said something like, "Yes, you have."

What an understatement.

I told him, yes, I would be interested in interviewing, and I made the trip to the Ohio campus. I met with their selection committee, and they made me feel right at home. I conferred for two hours with Dr. Robert White, the president, and we got along famously. I answered all their questions, and by now I had made up my mind that I really wanted the job. But no offer came.

I waited. I waited some more. The longer I waited the more bored I got selling real estate. I'd come home and my wife, Rena, would ask me how things were going and I'd say, "Just great, really terrific, everything's fine." And she would say, "Mike Lude, I've lived with you a long time. You're not happy." And after the unexpected death of Max Moore, the Denver realtor who had hired me after I lost the Colorado State coaching job, I knew real estate was not for me.

Fall came. Football season was under way. And I was having withdrawal pains being away from the work I had thrived on from the day in 1947 when I joined the football coaching staff at Hillsdale College. On a Tuesday in late October 1970, Dr. White, the Kent State president, finally called. His words were simple, but they meant a lot to an unemployed football coach who had one daughter in college and two more in the wings.

"Mike, we would like to have you as our athletic director," Dr. White said. My response was equally brief: "Dr. White, you just hired an athletic director."

I had accepted without even knowing how much the job would pay. It appeared that Dr. White wasn't certain, either, because before we finished talking he asked me: "Uh, Mike, when you were here for an interview and we talked about the job last July, what did I tell you the pay would be?"

As I recall he had proposed a range. I said the low number wasn't nearly enough and that I had hoped to get more than the high. He agreed to give me the high and offered to try to help me "in a lot of other ways."

After working out the logistics of travel, I packed my bag and hopped a plane to Cleveland, then drove to Kent, a pleasant city of about 30,000 in northern Ohio. I was anxious to get started on my first job in a new career. I was back in sports and still at the college level but I had a whole new range of responsibilities.

The first day on the job, I discovered I didn't have an office. My hiring was to be the beginning of a reorganization that would separate the athletic program from the physical education department. President White found temporary space for me across the hall from his office, and the location worked to my advantage. It sent a strong message to the campus, especially administrators and faculty, that the hiring of a separate AD was important enough to station me close to the seat of power.

I wasn't even settled in when we had our first of many informal chats. It was the start of a relationship in which Dr. White became my mentor, my adviser, and my friend.

"Mike," he said, "we've made fifty years of poor decisions here about the administration of intercollegiate athletics. I want you to take this and run with it. Put it together and fashion a department that you and I will be proud of. We don't have a lot of resources [that sounded a lot like what I had heard at Colorado State], but I have a lot of desire to help you be successful."

And I had a lot to learn.

Dr. White was not on the campus during the infamous Kent State shootings back in May; he was on a trip to Iowa at the time. But he was taking a lot of criticism over the incident, and a lot of questions were being asked about what had caused the tragedy. Actually, the governor had made the decision to send in the National Guard, and when the Guardsmen felt threatened they panicked.

The mood on the campus that first year was hardly festive. The incident cast a long shadow at Kent State, and the date, May 4, 1970, remained etched as clearly as Dec. 7, 1941, or 9/11/01 for those who were there at the time.

The atmosphere was not like any I had experienced at the schools where I had coached earlier in my career. The place was depressed and subdued, almost morbid. It seemed to lack a soul.

My approach with Dr. White was that we must try to give the students something to get excited about besides Vietnam, Cambodia, ROTC, and other issues that left such indelible scars.

I wanted to create a chance for those on campus to explode— a healthy psychological explosion about cheering for the football team or the basketball team, maybe even something that they didn't want to be a part of. It took a while but they did. It was a tough sell, you bet, and I never once thought it would be easy. But you get the direction and you keep going with it.

At the press conference when I was introduced as the new AD, I made a strong effort to be enthusiastic and optimistic—traits that have been ingrained in me in every job I have held. This was especially important in the Kent State situation. In newspaper articles I've been called Mr. Enthusiasm and the Good Humor Man because of my personality. And I was smart enough to keep from shooting my mouth off about possible solutions of problems I didn't yet know existed.

One of the top faculty leaders I apparently had made an impression on was Dr. Gerald (Jug) Ridinger, chairman of the search committee that helped pick me as AD. Ridinger, who later became the Kent State faculty representative, told me I was the only person interviewed who also interviewed the committee. And the selection group seemed to be impressed by the host of my friends who called to volunteer recommendations. They included some well-known names in the ranks of collegiate football: Frank Broyles, Paul Dietzel, Dave Nelson, Bump Elliott, Wiles Hallock, Lou Holtz, Joe Paterno, Lou Sabin, Biggie Munn, Johnny Majors, and Bill Murray, former Duke coach who was executive director of the American Football Coaches Association.

I joked later that the reason they recommended me was they just wanted to get me out of the coaching profession.

I spent a lot of time in the early weeks with Carl Erickson, dean of the PE department, who had run the athletic department, picking his brain about the inner workings of the program, going over personnel, interviewing and interrogating him in every way. Before I had time to give much thought to the coaching staff, Dave Puddington, the head football coach, volunteered to quit if I wanted to bring in my own man. I wasn't anxious to make a change with just a few games remaining in the season. But the second time he came to my hotel with his letter of resignation—after a late-season defeat—I agreed. His departure was announced after the final game of the 1971 season.

The news traveled rapidly. A day later I received a call from a Colorado assistant I had met in Boulder several months earlier. His name: Don James. I had in my briefcase a list of coaches I wanted to talk to about the possibility of being Kent State's new head coach. There were two guys from Wyoming but the name at the top of the list was Don James. He had superb regional ties, having played quarterback in Masillon, Ohio, home of a celebrated high school football program. The father of one of Don's good friends was Paul Brown, who became a pro football legend with the Cleveland Browns.

James had an impressive coaching background; he was an assistant at Florida State, Kansas and Michigan before becoming defensive coordinator at Colorado with Eddie Crowder. From a recruiting standpoint, Don had great credibility in northern Ohio.

I invited Don to visit. He wasn't concerned about the salary, which was very low; he was eager to become a head coach. I told him the job was his. Don stayed with Colorado through that team's Liberty Bowl appearance, and then he and wife Carol and their three children moved back to Ohio.

We had a new stadium at Kent State with permanent concrete seating on one side and temporary bleachers on the other side. It seated 30,000, although they didn't need more than 3,000 seats to handle Kent's biggest crowds when we started. There were no offices for the coaches or for the staff of the new athletic department I was putting together. We took some of the rooms underneath the new stadium and compartmentalized the space for the football coaches.

My first working office was the president's box in the press box. It was pretty basic, no heat and no frills. During games we would put a tablecloth over my desk when lunch was served to the president's party. We also created office space in the stadium press box for two newly hired assistants and simply shifted furniture and covered desks with sheets on game days.

Those first hires were an assistant AD and a sports information director and both were superstars. I knew that Dick Tamburo, an assistant football coach at Iowa, wanted to go into administration and I hired him as my No. 2 person. Dick proved to be just what I needed. When I called David Price at the Western Athletic Conference office and told him I was looking for an SID, he said Eddie Mullins might be available.

Eddie had made a national reputation at the University of Texas-El Paso (UTEP) for his creative press releases which always featured one or more colorful similes. Describing a receiver's talents, Eddie once wrote, "He has more moves than a can of worms." After years as a student and sports publicist at UTEP, Mullins was ready to make a change, and when I called he said yes.

Mullins was a real pro and had good contacts in the media nationally as a result of his work at UTEP. He wanted to bring with him a kid named Jim Paul, who had impressed Eddie as a student assistant in El Paso. I agreed. From his start at Kent, Jim went on to become a well-regarded baseball executive and at one point was athletic director at New Mexico State University at Las Cruces.

This fledgling athletic staff established great camaraderie, as often happens when people work long and hard in difficult situations. Almost daily, about 6:30 p.m., they would come up to my office, and we would go someplace to have a beer and talk over the day's activities. Besides being my valued consultants, Tamburo and Mullins got involved in fund-raising and putting on booster club events.

Getting my family moved from Colorado and settled down posed a more perplexing and, at first, odorous assignment. My wife, Rena, had made a passing comment that perhaps it would be nice to find a house on a lake. We had always enjoyed her parents' lake house back in Michigan.

There were two lakes just outside of Kent and Bob Wilbur, a college booster who was a real estate broker as well as owner of a hotel and restaurant, heard about a listing on East Twin Lake. We went to check it out.

We opened the door and the stench knocked us over. There were animal feces all over. The doors and window sills had been chewed and scratched. A bunch of dogs and cats had been kept inside the house for some time while the woman who owned the house was gone indefinitely. The people who were supposed to care for the animals apparently just threw food in, but nobody let the animals out so they had done their bathroom duties inside the house. It was a mess.

But the house was a great buy, if we could just clean it up and get rid of the overpowering stink before my family arrived. Wilbur put a cleaning crew to work the next day and progress was being made, but the place still smelled. He also had a carpenter doing major refinishing work.

Before Thanksgiving, Rena and the girls came out to join me from Denver and checked into the hotel suite where I had been staying. I told them *do not* go out to the house; the cleaning job had not been finished. No, I didn't tell them what a stinking mess it had been.

When I came back from the office that night about 6:30 or 7 o'clock, Rena and the girls were sitting in the middle of the floor, and all of them were sobbing. They had ignored my advice and decided they just had to go check out the place where they'd be living.

Rena just glared at me and said, "Mike, how can you put us in that shithouse?"

In just a few days the cleanup was complete, and we moved in Thanksgiving Day. The house had been completely transformed, and it turned out to be a great home for us. It was perfect for entertaining and ideal for gatherings of the soon-to-be-organized Kent State University Blue and Gold Club boosters organization.

After the NCAA decision that allowed an additional football game each season, there was a lot of scrambling by most colleges to find an eleventh opponent. I called Earl Edwards, the head coach at North Carolina State, hoping to add a game and the revenue that went with it. I had a great coaching relationship with Edwards, sharing offensive ideas and concepts.

I told Edwards I didn't expect to win because N.C. State would be a huge favorite. Our Golden Flashes may have been out of their class, but that didn't seem to make much difference and Don James pulled off a major upset, 23-21. Edwards never let me forget that game, joking that I had set him up.

At least a few people on campus took notice. No one was more enthusiastic than Tony Adamlee, our team physician, who earlier had played with the Ohio State Buckeyes and the Cleveland Browns. When the team flight arrived home in a downpour about midnight after the victory over North Carolina State, a small but happy group of family and friends showed up at the airport. Tony grabbed an umbrella that had been provided by the airline and said: "Here's your gift to remind you of our first great victory." I kept it until it finally fell apart a year or so ago.

That opening was probably the high point of the season. For Don James, the win-loss record of 3-8 in that first year at Kent State was the worst of his head-coaching career. Don and his staff just worked that much harder in the off-season, mounting a concentrated recruiting effort that was critical in the revival of the football program.

It came quicker than most of us anticipated. In his second season Don's team won the Mid-American Conference championship and a trip to the Tangerine Bowl. Don was named Coach of the Year in the MAC. The next season, with many of the same players, Kent cruised to a 9-2 record. That team's defense, led by Jack Lambert, held all conference rivals to fourteen points or less. Lambert was to become a pro football Hall of Fame linebacker with the Pittsburgh Steelers' famed Steel Curtain defense.

The success of the football team gave our entire program a lift, on our own campus and in other parts of the intercollegiate athletic ranks. I felt strongly that a winning football program would trigger the momentum to help the rest of the Kent State student body and faculty out of the doldrums and revive support from our alumni and Kent-area fans. We encouraged pregame tailgate gatherings, and we started a Blue and Gold booster club. Our attendance had yet to fill all 30,000 seats, but we were making progress and we were winning.

*Football coach Don James (left), and Fred Jacoby, Mid-American Conference commissioner, join Mike for Kent State golf outing*

We got people talking with the upset of North Carolina State, and when the wins began to come more consistently in 1972, leading to a bowl game, and in '73, the students and alums got excited—hey, this thing is for real. They didn't forget about May 4 but they had something to bring them together.

When we played Miami with the conference championship on the line in 1973, there was a big crowd, even though it had started snowing several days earlier and we were plowing off the field the morning of the game. I went out there at 3 a.m. Saturday to check things out because not many of our grounds crew had much experience clearing the white stuff from a football field. I had faced the same challenge at both Maine and Delaware.

We had the tarp over the field, but the darn thing froze. So we had one tough job to get that field in shape to play on. I recall a picture of me sitting at the top of the stadium in my stocking cap after I'd worked some long, long hours with that maintenance crew. It wasn't enough to win, though, and Miami prevented a second straight championship.

Off the playing field, we started raising funds from our newly devoted boosters. Dick Tamburo, helped by Eddie Mullins, began calling on prospective donors in the community. One of them was Ken Hiney, who owned an Akron printing business. Ken routinely arrived at his shop early, usually by 6 a.m. He would go to lunch, often consuming several cocktails, and never return to the office.

Eddie and Dick set up an appointment for lunch with Hiney to see if he might make a contribution to the athletic department. About 7 p.m. I got a call at home from Tamburo. "Hey boss, will you come and get us?"

Why, I asked.

"Well, the monkey stole the keys to my car and we can't come home."

"The monkey? What are you talking about?"

Hiney had a pet monkey in his shop, and as Dick walked by the cage he waved his keys in front of the cage. The monkey snatched the keys out of Dick's hand and refused to give them back. That was before they started drinking.

It turned out they had joined Ken for lunch and a drink, and that led to another drink, and so it went, on into the late afternoon. By the time they were ready to go home they were in no shape to wrestle a monkey for a set of car keys. I went and picked them up. Mullins, a talented story teller, later recited the details of the monkey episode with such élan at the annual gathering of college sports information directors that he won the best story award for the year, a television set.

Tamburo had a management style of his own. I would outline a project and explain it to Dick. If he ran into opposition when it - came to implementing an idea, he could be somewhat blunt.

"That's the way Mike wants it," Tamburo would say. "And dammit that's the way we're going to do it. If you don't like it you gotta fight me first." Former linebackers can be persuasive if they try.

As I got better established I pushed hard to create a program for athletic development and began raising cash to be used exclusively for our department. I hired a young guy, a former Kent football player, Doug Smith, who had worked in several previous jobs on campus. He proved to be a premier fund raiser and currently works at Baylor University in Waco, Texas.

Unfortunately, Tamburo departed Kent State after about two years when he was offered a job as an associate AD at Illinois. Cecil Coleman, the athletic director, knew Dick when both were at Arizona State, and I couldn't come close to matching the salary he would receive at Illinois.

Not everything was going as well as the football program. In basketball I inherited Frank Truitt, who had come a year earlier from being head coach at Louisiana State University for just one year. Earlier he had been the top assistant at Ohio State when the Buckeyes won the NCAA championship. He was a good coach but had a hard time disciplining his players. I was going to have to make a change.

I hired Stan Albeck, a bright, promising basketball coach. Twice. The first time was as a replacement for Tamburo. But he left after a few months to take an assistant coaching job in the pro ranks. After the departure of Truitt, I hired Albeck back—this time as head basketball coach. But shortly before practices were about to begin he bailed again for another NBA job.

I was frantic to find a coach. When I made a hurried decision things didn't get much better. The new guy was Rex Hughes, who had been an assistant at the University of Southern California. He was volatile, to the point of challenging anyone and everyone—including me—when he got riled up.

I found Hughes through Dean Smith, the incomparable North Carolina coach and a person I had been close to in the Fellowship of Christian Athletes. Smith said John Lotz, one of his assistants, thought highly of Hughes.

After getting permission from Bob Boyd, the head coach at USC, to talk to Hughes, I was off to Los Angeles for an interview. I met Rex and his wife, a delightful lady, and hired him on the spot.

Off the court, he loved to sing Christian hymns, and he had a nice voice. At basketball practice he would lock the doors, and what came out of his mouth couldn't be repeated in church. He used a full vocabulary of four-letter words, including some he may have invented.

Rex was never shy about turning loose his rage on officials. In those days a starting pistol with blanks was used to end a period. One night Rex was giving a referee a lot of verbal abuse and had already been whistled for one technical foul. Enraged over another call, he went to the scorer's table, picked up the pistol, aimed it at the official and fired the blank.

Rex was quickly ejected but he refused to leave. I came out of the stands and finally got him out in the hall of the gymnasium, but he was still ranting. Now he wanted to fight me. I told him bluntly: "Rex, let me tell you something. You have never fought me, and you don't know that you can lick me. So let's just put it this way: it's better not to try than to be embarrassed."

He calmed somewhat but instead of retreating to the locker room he wanted to go up in the balcony to signal instructions to his assistant down on the bench. Of course, he couldn't do that. Well, I finally got him out of there. Yes, Rex's antics entertained the crowd, but Fred Jacoby, commissioner of the Mid-American Conference, was less than amused. After I left Kent State Rex lost his job and did some coaching in the Continental League.

One of my better hires was Tod Boyle, who coached swimming

and was assistant athletic director, picking up many of the things handled before by Dick Tamburo. Tod won several conference championships, and he was the epitome of a team player. He'd do anything that needed to be done, usually without being asked.

Our track and field coach, Doug Raymond, was another of my favorites, a loveable type as well as being a fine coach. When the students clashed with National Guardsmen five months before I arrived on campus, Raymond was right out in the middle of it, trying to dissuade the demonstrators before shots were fired.

Doug's choice of beverage was Teacher's Highland Cream scotch, and I'm sure he took a few sips before his annual New Year's Eve ritual. He lived on West Twin Lake not far from our home, and at twelve o'clock he would get out his old trombone and play Auld Lang Syne.

One day he came into my office to make a strongly worded request, to which I had to say no, and he was not pleased. He got to the door, pulled it open, and seemed on the verge of slamming it. Then he turned around, smiled broadly, blew a kiss to me and said: "I love you, Mike."

Then I got a new boss and the job got a lot tougher.

Dr. White wanted to give up the college presidency to return to the School of Education. One of those being considered as a possible replacement was Dr. Glenn Olds, the president of Springfield College in Springfield, Massachusetts. Cy Porthouse, one of the Kent trustees and the owner of a rubber factory in nearby Ravenna, Ohio, had asked me to get a scouting report on Olds from the Springfield athletic director, Ed Stietz. The report was not good, at least from my standpoint.

Stietz, the longtime secretary and editor for the NCAA Basketball Rules Committee, said Olds was not the least bit sympathetic to intercollegiate sports. Tell your trustee not to hire him, Stietz said. I passed this information along to Porthouse, but he didn't have the votes to block Olds from getting the job. It didn't help my situation when Olds found out I had been checking up on him.

Olds seemed to have great ideas about development of the university, but none of them had anything to do with the athletic department. Often I heard him say, "Mike, you've just got to learn to do more with less." Glenn Olds was one of those people who liked athletics when everything was going right but he wasn't interested in providing the resources to make the program viable.

Maybe he had been in some sort of intellectual cocoon—far from the reality of college sports—but Olds invited Don James and me to his home one night and explained at length a theory he had been pondering for some time. He felt strongly that football coaches should not be on the field during a game; the game should be turned over to the athletes, and the coaches should sit in the stands like the rest of the spectators.

Don and I tried to answer seriously, pointing out that we would be put at a huge disadvantage because the opposition would never agree to such a restriction. We left, shaking our heads, not certain whether we should laugh or cry.

When it was announced that I was leaving Kent State to go to the University of Washington, I got a call from Dick Shrider, the AD at Miami of Ohio, a highly respected colleague with whom I shared some of my feelings about the Glenn Olds administration. Shrider called and his first words were: "Mike, tell him to go to hell, baby," a reference, of course, to Olds.

What made the Kent State job such a huge undertaking was that most of the organizing of the athletic department had to be done from scratch. Almost everything we did was a new adventure. The hardest part was trying to come up with the resources—the cupboard was oh, so bare—to get all the things done that were needed to bring the program from the Dark Ages to the real world.

Early on, I interviewed each member of the staff to get his or her insight to the situation; then I compiled and distributed a staff-wide memo titled "How we can be successful." It enumerated all the things we needed to do to reach that goal. One of those things was loyalty to one another and being team players. That involved not only the staff members but their spouses. The memo was enthusiastically received.

In an effort to give our program more public exposure in the greater Cleveland area, I got acquainted with Art Modell, then owner of the Cleveland Browns of the National Football League. The relationship was highly productive. It didn't take too much persuasion to get him to move the Browns' summer training camp to the Kent State campus facilities from Hiram College.

The move helped us financially in the form of rent for the use of our fields and other facilities and also gave us a significant boost in public relations. Members of the media who may have ignored us for years were on our campus regularly, covering the Browns' preseason workouts and every story written for more than a month carried the Kent, Ohio, dateline.

Modell also helped put together a collegiate football double-header in Cleveland Stadium—which proved to be a disaster, at least at the box office. And when I applied for the job of athletic director at the University of Washington Art wrote a superb letter of recommendation.

When the job of commissioner of the Mid-American Conference became vacant I had recommended Joe Kearney, whom I later succeeded as athletic director at the University of Washington. Kearney would have been a good choice—he later served as commissioner of the Western Athletic Conference for many years—but the MAC selected Fred Jacoby for its vacancy.

Fred served us well; he was a bright, hard-working guy, totally honest and highly respected by all of his colleagues. Later he moved up to become commissioner of the Southwest Conference. He was an extremely close friend and I respect him greatly. Many of the athletic directors and coaches in the MAC I admired and worked with became lifelong friends, including Joe Hoy at Western Michigan, Bill Rohr at Ohio University, Dick Shrider at Miami of Ohio, and Dick Young, who became AD at Bowling Green the same year I got the Kent State job. Dick later moved to Oklahoma State and then Washington State.

My path crossed with that of Joe Kearney again shortly after the 1974 football season ended. His head coach at Washington, Jim Owens, was retiring. After listening to me rave on and on about Don James, Kearney called to ask permission to talk to James about moving to the Northwest. James left behind a lot of good memories and a record of 25-19-1 in four seasons.

After accepting the UW job, Don recommended his defensive coordinator, Dennis Fitzgerald, as his Kent State replacement. I wasn't totally convinced, but I respected Don's opinion and said OK. Dennis was a terrific assistant coach and an outstanding coordinator, but he didn't have the leadership and personality and the overall concept of what it took and how to administer a program as the head coach. His first season of 1975 was a disaster.

Meanwhile, Kearney was growing disenchanted at Washington, and it didn't take him long to land the athletic directorship at Michigan State. He even offered to take Don James with him, but Don had completed only one season in Seattle and liked it there. When Washington officials started searching for a new AD, James asked if he could offer a suggestion. That's when my phone rang.

Al Ulbrickson Jr., vice president for student affairs, asked me to send a resumé and I agreed to meet him in Ann Arbor, Mich., for an interview. We talked for three hours, discussing the job. I was sold, but it took Ulbrickson a while to agree. In March, Don and Carol James visited us at Kent, and we talked about the vacancy in Seattle. While they were staying at our house, Don called Dave Cohn, one of the Washington program's biggest boosters, and I talked with him. Subsequently, I visited Seattle for an interview and was offered the job.

Purple and gold would become my favorite colors for the next fifteen and a half years, the longest tenure of any University of Washington athletic director.

# 10
## BOWING DOWN WITH THE PURPLE AND GOLD

◆ ◆ ◆

The camera sweeps from the stadium to a panoramic view of Lake Washington. The lush green background, bathed in afternoon sunshine, reaches south to the brilliant image of Mount Rainier, its snow-capped peak stretching 14,410 feet into the sky. On the lake several hundred boats, an elite and popular mode of transportation to University of Washington football games, bob at anchor.

At some point during most football games televised nationally from Husky Stadium in Seattle, viewers from Bangor to Bakersfield are teased with a peek at the surrounding landscape. The image is something indelible, quite often far more so than the game itself. Those living in less scenic precincts could be forgiven for feeling a bit envious.

Few college campuses in the United States occupy such an attractive location. And by almost every other measuring stick, the University of Washington ranks with the elite colleges in America: great academics, respected faculty, and outstanding facilities situated in a city ranked among America's "most livable."

In the realm of intercollegiate athletics, the Huskies have a long and successful tradition, and the school belongs to one of the most prestigious conferences in the land. This is the big time.

I was part of it for 15 plus years as director of athletics, definitely a career highlight.

Before landing the Seattle job, during my five and one-half years as athletic director at Kent State, I became acquainted with two prominent University of Washington officials. One of them stole my football coach, and the other one frightened me to death. Both of them have since become close friends and respected colleagues.

Joe Kearney, the athletic director I succeeded, had listened to me sing so many choruses praising Don James, the Kent State football coach, that Kearney hired Don at Washington. It was a strong recommendation by James that helped me rejoin him as the Huskies' athletic director.

When I was at Kent State, I remember attending NCAA meetings and observing Harry Cross, Washington's faculty representative. As that body's president and later its parliamentarian, he was intimidating. He came across as a hard-nosed lawyer—tough and rigid, not someone you wanted as an adversary. After accepting the job as Washington's athletic director, I was concerned about how I would get along with Cross. Not to worry. He became my advisor, confidant, and an expert on all the nuances of the workings of the NCAA. He was as helpful as any faculty rep could be.

During the three-hour interview I had with the selection committee at Washington, I was asked some pointed questions about racial unrest and problems that resulted in student protests on many college campuses. I found out later that in 1969 four black football players at Washington had been suspended, resulting in a boycott of the UCLA game by other African Americans on the team. As a result of this incident, the UW administration had become increasingly sensitive to the diversity issue. After my formal interview, my wife and I were invited to a casual social gathering to meet leaders of the minority community. At first, things seemed a little stiff; then the door opened and a big African American filled the room.

Rena and I immediately recognized the latecomer as Isaiah Kelley, one of my former players at Colorado State. He was married to an airline flight attendant who had grown up in Seattle. When Isaiah heard I was being interviewed, he asked if he could be on hand to welcome me. When Rena saw him she ran to him, jumped into his arms, hugged him, and kissed him.

That was a bigger icebreaker than one of those ships they send from Seattle to Antarctica. A week or so after I returned to Kent State, I received a telephone call from Al Ulbrickson Jr., the vice president of student affairs, offering me the job.

I was ecstatic about being picked for the Washington job. Now it was time to go to work on some potentially serious long-range problems in the Husky program. The first day on the job I met briefly with Dr. John Hogness, the school president, and he was blunt.

"I have just one major request of you. Get us out of the red ink and into the black. That's the most important thing now."

I was taking over a department of intercollegiate athletics that was in debt by more than $400,000 and it appeared the situation could be going from bad to worse.

Seattle was going through a major transition in terms of spectator sports, and I wasn't the only new arrival. The city's sole major league franchise, the Seattle Sonics of the National Basketball Association, was about to be joined by two new teams, the Seahawks of the National Football League and the Mariners of Major League Baseball. The teams would share a new domed sports facility, the recently completed Kingdome.

In the big picture, my biggest challenge would be keeping the Huskies in a leading role in the rapidly changing local sports scenario. How I performed would be the measure of my success or failure as an athletic director. Nothing I accomplished has caused me more pride than my role in the way the UW sports program was able not just to survive but to prosper through this dramatic facelift of Seattle sports.

For many years Husky football had no serious competition for the entertainment dollars of Seattle-area fans. Minor league baseball and hockey had long-established niches; so did Seattle University's basketball program, highlighted by a trip to the Final Four of college hoops when Elgin Baylor was playing there. Every August the locals stage a civic celebration called Seafair, a nautical theme event with pirates and parades and an unlimited hydroplane race—boats racing around a course at speeds approaching 200 mph.

Seattle fans had thirsted for a professional football team for at least a quarter of a century. In the late 1950s there were attempts to bring a team in the fledgling American Football League to the Northwest and use Husky Stadium as its home. University regents, wary of the impact a pro team might have on the box-office success of the Huskies, turned down the plan.

The regents expressed a dim view of mixing professional and intercollegiate football in the same venue, and if I had been there at the time I would have totally supported their decision. I think it's absolutely wrong; professional and college teams in the same facility are not compatible.

The funding to construct a multipurpose Seattle stadium was turned down a couple of times by voters as the NFL cast a longing eye at expanding to the Pacific Northwest. Finally, the Kingdome project got a green light from the electorate.

Arriving as athletic director in the spring of 1976, I faced a head-to-head battle with the Seahawks, starting with ticket sales for the coming season. Sellout crowds appeared likely for the expansion franchise despite the unlikelihood of much success on the field. Ticket sales were booming, partly at the expense of UW attendance.

In the previous year, the first for Don James as head coach, the Huskies won four of their last five games to salvage a winning season, barely (six victories and five losses). Jim Owens, James' predecessor, had transformed the Washington program as well as the prestige of West Coast collegiate football early in his UW career. After back-to-back Rose Bowl victories over favored Big Ten opponents in 1960 and '61, Owens' popularity was unparalleled. Adoring fans suggested the coach, who lived on the shores of Lake Washington not far from the campus, could have walked (on water) to work.

But the metaphors invoking deification became less frequent in the later years of the Owens regime. Some of the luster of those magnificent single-platoon conquests was dulled by a string of seasons in which the Huskies lost four or five games.

In my first year at Washington and the inaugural season of the Seahawks, Husky football attendance sagged about as we had projected. It fell to 42,595 per game, down from 51,383 a year earlier. Don James was making strides in regrouping his program but it didn't show in the win-loss column. The 5-6 record of 1976 evened his two-year totals to 11 wins and 11 losses.

If we didn't do something in a hurry we were headed for big trouble.

The turnaround came almost exactly a year later. After a slow start, the Huskies finished with six wins in their final seven games, capped with a routine thumping of arch rival Washington State. But UCLA could clinch the conference title and a Rose Bowl invitation by beating University of Southern California in the final game of the season.

I will never forget sitting in the James living room in Bellevue with a bunch of Seattle media types watching the USC-UCLA game on television. The unlikely hero in this whole scenario was Frank Jordan, the USC place kicker.

With time running out, Jordan kicked a field goal to give the Trojans a 29-27 victory over the Bruins. The UCLA loss put the Huskies in the Rose Bowl for the first time in fourteen seasons. To cap an already wonderful season, Washington scored a huge upset in Pasadena, 27-20 over Michigan. It was the first of what would be fourteen bowl game appearances by Don James-coached Washington teams. Our program, despite the shadow cast by the Seahawks, was on its way to becoming one of the most successful in the country.

That Rose Bowl victory revived season ticket sales. It attracted new members to the Tyee Club, our booster organization. It convinced fans to get out their checkbooks to support the Huskies' sports program across the board. We attracted more radio and television sponsors and the Pasadena victory gave a big push to our promotional brainchild, Husky Fever, to become a million-dollar fund-raiser.

Despite competition with the Seahawks for fans and media attention, I had a good relationship with the team's original owners. Most of them were University of Washington alums, including members of the Nordstrom family who owned and ran the chain of upscale clothing stores, and Herman Sarkowsky, a prominent developer. John Thompson, the first general manager, was a UW product and former staff member in the Department of Athletics. John and I met regularly, and we created a good feeling of coexistence.

For the most part, the staff I inherited at Washington was outstanding. The head coaches in our high exposure sports, football and men's basketball, ranked with the best in the country. I knew all about Don James from our relationship at Kent State, and I was confident he was headed for a long, successful career.

Joe Kearney had high praise for Marv Harshman, the basketball coach, and it took less than one season of watching him in action to realize he was a class individual and a fine coach. Marv was highly respected by his colleagues, a consummate teacher. He had strong ties to the state's high school coaching ranks and knew most of them on a first-name basis. He had coached thirteen years at his alma mater, Pacific Lutheran University, another thirteen at Washington State, and was closing in on thirteen more years at Washington.

With a few exceptions, I was impressed with the rest of the UW staff, but it didn't take me long to make a couple of major additions. When I made a tour of media outlets—sports editors, TV sports directors, publishers, and the like—I had two things in mind: I always got along well with the press, and I wanted to let the media of Seattle know I would always be accessible. I also wanted its help in finding a sports information director. The strong consensus was Mike Wilson, who was the SID at archrival Washington State. Mike and I talked by phone, but he was just leaving with the Cougar baseball team for the College World Series in Omaha. To get the process moving, I arranged a dinner with Mike's wife, Pat, in Seattle. Rena and I were impressed. I never forget to remind Mike that he got the job because of Pat's interview.

Another big step forward was the hiring of Judy Cadman Biondi as development director. She had impressed me at a meeting with top executives at the public television station. We were trying to find a spot for a weekly TV show for Marv Harshman, and Judy was head of development at the station. I concluded if she could raise money for public TV she could do an even better job for the athletic department. Judy got our development program into high gear, greatly increasing the flow of much-needed funds that helped put us in the black.

At many of the meetings I attended with Husky alumni, I noticed that an inordinate number of the men were unusually tall. I finally figured out why: Washington is one of the hotbeds of collegiate rowing, dating back to the Hiram Conibear era in the early 1900s. Through the years, the Husky crew program has won numerous national championships and Olympic medals, and produced coaches for many other schools. At one time, most of the shells used by college rowing programs were made in the Seattle workshop of George Pocock.

When female rowers were added to the program, Washington's domination of national rowing also expanded. The men's coach when I arrived, Dick Erickson, was a special member of the staff. He lived the tradition of Husky sports, as a champion Husky rower, as a coach who won numerous honors, including the world-class Grand Challenge event at the Henley Royal Regatta in England, and as a trusted and loyal staff member after he left the coaching ranks.

Most of the thousands of people who attend the Windermere Cup Regatta and Opening Day of the Northwest yachting season each May are unaware that it was the creation of the fertile imagination of Erickson. He combined crew racing with the colorful boat parade marking the opening of the yachting season. Boats jammed on a log boom along the Mountlake Cut's 2,000-meter race course add to the festivities. Windermere Real Estate then stepped forward as a major sponsor, inviting top crews from around the globe to the annual May event—international rowing's biggest spectator attraction.

Bob Ernst, the coach Dick attracted to Washington and who later succeeded Erickson as men's coach and coordinator of the rowing program, won several national championships as the Huskies' first women's coach, then turned the job over to Jan Harville. She sustained that success for years before retiring in 2003.

A year before Don James' first Pasadena trip, Rena and I joined other conference athletic directors and wives at the Rose Bowl. Rena and I got up early New Year's Day morning for the Tournament of Roses parade. As the Big 10 band turned the corner at Orange Grove and Colorado Avenue, I told Rena, "When the day comes that our Husky band marches around that corner, I'm going to cry like a baby." I just didn't think that would happen as soon as it did.

Sure enough, tears of joy filled my eyes on the morning of January 1, 1978, when the Husky band hit that corner playing the Husky fight song, "Bow Down to Washington." I was proud of our band and its director, Bill Bissell. When I arrived at the UW, the marching band was funded by the music department but there was a lot of hand-wringing about lack of money. The squeeze was on me to make the band a part of the athletic department. Eventually, we took over all band expenses—uniforms, instruments, travel, and Bissell's salary.

Bissell transformed the band into an elite Husky rooting section. From that first Pasadena march, the band was always there wherever the Husky teams went bowling—capped by a national championship in the 1992 Rose Bowl.

I used to tease Bill that I didn't want some monster-size band with an army of musicians standing in the middle of the field and barely moving back and forth, turning their butts to the sidelines. I wanted a real marching band, like the one in *The Music Man*. He agreed—not the biggest but a band with a touch of class. He made it happen. The band's rendition of "Tequila" became a Washington trademark.

*Giving a pep talk to members of the Washington Husky band with popular director Bill Bissell before going on 1990 bowl trip*

"Louie Louie" became so popular in the early 1980s that Husky fans tried to get it adopted by the state legislature as the official state song.

An avid fan of vaudeville, Bill considered himself an entertainer as much as a band director. He was innovative and loved to poke fun but never crossed the line of bad taste with the band's routines. I had a terrific rapport with Bill and with the band: on my regular morning rounds before home football games I would often give them a pep talk. I still have a photo of me with the tuba section and I'll never forget when the band did a "MIKE LUDE" spellout on the stadium turf.

Another staff member who impressed me from our first meeting until the day I left was Gertrude Peoples, who was in charge of the academic counseling and tutorial programs. When I arrived she was a one-person department handling all the athletes in the program and doing a magnificent job. She is responsible for more University of Washington athletes finishing their degrees than any other individual.

Some of the academic snobs in the Administration Building were skeptical of Gertrude because she left college to take care of her family before getting a degree. She couldn't have been better prepared and more effective if she'd had a masters and a PhD. They didn't come any better.

One coach who disappointed me was the baseball coach, Bubba Morton, a former professional player. I wasn't pleased when a group of Husky players came to me to complain that Bubba had missed prac-

*Chatting with Gertrude Peoples, who did a great job as Washington's head of academic counseling program for athletes*

tices and on one road trip had failed to show up for a game, leaving the players to manage themselves. He simply didn't fit what I was looking for in a work ethic— energy, enthusiasm, and dedication.

To replace Morton I brought in Bob MacDonald, a former Husky pitcher and UW alumnus who had been an assistant at Washington State University. MacDonald did a fine coaching job through my fifteen years at Washington. He never lost his enthusiasm or shrugged off an assignment. Besides coaching, he was a major player in carrying out the details of every bowl trip we made. Bob worked as our liaison with the hotels and with rooming and food services. His regular partner in bowl planning was Allen Stover, a former high school teacher and coach in Renton.

Stover started out as an unpaid intern, but he handled every assignment amazingly well. When we went to a bowl game, I put him in charge of transportation, to make sure the buses were on time at the right place, and to handle the tricky job of assigning courtesy cars. Whether it was a Rose Bowl in California, an Orange Bowl in Miami, or an Aloha Bowl in Hawaii, Allen and Bob would attend our daily planning meeting. We started at 6:30 a.m. in my hotel suite. The team also included Don Smith, associate athletic director, and our directors of sports information, tickets, strength and conditioning, facilities, and development. We wanted to make sure nobody got embarrassed and things happened the way they were planned.

To be competitive with the new pro football and baseball teams in Seattle, I wanted to upgrade our marketing, but I lacked a budget for any kind of a serious media blitz. I mentioned my problem to Al Thompson, president of a supermarket chain that was a radio sponsor of football and basketball broadcasts. Thompson offered an alternative plan: promote Husky sports through the region's grocery stores.

"Not everybody reads a newspaper but everybody eats," Thompson said. He volunteered to enlist the help of suppliers, retail grocery stores, and food industry employees, and called them together to brainstorm the concept.

Thompson took the lead in planning an event we billed as the world's biggest tailgate party. Mike Wilson, our sports information director, came up with the name, Husky Fever. The grocery suppliers provided the food and also created a blitz of decorations, bumper stickers and promotional material in the stores and in their advertising. Consolidated Restaurants, owned by Dave Cohn, one of our most loyal supporters and UW regent, prepared and served the food to several thousand fans. We borrowed army tents and tables, courtesy of General James Shelton, a former player of mine at Delaware who was then the ROTC commandant at Fort Lewis, near Tacoma. Later we bought a huge purple-and-gold tent.

Participants that first year included Thompson's Tradewell stores, Golden Grain, Johnson and Lieber food brokers, Crescent Foods, S&W, Coca-Cola, and no doubt some others I have forgotten. By the second year, more food suppliers were lining up to take part—QFC, Pepsico, Johnny's Supermarkets, and many others. It helped get our Purple and Gold program out of the red and remains a popular and significant fund raiser for the UW. Husky Fever was another step forward in putting together a well-rounded program. I felt we were making progress. Yet I never lost sight of the fact that football provides the fuel that makes the engine roar in the world of intercollegiate athletics. Football creates the revenue—ticket sales, contributions, radio and television contracts, and gate guarantees for road games—to support itself and all other areas of the program.

So thanks to the success of Don James' staff and players in that first Rose Bowl season —with an assist from the foot of Frank Jordan—we were on our way.

# 11

# (1) DON JAMES, (2) DON JAMES, (3) DON JAMES

◆ ◆ ◆

Long after Don James was hired to be the head football coach at the University of Washington, he still could laugh about the welcoming message on a hotel lobby reader board as he was checking in.

The sign proclaimed: "Welcome Don Jones, new Husky coach." Too frequently James found himself correcting well wishers about the name of the school where he had coached previously. "Not Penn State," Don would say, "It's Kent State. You know, in Ohio."

Most Washington fans *didn't* know. James or Jones. Kent State or Penn State. The UW boosters had never heard of Don James and all they knew about Kent State was that it had been the scene of a tragic shooting five years earlier, where four students had died and others had been wounded, the aftermath of a campus protest.

But those University of Washington fans soon found out all about Don James, the coach who would be nicknamed the Dawgfather of Husky football. So did opponents of Husky teams: the traditional rivals in the Pacific Northwest, the other conference opponents, and many of the great football teams of intercollegiate football which competed against the James Gang in bowl games and in intersectional matchups.

The national recognition and respect James earned during

his eighteen-year career at Washington is reflected in a *Sports Illustrated* article at the height of his career. In a preview of the 1984 season the magazine listed the top three football coaches in America. The S-I list: (1) Don James, (2) Don James, (3) Don James.

I couldn't disagree. From the first time I had a chance to meet and talk football with Don James, when he was an assistant at the University of Colorado, I was convinced he was destined to be a premier head coach—if given the chance.

When I had that chance as the athletic director at Kent State, I hired him to run the football program and he has been making me look good ever since.

By his second season at Kent State, he was taking what had been a rundown, woebegone program to a bowl game. By his third season at Washington, he was winning the conference championship, capped by an upset victory in the first of six Rose Bowl appearances. It was the start of what soon became a routine series of post-season games that created a national power. Once dominated by the traditional West Coast juggernauts in Los Angeles—USC and UCLA—the Huskies went head-to-head in the recruiting war for the top talent in Southern California and became a major force in West Coast football.

You may have noticed I have a tendency to lapse into superlatives when I talk about Don James. But let's look at the record over his eighteen seasons at Washington:

James won more games (153) than any coach in UW history. He won more conference games (99) than any coach in Pac-10 play. Among Washington coaches (on the job for at least five seasons), James is second behind Gil Dobie in winning percentage (.726, 153 wins, 57 losses and 2 ties). Dobie's mark of 58-0-3 (1908-1916) likely will never be broken.

James led Washington to a national championship in 1991 with a 12-0 record.

James took the Huskies to the ultimate Big Game, the Rose

Bowl, six times and won four of those national showcase contests in Pasadena.

James-coached Husky teams went to 14 bowl games in 18 seasons, winning 10 of those post-season appearances.

He was named national Coach of the Year in 1984 and 1991.

Against traditional Northwest rivals, Washington State, Oregon, and Oregon State, James' record was an overwhelming 43-9. Dominating the region became a strong selling point in recruiting, keeping top players from straying elsewhere.

In the decade of the 1980s, the Huskies won more games than any other conference school, 84. Four of those UW teams were ranked No. 1 at some point of the season by at least one major poll or publication.

The success Don James' teams had on the playing field was critical in everything I did to make the intercollegiate athletic program financially healthy at a time it could have lapsed into a death spiral. Washington consistently has led the Pac-10 schools in football attendance, despite head-to-head competition from three major league professional franchises in the Seattle market—for both ticket sales and media attention.

In my years in sports, I've been around some great, great coaches, and as far as I'm concerned Don James is the best. There are many reasons I believe this, encompassing a wide range of qualities.

Nobody was ever better organized. He put a premium on precision organization and on coaching his coaches. There was no standing around or wasted moments on the practice field. He made sure his staff and his players paid attention to detail. He was relentless about going back over all the things that got his teams to the point that they were when they were successful. He put a premium on not accepting mistakes; he was obsessed with correcting mistakes, fixing the things that didn't work.

The attention James demonstrated to all three parts of the game created a national reputation for teams featuring disciplined offenses, tough, aggressive defenses and well-schooled special teams.

He never forgot the importance of the last thirty-six hours before a game, the fine-tuning of reviewing with the staff every possible situation and being ready for it. He went over details of the substitution plan so there never could be too many men on the field.

He knew how to set priorities and set goals and how to work to take care of those priorities and achieve the goals.

There was some joking about him being a "tower" coach, a reference to the twenty-foot-high platform he often used during practices in Husky stadium. But it worked well for him. The tower was a great vantage point from which to watch his assistants and his players and he didn't miss a thing. He made extensive notes and later he would critique each practice at staff meetings.

Don made no effort to be buddy-buddy with the players. He was a strong disciplinarian. It took many of those who played for Don James a little time and some perspective to fully appreciate him as a coach. The players often felt, until after they graduated, that he was a little on the aloof side. Maybe that word is a bit strong, but he wasn't trying to be the players' pal, not at all. And the athletes' reaction was confirmed by the distance of his tower from the practice field. There was no hint that Don was trying to tell his team, "Hey, fellas, I'm a good guy. I want to be loved." He wasn't that way.

If a player got a message from Don saying "I want to see you in my office," it was like a summons to the guillotine.

Discipline is important in life, and I think every player who played for Don James will at some point agree there's nothing wrong with discipline. Don didn't make a lot of speeches or demands, but they knew that you played by the rules: the playing rules, the academic rules, and the social rules. If anything, he was a master of presenting the image of a head coach who was respected from every angle.

One of the greatest things about Don was that he never blew his own horn. That was not his style. He let his success and accomplishments stand on the record. One of the things every successful coach I've been around preached was paying attention to detail. And don't ever forget what got you where you are after becoming successful.

His presence and the strength of character and faith in what he did and how he prepared—from the start of his coaching career and as a head coach—was a significant example for the University of Washington and the Seattle area.

The concepts and philosophies James used so successfully to pre-

*Reunited at Washington with football coach Don James who built the Huskies into a national power*

pare for being a head coach came about through a series of mentors, including Bill Peterson at Florida State, Eddie Crowder at Colorado, Bump Elliott at Michigan and a couple of disciples of Bear Bryant and Paul Dietzel.

During Don's four seasons at Kent State we developed a strong bond of loyalty and mutual respect. When he told me he had been approached about the Washington job we had a long chat. I told him what a great situation that would be for him. The Husky program should be able to dominate the Northwest, break even with the California schools, and the final result would be a great season. Actually, it worked out better than that.

Oregon, Oregon State, and Washington State teams won just enough to keep the rivalries going but Don maintained a rather overwhelming superiority which was a boon to recruiting. I felt confident that Washington could recruit just about any player it wanted from the Northwest. Sure, some players went elsewhere. You couldn't keep them all. But on letter-of-intent day during Don's tenure, very few of the recruits the UW wanted slipped away.

As a recruiter, Don was no spin doctor who made a lot of promises he couldn't keep. He would go into the home of a recruit and be straightforward and honest. He didn't try to snow anybody and that came across, his total honesty. The reaction of most parents was positive: "I want my son to be coached by Don James." Some liked James because they felt their son needed stricter discipline and Don could "do with my son what I couldn't do."

I wouldn't say that Don truly enjoyed recruiting, but he considered it a critical part of his job. He knew that recruiting was a high priority in being a successful coach, that he would be a lot better if he had great material. He wasn't a typical salesman, but he was good at closing the deal.

He devised a system to get his entire staff involved in evaluating prospects. James used a numerical rating system to project how soon a prospect might be competing for the Huskies. A majority of the coaching staff would have to vote on the potential of each recruit before a scholarship was offered. This eliminated second-guessing should a player fail to live up to expectations down the road.

Don knew that I believed very strongly in the importance of having a successful football program and that I would do anything within reason to give him the support needed for football to thrive. Another thing means a lot to me: In the twenty years that we worked together, Don James and I never had a serious disagreement; we never had a fight about policies or procedures or the direction of the program.

He acknowledged I couldn't be oblivious to the needs of other sports, but he was confident in me and respected my experience as a head coach and an assistant. He respected my judgment, knowing that I had been in the trenches and faced just about every situation, those in which I had been successful and the one in which I had lost my job. The respect was mutual.

In meetings with other athletic directors they would quiz me about our relationship, and I could sense their envy. They'd ask, "who can I hire who would work as well with me as Don James works with you?" Our friendship never interfered with our professional responsibilities. He was supportive of the things in my job that dealt not only with football but all the other sports.

We were two guys with similar ideas and thoughts, similar values and ethics. We had come up during the Depression, and we knew what hard work was and were willing to do it; we knew the importance of honesty and integrity.

Don's office was just a short stroll down the hallway from my office, and we talked a lot. I would walk down to his office or he would come to visit me early in the morning before most of the staff had arrived. But as close as our friendship was, those meetings were rarely gab sessions. They were focused on a point that needed to be discussed. He was never big on chitchat; neither one of us was—just talking for the sake of talking.

The program James took over had a long tradition. University of Washington teams early in the 1900s under the legendary Gil Dobie, went undefeated for sixty-three straight games (including four ties), still an NCAA record. Dobie's thirty-nine straight victories (no ties) stood for forty years before being broken by Oklahoma's Bud Wilkinson. From Washington, Dobie went on to coach at Navy, Cornell and Boston College.

In another golden era for Washington, Enoch Bagshaw, one of Dobie's star players and a team captain, coached back-to-back Rose Bowl teams in 1924 and '25. His record of 63-22-5 in nine seasons was close behind James' mark.

Jimmy Phelan, Ralph (Pest) Welch and Howie Odell received mixed reviews as Husky coaches (all three were fired) through the better part of three decades before a tall, young (twenty-nine) Oklahoman took over the program in 1957.

Jim Owens had played at Oklahoma and coached with Bear Bryant at Kentucky and Texas A&M before Bryant's lengthy career at Alabama. Owens totally revamped the image of the Huskies and changed the face of the college game on the Pacific Coast.

NCAA rules had been revised to focus on a single-platoon style that limited substitution. It put the emphasis on tough, versatile, athletic players over specialists and situation players. Owens' 1959 team surprised the best in the West, winning the conference title with a 9-1 record, then shocked heavily favored Wisconsin in the Rose Bowl, 44-8. A year later the Huskies returned to Pasadena and overwhelmed No. 1-ranked Minnesota, 17-7. Back in Seattle, Owens could have been elected governor.

The bowl success, a testimonial to the team's "play it from the heart" dedication and its fierce pride, more than sheer talent, was a message to Western schools. It ended the Big 10's domination of the Rose Bowl—eleven victories in the previous twelve games in Pasadena. Most of those wins were by lopsided margins.

*Rose Bowl scoreboard shows final score in UW's upset win over Michigan marking turning point for UW football and athletic program*

At the time I was an assistant at Delaware, but we were well aware of Jim Owens and what was going on in Seattle. He had turned things around and had gained considerable respect in national football circles. When Don replaced Jim Owens in 1975, he was well aware of the legacy. The effort by a group of Owens' players and fans to commission and erect a statue of the coach outside Husky Stadium during Homecoming 2003 was a well-deserved tribute.

Part of Don James' detachment from his players—they almost never were exposed to his understated sense of humor—was his way of maintaining his objectivity. Because fans are great second-guessers of all coaches, Don's judgment came in for considerable scrutiny on the way to his first Rose Bowl in 1977.

After winning eleven games and losing eleven in his first two seasons, James still had a lot to prove to UW followers. So did Warren Moon, the quarterback whom James had installed as his starter in place of holdover Chris Rowland. After taking a lot of abuse, Moon emerged as the leader of the team that turned Husky fortunes around. He was named Pac-10 Conference Player of the Year and MVP of the Rose Bowl as a senior. As a professional QB, Moon helped Edmonton win five Canadian Football League championships and later won all-NFL honors with the Houston Oilers.

That Rose Bowl triumph was one of my favorite games as Husky athletic director. Another came in a rare Washington Orange Bowl appearance in Miami. The 1984 Huskies beat Oklahoma, 28-17, but had to settle for second in the national season-ending rankings behind a Brigham Young team that was unbeaten but played a rather dubious schedule.

As memorable as the win was the unusual penalty called against Oklahoma's Sooner Schooner, a wagon pulled by two ponies. After an apparently successful field goal, the Sooner Schooner charged onto the field in celebration. The driver didn't see the flag that nullified the play and the refs called a second penalty on the wagon for unsportsmanlike conduct.

On the replay, the field goal missed and the Huskies got a lift in momentum that carried them to victory.

Don's success at Washington won the respect of his coaching peers. He became active in the American Football Coaches Association (AFCA) and spoke at frequent coaching clinics around the country. He served on the board of the AFCA and later became president. Unlike some high-profile head coaches, Don often spent time in the lobby at coaching conventions, sharing his experience and answering the questions of young coaches on the way up. He has helped a lot of assistants get jobs at other schools. He recommended many of his own aides for head coaching posts, including the likes of Jim Mora (head coach at New Orleans and Indianapolis of the NFL); Dom Capers, a Kent State aide who went to the Houston Texans; Gary Pinkel, Toledo and Missouri; Ray Dorr, Southern Illinois; Bob Stull, Massachusetts and Missouri; Bill Wentworth, Denison; Skip Hall, Boise State; Jeff Woodruff, Eastern Michigan; and Chris Tormey, Idaho and Nevada-Reno. Others who left for NFL jobs as assistants include Chick Harris, Al Roberts, and John Pease.

Jim Lambright, one of the holdovers from Jim Owens' coaching staff, became a mainstay who helped create Washington's reputation as a defensive power. His loyalty was rewarded with the head coaching job when Don stepped down. Keith Gilbertson was the offensive coordinator with Don and later with Rick Neuheisel before becoming head coach in 2003.

As Don and the Washington program gained national attention, he was sought by other colleges and pro teams. When the Seahawks fired Jack Patera during the NFL strike in 1982, there was a lot of speculation that Don would become the new coach. John Nordstrom, one of the majority owners of the Seattle pro team and a University of Washington alumnus, told me the Seahawks were seriously interested. In my conversations with Don I think he felt his approach and coaching style were best suited to the college game.

Before the game at Stanford that season the Huskies were unbeaten in seven games and ranked No. 1 by the wire service polls. Speculation continued to build over the possibility of James moving to the Seahawks. To end the distraction, Don called an airport press conference and announced he would be staying at Washington as long as he was welcome. Still the Huskies were upset, 43-31.

Incidentally, the man I recommended to Nordstrom for the Seahawks was Chuck Knox, whom I had met years before while recruiting as an assistant at Delaware. Knox got the job, and I attended the Seahawks' press conference announcing his hiring.

Numerous well-known universities also eyed Don James for coaching vacancies. The most serious was Ohio State, as I recall, after the departure of Woody Hayes. Don and I talked about this when he was on the East-West All-Star coaching staff. But he told me then he wasn't going to move.

There was another point—and few people know about this—when Don was very discouraged. During the 1987 season we had tied Arizona and lost to UCLA, and somehow I had the feeling he might be thinking about retiring. I told him I would be in my job for no more than another five years and that at no time did I want to be shopping for another football coach.

I proposed that perhaps we both might retire at the same time. So hang in there. We crushed Washington State 34-19 and went to the Independence Bowl and defeated Tulane, 24-12. The crisis was over. Don's final three seasons featured a national title, three straight Rose Bowl appearances and a 31-5 record.

We had a great working relationship and a great personal friendship. Don and his wife, Carol, and Rena and I remain close friends. I'm sure that if I were in a serious accident and ended up in a hospital in a coma, when I regained consciousness I would find my wife, Rena, my three children, and my brother, Ron, at my bedside. And right there with them would be Don James. We have that kind of relationship; professional but also personal.

One of the biggest disappointments of my career was not being around for that exciting ride in the 1991 season when the Huskies went unbeaten and won the national title. University President Bill Gerberding decided not to honor the addendum to my contract that would have set my retirement date for June 1992. It was a downer not to have been part of that success. I had left several months earlier to run the Blockbuster Bowl in Fort Lauderdale, and spent most of the UW's dream season following the team by long distance from Florida.

Early on the morning after Washington's Rose Bowl victory, I was in my Fort Lauderdale office when the phone rang. Don James was on the line. "Mike, what size ring do you wear?" Don had just got the news the UW had been voted national champions, and he hadn't forgotten me.

That's the kind of guy Don James is, and it's why I consider him my best friend.

When I was leaving as athletic director there were those who encouraged Don James to seek the AD's job. With his background, his attention to detail, and his immense popularity with Washington fans and alumni, he would have been a good athletic director but he simply wasn't interested. He told me, "I don't need those twelve-month-a-year problems that the athletic director has. I'm plenty comfortable with the coaching situation."

Don's comfort level took a nosedive in 1992. It was a year of extreme contrasts for the Husky program: winning the Rose Bowl and the national championship on January 1 and then coming under conference scrutiny midway through the '92 football season. Billy Joe Hobert, the Rose Bowl hero, became the villain of the program. Hobert admitted accepting a series of loans and was suspended. Pac-10 investigators started digging. At a hearing the following summer, the Huskies lost scholarships and television revenue and were banned from bowl appearances for two years. James retired in protest.

Don felt that he was betrayed by the conference, and that he was not supported strongly by the University of Washington president. Don felt he could put up with the loss of scholarships and the loss of the TV revenue but not the loss of bowl appearances. That was something that hurt the whole squad.

The departure of Don James was a huge loss for the football program. It was a matter of principle for him. Considering the way he was treated, I don't blame him.

I totally agree with University of Washington fans who consider Don's coaching years as a benchmark of success for Husky football. It was fitting that the Tyee Center at Husky Stadium should be renamed the Don James Center in his honor.

And it's highly unlikely his name ever will be confused on hotel reader boards again, even in places like Pullman, Berkeley, or Tucson. Football fans in those Pac-10 outposts won't soon forget the Dawgfather of Pac-10 football.

# 12

# THE UNHERALDED PROFESSOR OF HUSKY HOOPS

◆ ◆ ◆

In the heat of what was a down-to-the-wire race for the Pac-10 basketball championship, University of Washington coach Marv Harshman lost his cool. This was the winter of 1984, and his Huskies were playing at UCLA, a game I was watching at home on television.

The TV monitor showed Harshman having some choice words with a referee, who then whistled him for a technical foul. When Marv persisted, he received a second technical and was kicked out of the game.

Soon my phone rang, and it was university president William Gerberding. He was incensed over Harshman's performance. He said he wanted me in his office early the next morning. "You and I have some serious decisions to discuss," he said.

At our meeting the next day he demanded that Harshman, a talented and popular coach, be ordered to return immediately to Seattle to be reprimanded, rather than stay with the team for another game later that weekend against Southern California. I talked and talked about how every basketball coach occasionally blows up at officials, but Gerberding remained adamant.

I proposed a compromise. Rather than make Harshman return to Seattle, I would hop a plane for Southern California. I would tell Marv the president was unhappy and that he was on thin ice. I told Gerberding I would guarantee there would be no more technicals. I said I would sit on the bench at the next game and make sure Harsh didn't lose his cool again. Gerberding finally relented.

I had a long meeting with Marv at the hotel before the game—it felt like a couple of hours—and we discussed how the administration seemed to have a vendetta going. I told him what I had committed to do, and he agreed I could sit on the bench with the team. I said it was not what I would prefer but that my goal was saving his job.

By the way, he was doing a great job. It probably was the best team Harshman produced in the 14 seasons he coached at the University of Washington. Those 1983-84 Huskies shared the Pac-10 championship with Oregon State and were ranked No. 15 nationally at the end of the season. In the NCAA tournament, Washington advanced to the Sweet Sixteen. After beating Nevada in the opening round, the Huskies came from behind to oust Duke, 80-78. Detlef Schrempf, who later had an outstanding pro career, scored 30 points and the team shot a school record 77.8 percent from the field.

That torrid shooting cooled off against Dayton and the Huskies went home with a 64-58 loss. But there was no reason to complain about a 24-7 record (15-3 in the conference). Unsung so long in his career, Harshman was named national Coach of the Year, and he boosted his career coaching victories to 620, the most of any active coach in the country. That number increased to 654 victories (including games coaching WSU and Pacific Lutheran) before he retired a year later, pushed out when he was doing some of his best work.

This didn't seem to impress Gerberding. He gave Marv no credit when he won championships and criticized him when his teams lost. He was anxious to get rid of Harshman, regardless of his success. A season that should have been totally enjoyable had been soured by the school president's lack of appreciation for the job Harshman was doing.

Not long after I became UW athletic director, Harshman had indicated he wanted to coach the Huskies at least thirteen years, matching his thirteen seasons at Pacific Lutheran and thirteen more at Washington State. As the season of 1983-84 wore on, Gerberding seemed determined to stick with that concept and told me that he expected this would be Harshman's last season.

I pointed out that Marv was having a sensational season and that he wanted to keep coaching. I had spent time watching his practices. I was fascinated by his teaching abilities. I was around when he was getting the team ready, and watched his presentation of the game plan. I observed him closely during games as he made adjustments. I watched him teach and coach and work with the players, and I said I didn't believe we could find a better coach anywhere.

Gerberding didn't agree. He didn't like Marv's bench demeanor. He didn't like the way Marv coached, how he hollered at his players, and, in Gerberding's opinion, degraded them. What Gerberding and most fans didn't know is that Marv had a far better relationship with his players than most coaches. When some kid is sitting on the bench and wants to find out how come, many coaches would send him packing with a nonresponse. Harsh would spend an hour talking to the player, explaining what he had to do to improve his status.

There was no reason Marv Harshman should not have been able to coach as long as he wished. He loved his job, and at a vibrant sixty-six he was still at the top of his game. He joked about coming to the gym with a cane in his declining years, but he was more than half-serious. He had just won a championship in one of the nation's toughest conferences and had a fine group of players returning for the coming year. I told Gerberding we would look ridiculous if he pushed Harshman into retirement against his wishes.

I never did fully understand Gerberding's feelings about Marv. There was speculation that when the UW president was vice chancellor at UCLA he heard coaching great John Wooden call Harsh the best coach of average talent in the country. I'm sure Wooden meant that as a compliment.

But Gerberding interpreted that comment to mean that Marv: (1) Could not recruit top players, or (2) If Marv got top recruits he couldn't coach them. Or perhaps Gerberding expected all coaches to be clones of the legendary John Wooden and Harshman didn't fit the pattern.

Harsh had agreed to let me sit on the bench after that late-season blowout in 1984, but any respect Marv had for Gerberding and Jim Collier, the school's VP for university relations, was long gone. Earlier it had been leaked to the press that Harshman would retire after the 1984 season. Harshman wrote a letter to the president expressing his concern that he was getting squeezed out.

In his book, *Harsh,* written with Terry Mosher, Marv revealed part of that letter: "The only way I'm not going to coach is if you are going to terminate me. And if you fire me, then I'm going to have the public on my side and you are going to have to have some justification, some cause."

I went to bat for Marv and got him at least one more year. I was able to increase his salary so his retirement benefits would be improved. When the president agreed to allow Harshman's return for 1984-85, he said he would make sure it was his last as the UW coach.

The next year, in his final season, Harshman's Huskies again shared the Pac-10 championship, after a wild and crazy finish. Down the homestretch in 1984-85, the Huskies had to win their final five games and USC had to lose once for Washington to gain a tie for the title. Thanks to an overtime victory by Oregon State over USC, it all fell into place and Washington was going back to the NCAA tournament.

Bracketed against Kentucky, the UW lost 66-58 and the

Harshman era was over. Detlef Schrempf and another German foreign student, Christian Welp, were the leaders on that team. Schrempf was probably Harsh's best player, but he coached some other UW standouts. Welp played four years and broke the ancient scoring record set in three seasons by Bob Houbregs (1951-'53). Center James Edwards went to the NBA and won championship rings in Detroit and Chicago.

Marv's record at Washington was 246 wins and 146 losses, second only to the celebrated Hec Edmundson, who was on the job twenty-seven years. Harshman ranks among the ten winningest coaches in Pac-10 history.

Marv Harshman was a superb coach in every respect. He was an outstanding teacher who thrived on schooling his players in every aspect of the game. He was a professor of basketball. For much of his career he was one of the best kept secrets in college hoops.

In his first season at Washington (1972) Harsh's team had a 20-6 record, the best mark since the Final Four team of Tippy Dye in 1953. He took three teams

*With Marv Harshman, a great teacher, superb strategist and highly successful in 14 seasons as Washington's basketball coach*

to the NCAA post-season action and one to the National Invitational Tournament, and probably would have had more tournament contenders except for the Pac-8/Pac-10 rule that for years allowed only one conference team to compete in tournament play. That restriction was quickly junked after television started heaping huge piles of money on schools that qualified for the NCAA event.

After his final regular season game, a gang of Marv's former players gathered to pay tribute to their coach. He was completely surprised when he came out of the Husky dressing room to be greeted by the cheers of 278 ex-players. I was amazed at how many he greeted by name.

The respect displayed at that gathering has been reflected across the country. Marv was held in the highest esteem by his peers in the Pac-10 and in the American Association of College Basketball Coaches, a group he once served as its president.

Joe Kearney hired Harshman from Washington State, and I'm certainly glad he did. This is a solid, solid individual. There is nothing phony about him. If all basketball coaches shared his high standards of honesty and integrity the NCAA wouldn't need a set of rules longer than an encyclopedia. He flatly refused to stretch his principles when he went recruiting.

A key to his success was being able to adjust his team's style of play to meet the individual skills of the players, helping them improve what they did best rather than forcing them into a totally foreign system.

One of the measures of respect for Marv Harshman as a basketball coach is a list of the jobs he turned down during his forty-year career. He was offered the Oregon State job when the legendary Slats Gill retired; he was courted by both the Seattle SuperSonics and Portland Trail Blazers early in the history of the Northwest pro basketball teams.

When Joe Kearney left the University of Washington to become athletic director at Michigan State, Harshman could have gone with him. He elected to stay at Washington, and I could not have been happier to have him coaching in the program I inherited. Of all the basketball coaches I worked with Harshman was No. 1.

When Marv Harshman was shoved out the door at Washington, I started a nationwide search for his successor. There were a lot of fine candidates. The coach I wanted turned me down.

The one the administration wanted was hired and he left four seasons later with the program in worse shape than the one he had inherited. The one who became a premier coach at a rival Pac-10 school slipped through the cracks of the selection process—much to my chagrin.

Gary Cunningham, who played for Wooden at UCLA and later coached there, was a big help and a confidant in my search. He knew what it took to run a clean program and be a good coach. It became apparent that if he were doing the hiring he would have two names on his list.

One was Don DeVoe, then the head coach at Tennessee. Gary said he was a great coach and a tremendous human being. And he was perhaps the only coach in the Southeastern Conference who was playing by the rules and was still successful. The other recommendation was Gary Colson at the University of New Mexico. Colson had cleaned up a program that had been in shambles because of rules violations, and he had outstanding coaching skills.

I assumed correctly that George Raveling, the USC head coach, had no plans to leave Los Angeles, but he made a couple of suggestions of likely minority candidates, Mike Jarvis at Boston University, Nolan Richardson at Arkansas, and Leonard Hamilton at Oklahoma State.

Another top candidate was Mike Montgomery, then a promising young coach at the University of Montana. He had been on the staff at Colorado State as an assistant, and I gave him high marks in every respect: good tactician, strong recruiter, fine teacher, and one who worked within the rules. My list also included John Chaney at Temple University and Rick Majerus, a former Al McGuire assistant at Marquette and then the head coach at Ball State.

At the time Louisiana Tech was having a great season, thanks to a superstar named Karl Malone. The coach was Andy Russo, who had cut his teeth with Don Haskins at Texas-El Paso.

And there were others I checked out as I spent that winter traversing the country, buying a ticket and sitting in the stands incognito, watching coaches. I took care to check out the way they related to officials because President Gerberding didn't want a person who would go running onto the floor to berate a referee.

I went to Ogden, Utah, to see Mongtomery's Montana team against Weber State and I was impressed. We had a two-hour lunch and interview, and he did a good job in the game. He was high on my list.

I got permission to talk to DeVoe from Tennessee AD Bob Woodruff. We arranged to meet at the Seattle airport when the Vols had a stopover on the way to play in the Alaska Shootout. We got along well, and before the winter was out I had made four trips to Knoxville to watch his team play. He seemed receptive to the Washington job and late in the season I took Jim Collier, my go-between to Gerberding, to Knoxville, and he seemed impressed.

When I went to Ruston, Louisiana, to see Andy Russo coach, the game was cancelled because of a huge ice storm. But I got to know him and his fiancée, Jacquie, later to become his wife—and in the NCAA tournament in Dallas I took Collier to see his team in action. Louisiana Tech lost but with Malone the game was close.

The weather was also a problem when I went to Philadelphia to meet John Chaney. The place was buried by a major snowstorm. Chaney was intrigued but couldn't imagine leaving the town where he grew up. Mike Jarvis wasn't in any position to depart Boston; two children were in school and receiving free tuition and fees because of his coaching ties to the university. Leonard Hamilton was making more money than we could afford and Nolan Richardson didn't seem to show much interest.

When the Washington football team went to Hawaii for the Aloha Bowl, I talked about the Husky vacancy with Gene Bartow, a longtime acquaintance whose Alabama-Birmingham basketball team was in the islands, competing in a preseason tournament. Bartow offered a strong endorsement of DeVoe, who had taken Tennessee teams to five straight NCAA tournaments in 1979-83.

As I neared a decision, my short list included DeVoe,

Montgomery, Colson and Russo. As we were getting ready to attend the Final Four in Lexington, Kentucky, we reached a consensus that Devoe was our No.1 choice, and he was agreeable to becoming the Husky coach. I had not sensed great enthusiasm from Gerberding, but he had not said no and we were set to make the announcement after the championship game. The day of the first semifinal game in Lexington, DeVoe called me and turned us down.

DeVoe, who was divorced, said his daughter was distraught when she learned he was considering moving to Seattle while she remained in Knoxville with her mother.

That didn't seem to bother Gerberding. He said he had been impressed with Andy Russo when he visited Seattle. Russo was a guest with the president, Collier, and some UW boosters on a yacht belonging to one of our major supporters during a Seattle visit.

I said, "Bill, I have at least three other coaches who at this point in their careers have much more experience and are better coaches than Andy Russo." I especially liked Gary Colson and Mike Montgomery. Then he said something about giving young people a chance.

"Are you telling me," I asked, "that we are to hire Andy Russo?"

Gerberding answered: "Well, I certainly wouldn't be disappointed."

I hung up, called Russo and asked how he would like to be the coach at the University of Washington. He said, "I would love it." Russo and Jacquie came to Seattle and were married at St. Joseph's Church, and their attendants were Rena and Mike Lude.

Mike Montgomery, who should have been the pick, left to become Stanford's head coach in 1986, and he's still there. His teams have been constant contenders for Pac-10 honors and he's been to a raft of NCAA tournaments. He would have been a great fit at Washington.

So we had the coach Gerberding and Collier wanted. In Russo's first season, 1985-86, the team of holdover talent from Marv Harshman won 19 games and lost 11. With a Pac-10 record of 13-5 the Huskies went to the NCAA tournament and lost to Michigan

State in the first round, 72-70, on two free throws with two seconds left by Scott Skills, who went on to play in the NBA and coach the Phoenix Suns.

In Andy's second season the Huskies finished 20-15 and made it to the third round of the National Invitational Tournament before losing. By 1987-88 our fortunes were starting to diminish. It was becoming obvious that some of the players were not paying attention to their coach. He'd take a time out, and the players would be looking around, up in the stands, or wherever. It was a tough year: 10 and 19.

Then I got a distressing report during the 1988-'89 season about an incident involving Russo and Eldridge Recasner, a talented player Andy had recruited from New Orleans. Besides being a good prospect, he was a decent student who had not had any academic troubles.

Andy had escorted Recasner to the office of academic services run by Gertrude Peoples. He was reprimanding Recasner about not being attentive in a particular class. Gertrude reported to me that at this meeting Eldridge stood up and told Russo in plain terms: "Go F— yourself."

I asked Gertrude to bring Recasner to my office as soon as possible. He came into my office, and I recounted the details of the incident as it happened. He said, "yes sir, Mr. Lude, that's right, that's what I said."

I said, "Eldridge, let me tell you something. If you did that to me, I'd knock you right on your ass."

He responded, "Yes sir, Mr. Lude. I know you would. But he [Russo] wouldn't."

I told him in plain English he must apologize to Coach Russo. "Tell him you are sorry and that's not the way you were brought up and not how you conduct yourself. And promise him you will go to class regularly and be attentive and that you're really sorry."

"Yes sir, Mr. Lude, you ask me to do that and I'll do it." To my knowledge, that's precisely what he did.

Russo's record that year was 12 wins and 17 losses, only slightly better than the previous season, and we had players who were disenchanted with the coach. The fans we had left, alumni and Tyee contributors, were disgruntled. It became obvious we had some decisions to make. Collier, Gerberding, and I had frequent meetings and I finally convinced them we had to change coaches. The president said in essence, well, it's your responsibility, go ahead.

To me it was fascinating that when it came to hiring, Gerberding thought Russo was a great idea but when it came to dismissing him the responsibility was mine alone. All I had ever wanted was the president's total support, which was not exactly what I got.

Russo, whose four-year record was 61-62, agreed it would be better that he resign rather than being fired. Still to be resolved was a settlement on the final year of his contract. The lawyers, Omar Parker for Russo and Elsa Cole of the Attorney General's office for the UW, and I met and came to an agreement. Gerberding was not happy when he was informed of the deal but finally agreed. At least that's what the lawyers and I thought after we left the meeting.

The next day he dug in his heels. He was adamant that the terms were wrong and we would not pay Andy according to the agreement. Elsa Cole and I tried to reason with him and said it was our impression that he had agreed. He wouldn't budge. So Elsa and I went back to Parker's Bellevue office to tell him that the deal was off. Parker was cool. He called Gerberding and said in so many words that if he reneged he'd see him in court.

Gerberding and Collier insisted there hadn't been any agreement and that Cole and I had fouled it up, but by then there was nothing we could do about it. That was good-bye and farewell to Andy Russo.

At about that time I was chairman of an NCAA committee studying ways to improve basketball officiating and one of the others involved was Bobby Knight. I asked him if he had any recommendations, and he gave me a couple of names. One was Bob Bender, who later became the Husky coach.

Meanwhile, I was getting good reports about a former Husky player, Lynn Nance. He had been an assistant at Washington, Kentucky, and Hawaii and head coach at St. Mary's. He also had worked as an FBI special agent and as an investigator for the NCAA Infractions Division. Lynn made a great impression on the screening committee, which included UW faculty representative Dick Dunn, former Husky basketball great Jack Nichols, and ex-player Charles Dudley.

When Bobby Knight came to Seattle for the Final Four in 1989 we had breakfast and he asked about our search. I told him we were leaning toward Nance. "Hell, Mike, Lynn Nance is a lot better than the two guys I mentioned to you."

Let me say this about Knight: he was one of the best possible members of that committee. He arrived early. He would cancel speaking engagements to make the meetings. He would stay late. He had good ideas but he would listen as well as talk. I was extremely impressed. I would never abide or make excuses for his childish tirades and temper tantrums, often laced with expletives. But Bobby obviously has two personalities, his coaching personality and his other one. The one that is a friend of Mike Lude's is one I cherish.

Nance was overjoyed at getting a chance to coach at his alma mater. But he never had time to get over the hump. In the first season (1989-90) his team went 11-17 and the next year it broke even at 14-14. Unfortunately, I wasn't around after that, and after two more losing seasons he was out the door.

I wanted to do everything possible to help Nance be successful. I would have supported him strongly. I truly think he was the right man for the job. He was a loyal Husky. He was the guy. But two more losing seasons (12-17 in 1991-92 and 13-14 in 1992-93) made him expendable.

So he went the way of Andy Russo and Marv Harshman, who,

at age 85, remained sharp and alert to the countless nuances of the game of basketball. In a newspaper interview with Bud Withers of the *Seattle Times* in 2003 Harsh offered the opinion he could have coached 10 more years after he retired and yes, he would loved to have spent that time at Washington.

You know what? I can't disagree. I wish it could have happened that way.

# 13
# TITLE IX: A NEW ERA
# IN COLLEGE SPORTS

◆ ◆ ◆

It didn't take Chris Gobrecht long to establish the University of Washington's women's basketball program as a Pac-10 Conference power.

It took even less time to make clear to conference referees that she would let them know in no uncertain terms if she was unhappy with their work—which was much of the time.

Chris taught an aggressive, attacking style of play from end line to end line and from whistle to whistle, and her courtside demeanor set the pace for her players. Her example was charismatic with her team and with a growing number of Husky women's basketball fans. I was one of them and have remained so long after I left the UW program in mid-1991.

Having been around a large number of basketball coaches in my career in intercollegiate athletics, I understood the frustrations they experienced, and generally I gave them wide latitude when it came to disagreeing with officials.

But there's a limit to my patience. Several years into her eleven-year stint as head coach of a women's program that won a wide range of recognition, Gobrecht received a series of reprimands from the conference office.

I felt it was time to have a heart-to-heart chat with our head coach. I summoned Chris to my office and closed the door. "Chris, it's about time that you straightened up," I told her. "You've simply got to take care of your responsibilities and do a better job in dealing with officials. You'd got to clean up your bench decorum."

Then, in what I admit was meant to be both stern but give our conversation a light touch, I offered a warning. "And if you don't do as I insist, the next time I get a complaint from the conference about you, I have a notion to turn you over my knee and give you a good spanking."

I don't think she took me literally but Chris didn't laugh, at least in my presence. "You know what?" she responded. "I think you might do that. Mike. You can count on me. I'll be under control."

*Feisty Chris Gobrecht made winners out of UW women's basketball team*

And she was under control, most of the time. That doesn't mean she stopped confronting referees, but she was somewhat more subdued and didn't push officials into undue penalties, and the reprimands from the Pac-10 office became far less frequent.

Gobrecht was just one of many women who were being hired at universities across the nation for the thousands of new jobs created by Title IX, the federal regulations that mandated equal opportunities in athletics for women students. It's unfortunate that it took an act of congress to give women the opportunity to participate in intercollegiate athletics, just as men are given that opportunity.

It's also unfortunate that so many college administrators—such as the University of Washington president at the time, William

Gerberding—talked a great game in support of women's athletics but did little or nothing to provide the funding to pay for what became a monumental price tag. All of the expenses involved—scholarships for players, team equipment, the cost of travel to play a competitive schedule, and development of new facilities—were a huge burden dumped on the backs of athletic departments that were already strapped for dollars.

Before Gobrecht, there had been a series of women's head basketball coaches at the University of Washington. Several moved on after just a year or two at the job. There was at least one player revolt. I had an open-door policy to players, coaches, and staff, with one qualifier: you had to follow the chain of command. Nobody could come to complain to me without first letting the person they were unhappy with know what they were doing.

Returning from lunch one day in 1979, I was visited in my office by a group of eleven players from our women's team. After making sure they had received the permission of their coach, Kathy Neir, to go over her head to the athletic director, I listened to their complaints. Kit Green, my senior associate athletic director for women's sports, and Linda Hopper, the assistant coach, were at the meeting, and I still have a tape of what was said. The message was clear: if Neir remained on the job they would refuse to play.

It didn't take long to reach a tough decision: the lack of respect on the part of her players had created a dead-end situation. Her contract was not renewed for the following season. Several coaches—Pat Dobritz, Sue Kruzewski (she left to go back to her native Michigan after a good effort in Seattle), and Joyce Sake—held the job briefly until Gobrecht took over and a new era began.

Gobrecht had been coaching at one of the California state schools in the Los Angeles area when Kit Green and I interviewed her for our women's basketball vacancy. I was impressed.

Chris was an excellent coach. She was a good recruiter. She had poise, concentration, and intelligence. She was very fiery and her teams played that way, working relentlessly and swarming on defense to force mistakes and turnovers. With the support of assistant coach Kathy Anderson, a former All-American at Southwest Missouri State, she built the UW women's program into one that won national respect.

One of her biggest fans was Gerberding, who rarely missed a home game. He seemed enamored of and energized by the women's basketball program. In contrast, he was often critical of our veteran and highly successful men's coach, Marv Harshman. He constantly pointed out that Marv's aggressive style resulted in technical fouls, but never, ever did he say one word when Gobrecht was whistled for her antics on the bench.

Chris made huge strides with our basketball program. The Huskies became a Pac-10 power and were regulars in post-season tournament action. In eleven seasons as head coach, Gobrecht's teams advanced to post-season play nine times. She won three conference titles and finished second in four other years. She was named Coach of the Year in 1987 and '88.

Only one other coach, Pat Summitt of Tennessee, reached the career 300-victory level faster than Gobrecht. At Washington her overall record was 243-89.

I recommended Chris when she decided to seek the Florida State job and was pleased to see her get a chance to return to her alma mater, USC, as the head coach.

The task of enlarging an intercollegiate athletic program to include women's teams in a wide range of sports, with all the same trappings offered to male athletes, became a critical part of my job.

I felt responsible for following the dictates of Title IX, but I also had the responsibility of keeping the athletic department from lapsing back into the red ink I had inherited. I was accountable to the campus administration, and I was concerned that moving too quickly could create expenses well beyond the revenue available to pay the additional costs. We had a plan that we would walk but not sprint into dramatically increased numbers of women participating in intercollegiate sports at Washington.

Still on the blueprint for the year after I left Washington were plans for adding programs in women's soccer and softball. My eventual successor, Barbara Hedges, did an outstanding job of establishing strong programs in those two sports. The soccer and softball coaches she hired and their respective facilities rank among the best in the country.

In the early years, women's teams were not part of the NCAA but competed under the aegis of the AAIW (Athletic Association of Intercollegiate Women). After the Title IX decision, the push for NCAA recognition of women's sports became a strident shove from an increasing number of aggressive women administrators, something I wholeheartedly endorsed. I believed in it then and I still do.

But the finances were skewed beyond all proportions and probably always will be difficult to sort out. The average major college sports program now has a dozen or so men's teams and a similar number of women's programs. In most cases, football is a cash cow; at some schools, men's basketball is also a significant earner. In isolated instances, hockey pays its own way, and other schools may budget minimal profits in a handful of sports.

Generally, though, football pays an overwhelming percentage of the entire budget. That's the way it has been at Washington for years—as long as I can remember. The situation puts increasing pressure on the football coach, his assistants, and the team.

I tried—quite often to no avail—to send a message to those who pushed and pushed for more and more things for women's programs: try to do something to generate income to help pay the bills. I thought Kit Green was an outstanding administrator, but there were times when she didn't seem to get it about funding.

She would say to me, "It's not my job to get the money; that's your job." I used to tell her she was doing a great job but sometimes lost perspective. "When you get with feminine activists on campus," I said, "you come back requesting things you know are somewhat impossible for us to do."

Under the circumstances at the time, I'm convinced the conservative path we took, not rushing into programs we couldn't afford, was the proper one and I'm extremely proud of what was accomplished.

The first women's program to achieve national stature was the same sport that had brought the Huskies international recognition since the turn of the twentieth century: rowing. Dick Erickson, whose men's crews were solid contenders for national championships year in, year out, had already expanded the program to include both sexes by the time I arrived in Seattle. Bob Ernst, later to succeed Erickson as the men's coach, moved from coaching the freshman crew to become head women's coach.

Ernst's crews dominated women's rowing nationally and he coached the U.S. women's eight-oared shell to an Olympic gold medal in 1984 at Lake Casitas in California.

Jan Harville was promoted to the women's head coaching job after Ernst replaced Erickson, and she continued to dominate national championship

*Bob Ernst and his successor as women's coach, Jan Harville, led UW crew program to national domination*

events for years before retiring in 2003. Both were exceptionally loyal team players on my staff.

It didn't take me long to realize the tremendous heritage of rowing at Washington and the significant role that sport and former rowers have played in the school's colorful athletic history, dating back more than a hundred years. Athletic directors at many schools look on crew as little more than a financial drain on the budget. Not at Washington. I made it a habit to be on hand at major rowing events, both men's and women's competition. I was honored when a new Husky shell was named for me after I left the UW.

Not all of our women's teams and their coaches were as successful as the crew. The women's track coach I inherited at Washington prompted a visit to my office by some members of the team. They told me the coach, Al Bonney, was having an affair with the team's superstar runner from Ireland, Regina Joyce. The women were concerned.

After determining there seemed to be some validity to the reports, I went to talk to my boss, the school's vice president for student affairs (an unfortunate title in this instance). He insisted we both meet with the VP for affirmative action. When we went to his office I suggested that the thing we had best do was ask for the coach's resignation.

He looked at me as if I had just climbed off a turnip truck and said: "We've had cases like this happening throughout the university—graduate students having affairs with professors and so on. I don't see a real problem here."

I didn't agree. "What if you had a daughter on the track team and she had a similar situation with her coach?" I asked. He didn't budge. "Well, I would say, 'Honey, you're old enough to make your own decisions; you do what you think is right.'" So I didn't get much support there.

Years later, after Bonney and Regina Joyce were married, he did resign. As far as I was concerned it wasn't what I would have preferred. Bonney and our women's gymnastics coach, Bob Ito, once had a meeting with Kit Green that made her feel very uncomfortable. They were less than respectful of her and gave her a very bad time.

Ito had been the target of criticism by the team's captain, Yumi Mordre, an All-American who had come to confer with me as the team's representative. I asked her if she had received Ito's permission to see me, and she said she had. Yumi said the other gymnasts were upset with Bob because he was far too familiar with some of the athletes. Shortly after that, the uncle of one of the gymnasts came to me at the request of her parents and said Bob was making overtures to his niece.

I called Ito into my office to talk about the situation, and he didn't deny what I had been told. He later married that outstanding young woman. Eventually, we suggested it was time for Ito to do something else that didn't involve the University of Washington. Ito felt strongly that we did not handle him fairly and hired a lawyer. After I had left the UW and was in Florida running the Blockbuster Bowl for Raycom, Ito's lawyers arrived to take depositions; they visited me again a year later when I was at Auburn. The UW ended up agreeing to a minor settlement with Ito on the grounds that he was not given total due process.

University officials also reached a settlement with Lindy Vivas, a women's volleyball coach we had hired from Texas A&M. She was bright, attractive, and energetic and made a good impression when she was interviewed. She was also disruptive and I decided she had to go. She filed a sexual discrimination and harassment grievance with the UW Ombudsman. Her complaint was based on a statement I made at a staff meeting. I said that to be successful it was my job to please President Gerberding and Vice President Jim Collier, and therefore you, the staff, are responsible to please me. She twisted that into the suggestion that I was asking for attention and that was sexual harassment. It couldn't have been further from the truth.

There were lengthy hearings and despite the efforts of Elsa Cole, the lawyer representing the UW from the attorney general's office, the university made a financial settlement—to Elsa's chagrin and mine.

Clyde Duncan, who replaced Bonney, also caused problems. After Kit Green and Don Smith, another senior associate AD, hired him, I learned Duncan didn't have a degree. That upset me greatly. How on earth can we be pushing so hard about graduation success rates and hire a coach who lacks a degree himself? Then I found out Duncan had been representing a sports agent in Tacoma, acting as what is known as a runner between some of our football players and the agent. When we found that out I ended our relationship with Clyde Duncan.

We finally got a winner in Orin Richburg, a former sprinter who had been an assistant at Kent State. At one time I had tried to recruit him to play football at Colorado State. Orin did a good job with the women's track team and later became Washington's men's coach after Ken Shannon retired.

After Chris Gobrecht's women's basketball teams became competitive with the best in the Pac-10 we moved their games to the same facility where the men's team played. But I faced resistance when I proposed selling season tickets to help pay the bills. I said we should charge the same ticket price that we charge for men's games. Kit Green was very much against that. She said no one will come.

I tried to point out that if the goal was to give the women's and men's basketball programs equal status we should treat both teams the same. I added that we also should charge for parking. Kit said, Oh, no. People won't come. We can't do that. They're just not going to show up.

My point, of course, was this: If we are going to offer equal treatment in terms of scholarships, coaching, travel, and equipment, we should have equality in ticket prices and charges for parking at the games.

The part of gender equity in sports with which I don't agree is the insistence on what I feel is a quota system. I don't think it is proper or necessary for the athletic programs to reflect, down to the last decimal point, a given school's enrollment percentages according to gender.

Courses that are required for graduation, like English 101,

should automatically reflect the ratio of men and women enrolled. The same goes for other required subjects.

But there's nothing mandatory about intercollegiate athletics. It is an elective activity. Therefore the demand for and interest in such a program should dictate the number of participants, just as with so many elective subjects within the curriculum of the university. When you have a so-called mandate for equality, it amounts to a quota system, pure and simple.

It's a fact of life that some college courses like nursing and home economics usually have more women students than men. The school of engineering has more men. Nobody mandates the gender makeup of those departmental enrollments. Why intercollegiate athletics? I tried to make this point with activists for women's sports, but they didn't want to listen.

So at Washington, we had to depend on football, the only sport to show a profit with any consistency, to pay the way for the new women's programs. President Gerberding had become a strong supporter of gender equity, but he pleaded poverty when it came to paying the additional expenses, which were considerable.

As far as I knew, there was no effort by feminists to put pressure on President Gerberding to help fund the widely expanding women's athletic programs. All the pressure was on the athletic director and the athletic department.

Gerberding did allow us to approach the state legislature and we were able to get some help in our budget crisis from some prominent legislators. Jim McDermott, now in Congress, joined in. Kit Green and I and others went to numerous meetings in Olympia to lobby for our case. At least Gerberding didn't stop us from seeking help for ourselves.

The legislature's allocation wasn't a lot, hardly hundreds of thousands of dollars, but it was far better than nothing.

# 14
## HUSKY STADIUM PLAYS
## HUMPTY DUMPTY

◆ ◆ ◆

The expression on the face of Helen Gullickson, my secretary, couldn't mask her anxiety over the telephone message she was about to deliver.."You've got to take this call," she said. "It's the foreman at the construction site."

I was wrapping up an administrative staff meeting in my office on the second floor of the Graves Building at the University of Washington when Helen interrupted with an urgent knock on the door.

The ambiance around the athletic facilities had been distracted of late, not by the familiar sound of a bat impacting a baseball, but by the alien clatter of ironworkers banging away in a cacophonous chorus of metal on metal. The construction team had been on the site for three months, laboring to complete a $17 million remodeling of the football stadium.

They were working under a strict schedule requiring completion before the opening kickoff of the first game of the football season in early September, just six months away.

I picked up the phone and listened to the calm but cautious voice of Wally Sharp, the project superintendent. "Mr. Lude, we've heard some groaning in the steel. I don't know what this means; I'm not sure. But here's what I've done: all the ironworkers are off the job. I've got your maintenance guys out of the building near where part of the work is going up. Things should be OK, but I wanted you to know."

I thanked him for the heads up and hung up, wondering where this brief but somewhat ominous message might lead.

I found out in a hurry and it was frightening. I glanced out the window in the direction of the new construction just in time to see one corner of the 130-foot-high steel framework start to twist and gyrate. In seconds it came crashing down. The noise was overwhelming, like what one might expect from a couple of huge sixteen-wheel rigs colliding at high speed on a California freeway.

It was classic Humpty Dumpty.

"Oh my gosh, I can't believe it," I gasped as I dashed down the stairs, adrenaline pumping, and sprinted toward the stadium. When I arrived I could see that the facade of what was to have been the first two sections of the new covered north grandstand of Husky Stadium had been reduced to a tangled mess of metal.

The pile of rubble, an estimated seven hundred tons of steel, reminded me of photographs of the war-ravaged cities of Germany after concentrated bombing raids by Allied planes in World

*Husky Stadium expansion collapse; 700 tons of steel framework comes tumbling down*

War II. Construction workers who had been evacuated soon arrived on the scene. They were happy to be alive and amazed at how quickly their giant erector set had been destroyed.

I hoped that what I had heard on the phone from Wally Sharp was correct and that no one was injured. Still, I was taking nothing for granted. Paul Lydig, the general contractor, was already there.

He reassured me that thanks to Sharp's quick thinking, what could have been a horrible disaster had been avoided.

That didn't avert the damage to my psyche: I had to wonder what would happen to the stadium expansion project I had been dreaming about and working on for nearly ten years.

Workers were still fencing off the crash site when the place was overrun by the media—television crews, radio reporters waving microphones and print reporters clutching notebooks. The next wave of visitors, descending on us from various corners of the campus, included experts from the School of Engineering, staff members from the UW maintenance department and, of course, my bosses from upper campus, school president William Gerberding and his vice president for university relations, Jim Collier. I can remember an earlier stop in my career when we didn't draw a crowd this big for a football game.

Lydig and I agreed it was critical to shut the job down. First we had to find out what had gone wrong. What caused the steel framework, stretching so high in the sky, to collapse? Was it a flaw in the design? Was something wrong with the steel? Did the ironworkers screw up? Or was there some other mystery cause?

I needed to find out, for certain, what had to be done to assure there would not be a repeat performance, how long would it take to determine the cause, and whether we might even end up going to court and face major legal fees.

I had another vital concern: the effect this construction setback might have on the UW's growing intercollegiate program. Simply, would the project I was counting on to help pay for rapidly rising expenses ever be completed or would this be the final chapter with the story only half-written?

Whoa. Let's wait for some answers. Only then could we go to the next step of returning the ironworkers to work.

The university appointed committees, hired consultants, and created a review group that stopped work for more than three weeks. The experts poked and probed, and their report thoroughly examined the mishap. They held blameless anything in the design work. Likewise, there was no problem with the steel, which had come from Korea.

The investigators zeroed in on a decision in procedure during construction. At the time of the crash, workers were erecting the second of eight sections that made up the steel framework for the new north stands. The sections were to be put up individually but connected together. The first section was in place; the second unit was about half-finished and was being supported by two sets of cables. One set of supporting lines stretched to the first section, and another set was attached to several anchors in the ground surrounding the work.

When the support lines to the ground anchors were removed, apparently prematurely, undue stress was put on the cable connected to the first unit, and both sections came crashing down.

It all happened midmorning on one of those rare bright and sunny February days in Seattle when an athletic director normally would be thinking about the coming of spring sports. Not today. The gloom cast a huge shadow far beyond the sunshine.

For those not familiar with the Seattle landscape, Husky Stadium is located on Union Bay, an arm of Lake Washington that makes up part of the waterfront of the UW campus. It is one of the few college football facilities in the nation accessible by pleasure boat. Several thousand Husky fans board an armada of vessels— ranging from small runabouts to luxurious yachts—to attend Husky home games. Other fans arrive via large tour boats, getting in the Purple and Gold pregame spirit at restaurants on Lake Union and Lake Washington before making the short cruise to the docks near the stadium.

The football facility is clearly visible to thousands of commuters who use the nearby Evergreen Point Bridge. The floating span is supported by concrete pontoons and stretches several miles across Lake Washington to the booming Eastside bedroom communities of Bellevue and Kirkland and several other cities and towns.

When I first came to the UW and was driving to work over the floating bridge, I would look at the stadium and think it resembled a seagull with only one wing. Built in 1920 with 30,000 seats the stadium was expanded to hold 40,000 in 1936. Then came the first wing at a cost of 1.7 million in 1950, a second deck over the south stands with 15,000 new seats. That expansion work sheltered many fans from Seattle's fabled precipitation. A minor addition on the stadium rim and portable bleachers boosted capacity to 59,000 in 1968. But the north stands remained wingless, uncovered.

You don't have to live in Seattle long to appreciate being able to sit on a dry seat in a covered stadium while viewing a football game. In the recognized drizzle capital of America it's understandable why the city's first major league stadium was domed. The NFL Seahawks and the baseball Mariners used the Kingdome for about twenty-five years until it was imploded and replaced by two separate taxpayer-supported facilities in downtown Seattle costing a total of roughly a billion bucks.

My objective for Husky Stadium was far less ambitious, at least in cost. But I was convinced that putting a matching wing over the north side grandstands to add another 13,500 seats would be a huge benefit to the program. It had everything to do with hard cash.

Shortly after I arrived on the Seattle campus in 1976, President John Hogness made clear that one of my first goals should be to get the athletic program out of debt. The red ink amounted to about $400,000, which translated to today's dollar would be about $4 million. Another development was going to cost much more money. The Title IX legislation mandating equal status for women athletes in the universities of America was gaining momentum. It would see the UW field NCAA-level teams in a dozen or so additional sports, part of the biggest expansion in the history of intercollegiate athletics.

The dilemma at Washington and at most other universities was the same: how do you pay for it? The UW athletic department prided itself on being self-supporting, paying the bills without funding from taxpayers or student fees. I detected no inclination from the UW administration to change this situation.

It was kind of like adopting a dozen new children without having any more income.

Former athletic director Joe Kearney had floated the idea of putting a matching upper deck on the north grandstands a decade or so earlier, but the suggestion was sidetracked by upper campus. Joe had warned about the difficulty of the bureaucracy at the UW, and as I found out later, he was right.

Joe told me he had obtained tentative commitments for contributions and was about to start the project, when the administration told him it was a no-go. He had some money—I can't tell you exactly how much—but it was refunded, and the plan was put in mothballs. He was told never to bring it up again.

When I started talking about stadium expansion in the mid-1970s, most people looked at me as though I'd lost my mind. Seattle had been targeted for major league teams in baseball and football, and the new franchises were gearing up to compete with the UW for fans and media attention. After the 1976 football season we projected losing about 10,000 season ticket holders to the fledgling Seahawks.

Then Don James stepped into the national spotlight of college football, and my dream of stadium expansion took on a touch of reality. It was 1977, my second year at Washington. The season had started badly—three losses in the first four games—but finished in sheer fantasy. When USC upset UCLA on the final play of their game in Los Angeles, the Huskies were heading for Pasadena and the Rose Bowl for the first time since 1963.

What happened on New Year's Day added to the excitement. Quarterback Warren Moon led an upset victory over Michigan, the first of ten post-season victories in fourteen bowl appearances by

James-coached UW teams. Besides returning the Huskies to national prominence, the victory was a message to Husky fans whose enthusiasm had been slipping in recent years. It was time to climb back aboard the bandwagon.

Going into the 1978 season, we were getting close to sold out for what fans would refer to as the "good" games, our major Pac-10 and big time intersectional opponents. The sale of season tickets was on the rise.

At this rate, despite competition with the Seahawks in the Seattle sports market, sellouts at Husky Stadium seemed very, very possible—make that probable—on a regular basis. Many of the new fans had their checkbooks out, anxious to help us expand our revenue base by becoming Tyee Club members, the athletic department boosters who paid a premium for the right to buy better football season tickets.

While I had started a seat-allocation plan, rewarding donors on the basis of sustained financial support, there was a serious problem: I didn't have any good seats available to allocate.

My first step was to enlist support for the stadium expansion plan from some of the big hitters in the community, people with high visibility and excellent resources. These longtime loyal UW backers included Bruce Nordstrom, Dave Cohn, Frank Orrico, Bob Behnke, Claude Bekins, Sam Stroum, and many, many others. They were all impressed. They quickly grasped the impact this project would have and wanted to see it happen.

I spent a lot of time selling the concept. The board of our Tyee group liked the idea and we had several influential members of the Board of Regents and many outstanding community leaders who believed the project would work.

There was opposition from most of the residential neighborhood organizations in the vicinity of Husky stadium—Montlake, Laurelhurst, View Ridge, Windermere, Hawthorne Hills—and some qualms on the part of the Seattle City Council.

I spent extensive time meeting with these groups in an attempt to convince them we wanted to be good neighbors and the University of Washington understood their concerns—about parking, more traffic congestion, noise, the glare of lights of night games, the clutter of trash, and other problems such as using residential shrubbery for toilet facilities after staying too long at a post game tailgate party.

Mike Heavey, a lawyer who became a member of the legislature and then a judge, helped us tell our story to convince the nearby residents that we could be good neighbors and keep disruption to their lifestyles at a minimum. Some of the public meetings got rather heated, and Heavey, who headed the Montlake association, did his best to calm the rhetoric.

A couple of things helped us become more credible. Montlake needed a paved footpath and bike route from the playfield to the Montlake Bridge, and I found some athletic department money to build the footpath. And at a City Council session we agreed that night football games in Husky Stadium would be held no later in the season than the end of September.

We still had to convince President Gerberding and Jim Collier. They suggested a feasibility study. Jim had some previous experience with the Grenzebach group of Chicago. So we called this company to help us determine if what we wanted to do made sense.

The man who came to Seattle to do the study was Ed Dugan, a dynamic guy, a former small college president. He came back with a favorable report that, yes, this is a plan that might work. But the brass from upper campus had another valid question. How are you going to pay for it? We don't have the money for football stadium expansion, Gerberding said, and we can't see where you do, either.

Let's make this very, very clear: the University of Washington athletic department gets zero from the university. No tax money goes for fun and games. The department runs on the cash flow that the program generates. In fact, the athletic department didn't get to keep some of the funds it was able to generate, such as parking revenue at sports events.

And we always got a bill from the physical plant for any athletic department maintenance work. The university also collected a twenty-five percent fee for "administrative costs" for any new structure or remodeling project. So if a project cost $1 million, the school received $250,000.

In a light-hearted conversation I once had with President Gerberding I asked him, "Who cuts the grass in front of the other buildings around here, like the School of Business?" He said the physical plant people do that. I pursued the question. "Well, does the School of Business pay for that?" Of course not, he responded. I said then perhaps the physical plant crew should do the same for the lawn in front of the Graves Building (home of the athletic department administration) and the football practice field. I already knew the answer.

"No, we can't do that," Gerberding replied. "You're self-supporting." I didn't push further.

There were times I played hardball successfully to keep our finances intact. I remember when Charles Royer, then mayor of Seattle, served notice he wanted us to pay more for traffic control at our events, mainly football. When I went to City Hall to talk to him about the subject, I was well prepared. I had gathered the most recent numbers on how much tax we were paying, which was considerable. I also promised His Honor that I was ready to start a political campaign against the city administration to make the university tax exempt as a not-for-profit organization, thus eliminating the taxes we were paying. I also pointed out how the city, at least at that time, was giving tax breaks to the professional sports teams but not to the UW. End of discussion.

It turned out that Ed Dugan, the Chicago feasibility expert, had already calculated an answer about how we could pay for a stadium addition. In his report he made it clear we could do the job with a combination of revenue bonds and, in some form, alumni and booster contributions.

Before we started pitching supporters for help, we turned to

John Skilling, head of the prominent Seattle engineering firm of Skilling, Ward, Magnusson, Barkshire Inc. Skilling was a UW alumnus. So was Jon Magnusson, one of the other partners. We needed something to show, a model, some architectural sketches, and plans that would better demonstrate what the project was going to look like. And I put together some statistics on how it could reverse our budget deficit. Skilling's expertise produced a rendering of the proposed work that made it easy to visualize our goal.

At one point we considered the possibility of including skyboxes, private suites that could be sold or leased to individuals or companies. With the skyrocketing cost of player salaries for the pros and rising expenses for college programs, proposed arenas and stadiums were being designed to include luxury suites. President Gerberding didn't like that idea for Husky Stadium, not at all. It was out-and-out elitism, Gerberding said, and he wanted no part of it at the University of Washington.

As an alternative, I suggested setting up a large room in the new upper deck area, similar to a facility I had seen at the University of Arizona football stadium in Tucson. It could be used for pre-game meals for boosters, social events, and other special gatherings. There would be easy access to adjoining stadium seating with chair-back seats and cup holders and a variety of bells and whistles that could be marketed to the same well-heeled patrons who might have bought skyboxes or private suites.

Elitist? Perhaps. And I thought the room might raise an amount of money comparable to luxury suites.

Gerberding stamped his OK on the concept, although I'm not certain he realized at the time how spacious the "large room," labeled the Tyee Center, would be. The glass-enclosed reception area offers a view from goal line to goal line and has a capacity of about five hundred. It was later renamed the Don James Center, a tribute to Don's great UW coaching career.

After getting Gerberding's approval of the concept, our big

boosters lined up to reserve spots in the proposed stadium club facility. The starting contribution would be $50,000, which would cover ten years. Each Tyee Center supporter also would have to pay for four football seats in the adjoining seating area.

Most of the same alums who went to bat for the stadium expansion idea got right back in step. In two weeks we were fully subscribed. Lo and behold, we had raised more than $5 million. Think that was fast? It took just two days to sell revenue bonds that would finance the rest of the $17 million plus project. Those bonds would be paid off by part of the cash flow created by new Tyee members, who now could be rewarded with good seats in the expansion project.

Architects soon were working on the specifics of the project, and finally we were able to call for bids. Demolition was scheduled to start the day after the final home game of the season in November 1986.

We had hoped that Rick Redman, a former Husky All-American and president of a prominent Seattle construction firm, would get the job. But when the bids were opened he lost out to a well-regarded Spokane firm headed by Paul Lydig. Lydig was a tough, no-nonsense veteran of numerous major projects. It didn't surprise me when I learned he had served in the U.S. Marines. My kind of guy. He was anxious to take on the job, and I think he was intrigued by the extremely demanding deadline.

Because of the tight schedule, every stage had to be planned with precision. Major construction like this can be tricky. Any minor gaffe could become a major obstacle to the work schedule. The last thing I wanted to do was move or postpone the opening game of the season against Stanford. Can you picture me calling the Kingdome to inquire if a Husky game might be squeezed between a Seahawks exhibition and a late-season Mariner baseball contest?

Thanks to a relatively mild winter, construction was on schedule. We had finished all the pilings and the critical underground work and now we were moving toward the actual stadium work, the towering superstructure.

At least until that pleasant winter morning of February 25, 1987.

The turmoil at the crash site had not subsided when Lydig took me aside for a private chat. "We can make this thing happen," he said. "I'll make you a deal. You keep those SOBs from upper campus away from me and I'll bring this thing in." That's precisely what happened.

It seemed as though the investigation of the crash was taking forever, and with each workless day I was becoming more worried about having the stadium ready for the September opener. It was hard to cope with the red tape, but nobody wanted a repeat performance. Dee Glueck, the associate athletic director whom I hired to be our department's chief liaison for the project, and some of the Tyee board members helped me work through the bureaucracy.

While investigators deliberated, Lydig's crews cleared the tons of twisted metal from the work site so it would be ready once he got a green light. The cleanup was potentially dangerous, according to experts, because of the "energy" in the steel. It could "explode" if not handled with some delicacy. The work was done with care and without incident.

Lydig and his engineers huddled to devise a totally new construction strategy designed to make up for lost time. He doubled the number of work crews. Each crew would labor ten hours a day, seven days a week, a demanding schedule that would begin from the resumption of construction until the work was completed, hopefully on time.

It would be a race against the clock, and the Lydig crew was ready for the starting gun. The pace of the race had been stepped up from a distance event to a sprint. The ironworkers put on their track shoes and went to work. At first, chances for success seemed like a longshot. After a couple of months I think the odds slipped to even money. We were catching up.

A lot of people missed vacations that summer. Dee Glueck and

I spent endless hours following the progress being made on the job site and developed a tremendous admiration for the ironworkers. They have no fear, walking on an I beam or anywhere they could get a six-inch footing. These are brave, tough guys who take risk in stride, climbing over a web of steel, welding, riveting, and bolting.

We had a special rapport. They called me Coach, and we had at least one similarity: we all wore hard hats. I gave them Husky decals for their headgear and they loved it. These were my kind of guys. They were much like football players. They had the same competitive instincts. And they kept telling me, "Don't worry, Coach, we're going to bring this SOB in for you."

I loved their enthusiasm and pride, especially when they topped out the steelwork and hoisted an American flag to the highest point of the new stadium wing. The celebration over completing the project—marked with the pop of champagne corks—was extremely satisfying; it was as if we had won a championship on the playing field.

Compared to what those iron workers had done, a championship would have been a breeze.

If the workers were the players, Lydig and his subcontractors were the coaches. They deserve a tremendous amount of credit, mapping out the week-by-week,

*UW top brass (left to right) Tallman Trask, William Gerberding and Jim Collier don hard hats and join me for a tour of the Husky Stadium addition*

day-by-day schedule of work and then making sure it was completed. As it turned out, the insurance took care of the extra expense of rebuilding after the crash. Our concerns and questions were answered without legal intervention, and Lydig might even have made some money on the job. Other contractors have faced bankruptcy in similar situations, but Lydig's company remained in business long after the stadium work was history.

During most of the summer Dee Glueck attended every daily morning meeting with the contractors, and he had a major role in keeping things on track. Another hero was Al Tarr, who ran the UW's physical plant. When it came to fielding every imaginable question from all sides, he was like an outfielder with three arms. Al loved a sip of Wild Turkey to relax from the pressure of many long days on a difficult job, and we became close friends.

As the Stanford game deadline neared we still had a few unexpected hurdles to clear. One of the last things left to do was installation of the guardrails along the ramps winding up to the upper deck. The railing arrived on schedule but the pieces didn't fit. Attempts to modify the parts failed. Since we were not eager to have Husky fans fall off the ramps as they arrived to find their new seats we installed temporary posts and chain link fencing.

As we put the finishing touches on opening game festivities, we had a mini-crisis. None of the seats or aisles in the new north stands had numbers on them. We found the decals that had been ordered but had not been attached. I quickly organized a big crew from the athletic department and our maintenance ranks. Can you imagine if all those fans had gone looking for their new seats with no way to identify them? It was a routine but important job that had to be done precisely. As far as I know, not a single ticket holder complained. An overflow crowd of 73,676 turned out to see the Huskies beat Stanford that afternoon, 31-21.

The stadium expansion helped avoid a serious financial crisis. With a budget deficit and the dawning of a new era in women's sports there was no way we could have kept our full program intact. Joe Kearney, my predecessor, had made a lot of cuts in the budgets of individual sports before he left. Reluctantly, I eliminated men's gymnastics and wrestling.

For the athletic program to remain self-sufficient and pay for the added women's sports required by Title IX, we needed the added revenue that would come via stadium expansion. I think it needs to be said that yes, I was a football coach; yes, I understand football. But this was a benefit to all sports because the expanded stadium would generate funds to pay for the non-revenue-producing sports.

I remember asking Al Thompson, a former grocery chain executive who was one of our radio sponsors, what he would do if he had a store that just wasn't producing and had to pour money into it every week of every year. He said, "I'd close it."

In athletics we had one huge supermarket, football. All the other stores were losing money. But unlike a grocery store that lost money, I couldn't shut them down.

One word best defines the impact of adding 13,500 new seats to Husky Stadium: solvency. From a sheer business standpoint, I consider it my most significant accomplishment at Washington. It did a lot more than wipe out the $400,000 debt I inherited. When I retired in 1991 there was roughly $18 million in reserve, give or take a million.

In 2001 *The Sporting News* included Husky Stadium in its tribute to "Our Saturday Cathedrals," ranking it among the top five college football stadiums in the country with Tennessee's Neyland Stadium, Notre Dame Stadium, Florida Field, and Kyle Field at Texas A&M. TSN said Husky Stadium "stretches high into the sky, giving it a bigger-than-life feel and almost all the seats are between the end zones . . . Planners also wanted to make sure to maximize the views of Lake Washington and surrounding mountains."

The expansion boosted the stadium's listed capacity to 72,500, giving the UW the fiscal clout to attract the nation's most prestigious college teams—Michigan, Miami, Ohio State, Notre Dame, Alabama, to name a few—as intersectional opponents. The Huskies have led the Pac-10 in attendance consistently in the past two decades.

Several months after the stadium had opened, Don James and I joined a Husky booster gathering. When Don got up to speak, he reflected on the way we pushed the construction job to completion. "You know," Don said with a wide grin, "Mike got that stadium up, and it was his last erection."

The laughter had barely stopped when my wife, Rena, yelled from out of the crowd, "That's not true." More laughs. Yes, finally, with relief, we could all laugh.

# 15

## THE GERBERDING YEARS:
## A GOOD MARRIAGE GONE BAD

◆ ◆ ◆

One of the last things William P. Gerberding did before departing the University of Illinois to become president of the University of Washington seemed rather unusual to me. No, it was more than that. It was a shocker.

He fired the Illinois athletic director.

The action came after Gerberding had accepted the job in Seattle when he returned to wrap up his duties on the Illinois campus. It turned my normal concern about getting a new boss to abnormal apprehension.

I was well acquainted with Cecil Coleman, professionally and as a personal friend. He was well regarded nationally and had served as president of the National Association of Collegiate Directors of Athletics a few years earlier. From everything I knew and had observed he was highly respected in the Big 10 Conference for the program he headed at Illinois.

I knew very little about Bill Gerberding. My new boss had taught at UCLA and studied at the University of Chicago, schools separated by a deep philosophical chasm when it comes to athletics. UCLA has a reputation as a national all-sports power; Chicago is well known as the school that dropped its football program because it distracted from the institution's academics. Which would it be at Washington with Gerberding in command?

Then I got a call from Karol Kahrs, a member of Coleman's athletic staff at Illinois, and what she said only intensified my anxieties.

"If you ever have the opportunity to play golf with Bill Gerberding," Ms. Kahrs advised me, "just make sure you don't beat him. He doesn't take that kindly." Hmmm. Is that what cost Cecil Coleman his job? Beating the boss on the golf course? Come on. But I wasn't quick-witted enough to ask. Then again, maybe I didn't really want the answer.

After Dr. Gerberding arrived and had settled into his new office in the UW Administration Building, I did organize a golf game at Seattle Golf Club with the two of us and a couple of prominent boosters. Coming to the eighteenth green, the match was tied. Competitor that I am—former football coaches and ex-Marines are like that—I managed to sink a lucky thirty-foot putt to win the hole and the match.

Yes, I remembered the words of Ms. Kahrs. But as far as I know, sinking that putt never proved to be a liability in my association with Gerberding.

At least through the first nine or ten years of our relationship.

In fact, those years were among the most satisfying and successful of my career. The football team—which is the huge engine that makes almost every big-time college athletic program successful—was already winning: two bowl games in the first three years I was on the job in Seattle. It got better and better as Coach Don James established our football program as a national powerhouse.

Gerberding quickly made it clear he had no inclination to change the fiscal relationship of the school and the Washington athletic program. He was adamant about keeping the athletic department on a self-sustaining basis—no taxpayer or student funds would be diverted for frivolities such as throwing passes, shooting baskets, or rowing shells around the lake.

He was supportive—albeit that backing often was reluctant—

in allowing me to make some dramatic strides, including expanding our football stadium and adding other sports facilities. I eliminated the debt I had inherited and put our program on a strong financial footing despite the strain of launching an entire women's intercollegiate program as mandated by the Title IX gender-equity legislation.

That was before the marriage started to crumble.

When it did come unraveled, all of the letters, notes, and memos from President Gerberding that praised my efforts, telling me how lucky the University was to have me running the Department of Intercollegiate Athletics and what a great job I had done with a wide variety of projects and programs seemed worthless.

The Bill Gerberding I got to know was far different from the picture of composure and control he projected in public. I remember too vividly the Gerberding who fumed and criticized and who could be hostile to the point of insulting in the presence of someone with whom he disagreed.

*William Gerberding's praises turned to criticism*

In my experience he had an extremely low boiling point.

Not long before Gerberding retired—he was 65 and in his final year as UW president—a *Seattle Post-Intelligencer* feature story examined his regime. The article quoted him as saying: "I try to listen to people and accommodate. It's my opinion most quarrels, most shootouts in academe are unnecessary. They result from a failure to communicate with a failure to be tolerant."

The article pointed out that despite his achievements Gerberding "is neither evangelistic in style or a man given to grand visions. He attributes his success to being realistic, communicating honestly and working hard."

I just about choked on my Wheaties. Sure, the man worked hard. Certainly, he had to deal with a lot of issues, most of which he probably felt had a higher priority than the athletic program. As for the part about communicating honestly, though, let me put it this way: there were times I thought that he had either strong memory lapses or he handled the truth imprecisely.

It's hard to measure exactly how much damage was caused by Gerberding's severe criticism of some commonly accepted programs and practices and his flat opposition to others. Needless to say, if some of his ideas and opinions had been followed, the University of Washington would have been far less successful in the fiercely competitive world of intercollegiate athletics.

Gerberding grated over rewarding coaches with bonuses when University of Washington teams performed at a high level—bowl games and post-season tournament appearances. Such incentives are common practice throughout the business world. He fumed about our agreement with area auto dealers to have them provide courtesy cars to coaches and administrators, a plan similar to those used by almost every college athletic department in the country.

He criticized beloved Marv Harshman, the men's basketball coach, when Marv blew his cork at referees but Gerberding never said a word when women's coach Chris Gobrecht did the same thing. He rejected an offer—at little or no cost to the school—to have a world-class competitive swimming venue built on the UW campus, a much-needed facility that ended up being located in the far corner of King County, Federal Way.

He embarrassed me time and again—in Pac-10 Conference meetings and in negotiating with those outside the university, such as the Seattle SuperSonics. He let me take much of the heat, unfairly so, for the infamous melee when students were sprayed with Mace while trying to tear down the goal posts after Washington won the Apple Cup football game in 1989.

He brusquely vetoed the recommendation that John Price, head of the UW Law School, should replace law professor Harry Cross as our faculty athletic representative. I had gone to Gerberding's office with Cross, who had served with distinction for twenty-two years, including a term as president of the NCAA, to urge Price's appointment. Gerberding told us bluntly:

"I don't want any damn lawyer as our faculty rep."

Cross and I were speechless.

Gerberding was less than elated when the football coach showed up in separate appearances on the same platform with the president and vice president of the United States.

But the Gerberding era didn't start out like that.

In the first nine years I felt the president and I worked effectively together. My wife, Rena, and I enjoyed the company of Bill and Ruth Gerberding at a number of social activities, some of which were at their home. I felt blessed to have such a good CEO. I made a point to see he was well taken care of whenever I had the opportunity. He was a busy person, but I kept him informed about all the projects we were working on in the Department of Intercollegiate Athletics. I know he liked what I was doing, and he told me so.

Listen to this vote of support Gerberding gave me less than two years after he arrived on the Washington campus. He wrote: "My comments to the regents in January regarding the quality of the management of our athletic program . . . grow out of my genuine conviction that you are a fine athletic director. As I have had occasion to indicate to you in another connection recently, the woods are not full of such people and we are fortunate to have you."

He also made clear that he understood that it wasn't necessary for the president and the athletic director to agree on every issue. "I do not expect that our perspectives on everything will be the same," Gerberding wrote. "That is extremely unlikely in an area of such complexity when two intelligent, independent individuals are involved. All I expect is that we will be candid with each other and that has been my experience."

In another letter, dispatched after a football trip to the Freedom Bowl, he offered the thanks of the board of regents and his staff for the first-class treatment the presidential party had received. Gerberding wrote:

"You are a remarkable organizer of complex events. The myriad of tasks that need to be done are accomplished smoothly and quietly—and not effortlessly—by you and your staff. I want you to know that these achievements do not go unnoticed or unappreciated.

"Such logistical skills are, of course, not the only—or perhaps even the most important—attributes of a successful athletic director. It is true, however, that such skills would not so frequently be utilized if you were not also proficient in the other aspects of your job."

In another memo to Don James, the head football coach, and me, Gerberding wrote: "I have made a number of changes in the administration of this university. It is a source of great satisfaction to me that none are or will be needed in intercollegiate sports. I'm lucky and proud to be associated with both of you."

That was long before our relationship began to come apart.

In the year or two before I was pushed out of my job as athletic director—it was announced as a "retirement"—Gerberding became increasingly distant from me and from the athletic program. At one point, we were staying at the same hotel in Philadelphia. He was attending a meeting of research university presidents and I was chairman of a Pac-10 Television Committee session. But I never saw him, even after I voiced a desire to meet with him. He completely avoided me the entire three-days. This was at a critical time when Chuck Armstrong was considering Gerberding's offer to be interim athletic director.

Certainly, Gerberding had been faced with a full range of responsibilities and issues. College presidents are required to perform a delicate balancing act—satisfying the needs and egos of the intellectual community, facing the demands of students at a stage in life when they question everything, and constantly selling legislators on the pressing budget needs of higher education.

Thus, I felt when Gerberding and I attended Pac-10 Conference meetings we were fortunate to have with us the experience and expertise of Harry Cross, the University of Washington's veteran faculty representative. No one was more helpful to me than Cross, associate dean of the UW law school. He was a shrewd veteran of many, many conference meetings. Harry brought a huge depth of understanding from a faculty point of view, the administration point of view, and the athletic point of view.

On occasion, Gerberding could be extremely forceful—even antagonistic—in expressing opinions at conference meetings. His candor sometimes had Harry and me scrambling to play the role of mediator with the targets of his comments. I felt then and still do that Harry Cross was the best thing the University of Washington had going for it in intercollegiate athletics.

That's why I thought Gerberding's comment about not wanting another lawyer as Harry's replacement was especially distasteful. I had tried to talk Cross into remaining in the role he held for so long until I was scheduled to retire. I even promised to provide him an unlimited supply of his favorite bourbon. He had a reputation as being an all-American connoisseur.

Before making a recommendation to Gerberding, Harry and I discussed the job at length and concluded it would be wise to have another law professor in this position. We agreed that Price, the law school dean, would be ideal. He was reluctant, though, so Harry and I plotted to sell him on the idea. We discovered the faculty athletic representative at Minnesota was also the dean of that school's law school, someone Price liked and respected. We got him to call John Price to convince him to take the job. It worked.

Price agreed to accept, but then Gerberding shot down our strategy. Price didn't seem totally surprised when we informed him the president didn't want a "damn lawyer" in that role and was launching a search of his own on campus. Gerberding, with the agreement of Jim Collier, vice president for university relations, had zeroed in on Dick Dunn, an English professor whose scholarly focus was Charles Dickens. The UW administrators didn't know much about Dunn, but I think they felt he might be less than positive about athletics because of his academic background.

As it turned out, Dunn had played football and wrestled in high school and college and had coached wrestling at the Air Force Academy while stationed there. To the shock of Gerberding and Collier, Professor Dunn was a strong supporter of intercollegiate athletics. He went on to serve for ten years as Harry Cross's successor. He had some uneasy moments serving at the pleasure of Gerberding, but I consider him a close friend and a good faculty athletic representative.

It became routine before each conference meeting for the faculty rep and me to brief Dr. Gerberding on the issues that were on the agenda and sit on either side of him at the appropriate meetings to keep him up to speed. I would be the first to realize that most college presidents have higher priorities than the athletic program. But, like Gerberding, their intellectual prowess enables them to be a quick read of most issues.

Sometimes, though, an opinion or a stand on a particular matter came too quickly. One of those decisions by Dr. Gerberding cost the University of Washington a new swimming and diving facility.

When Bob Walsh brought the Goodwill Games to Seattle in 1990, the one major sports facility lacking in the city was a first-class venue for swimming and diving. When the Goodwill Games were over, Seattle still lacked such a venue. That's because it ended up being built in Federal Way.

The Goodwill Games, an Olympics-type international all-sports event, had been the brainchild of media mogul Ted Turner, who wanted to bring the former Soviet Union and the U.S. together athletically following back-to-back boycotts of the Olympics in 1980 (U.S.) and 1984 (USSR). Organizers of the Goodwill Games in Seattle wanted to build the pool on the UW campus, stage the international swimming and diving competition there, and then turn the facility over to the University of Washington to be an attractive new home for the Husky swimming program. It looked like a no-lose proposition to me.

The most likely campus location was at the site of the tennis courts between Edmundson Pavilion and the intramural building. The tennis courts could have been rebuilt over the pool. Dave Sabey, a prominent Seattle developer and a former Husky football player, had offered to build the pool at no cost to the university. Gerberding said flatly he wasn't interested; he didn't think Sabey could pull it off. End of discussion. Forget it. As a result there's a world-class natatorium in the south end of King County, miles from the campus and under used because of its location.

Gerberding was especially sensitive to anything that might create a negative impression of the University of Washington. I remember being at home, watching the Husky men's basketball team on television in a game against UCLA in Los Angeles. It was late in the season and the Huskies were in the thick of a championship run. UW Coach Marv Harshman protested an official's call at some length and was ejected from the game. Gerberding was not a happy president.

I tried my best to explain that getting frustrated and being tossed out of an occasional game is something all basketball coaches, both good and bad, go through. Gerberding wanted to call Harshman on the carpet and order him to return immediately from the California road trip. After a long meeting, Gerberding relented. I would join the team in Los Angeles and sit on the bench to make sure there were no more outbursts.

Gerberding fumed again when one of the Washington assistant basketball coaches was picked up for speeding on the freeway to Portland to visit a high school recruiting prospect. The coach was driving a vehicle that carried dealer license plates, and state officials started asking questions.

The car was one of several dozen that were part of our Car Coaches program, one of the fringe benefits offered to coaches and staff members at most major universities and by professional teams. Auto dealers actually loan the vehicles, and in return they receive game tickets, get a chance to make a road trip each season on the Husky football charter flight, and are feted with a banquet at the end of the season.

The president was extremely upset over the publicity when the basketball assistant was stopped in a car with dubious plates. Gerberding wanted to junk the entire automobile program. I didn't like the bad exposure, either, but being able to provide a free car is an attractive financial incentive in reducing turnover in the UW sports family.

The auto dealers who provide the loaner cars and their staff people, normally enthusiastic sports fans, like the idea of being affiliated with a successful program. The car people liked it even better if one of those coaches using a car enjoyed it enough to buy it for his wife or family.

Dropping the program would have put us in a non-competitive situation with almost every other major university in the country. After the emotions had subsided, Paul Cressman Sr., an outstanding Seattle attorney, worked out the legalities with the attorney general and the state auditor to save the Car Coaches program.

When Gerberding first arrived at Washington, I mentioned the possibility of arranging a vehicle for him through the Car Coaches program but he declined. So did Jim Collier, who followed him from Illinois to become vice president for university relations and the man between Gerberding and me in the chain of command. Collier later decided to take advantage of our dealer contacts, and I helped him lease a vehicle for about one-fourth of the retail rate through a Toyota dealer and a UW booster, Jerry Kenney.

Gerberding was not pleased when he picked up his morning newspaper and read about football coach Don James sharing a platform with Vice President George H. W. Bush during a campaign stop in Seattle. Don had felt honored when asked to present a football to the VP.

Gerberding didn't agree, but I'm not clear if his reasons were based on principle or politics. Born in Fargo, North Dakota the son of a Lutheran minister, Gerberding grew up in St. Paul, Minn. His academic forte was political science, and early in his career he worked for Senator Eugene McCarthy, an unabashed liberal Democrat from Minnesota. He was less than enthralled to see his football coach on the same platform with a conservative national figure.

James insisted he was only honoring the office rather than Bush. And Gerberding's reaction didn't stop the UW coach from a repeat performance at a Ronald Reagan re-election gathering a short time later. Originally, James had been asked to introduce the president, but protocol required that a prominent elected official handle those honors. So instead Don was asked to present President Reagan with a token gift and he agreed.

Religion also came into question, for a while. Early in Gerberding's presidency, I suggested that toward the end of each home football game he come down on the playing field, win or lose, and go into the locker room to get more acquainted with our coaches and players. Coincidentally, that also allowed him to witness one of the long-standing traditions of sports at most levels: a postgame prayer.

Gerberding didn't like it. I explained that we had two chaplains, one Catholic from the Newman Club on campus and a Protestant chaplain who was teaching Christian ethics in medicine at the medical school. The chaplains had never forced the players to pray; their message was pray in your own way—if you wish to pray.

Gerberding said that's not right. We might have Muslims, or Jewish players or atheists, whatever, he said. Yes, I countered, that well might be the case, but no one was forced to take part, that the prayers were all voluntary.

No matter, he reiterated that he didn't like the idea of having prayers and asked if other sports, like basketball, also had prayers. Of course, I said, prompting him to suggest that it would be his inclination to end locker room prayers in the men's basketball program after Marv Harshman stepped down as coach.

Before any edicts were issued regarding a prayer policy, though, I wanted to determine if our women's program had similar prayers. Yes we do, said women's coach Chris Gobrecht. While Gerberding barely tolerated the men's program, he and Collier were strong boosters of women's basketball. He was an enthusiastic follower of the women's program and of Gobrecht, a feisty, defense-oriented coach. Yes, I also respected and admired her style and success.

I informed Collier that prayers were also part of the regular routine of the women's team, before and after each game. I asked if the president wanted prayers to cease in the men's dressing room, should we not be consistent and also ban them for the women's team? Collier grimaced. "Oh, no. Are you sure?" Collier asked. He said he'd get back to me.

He didn't. And after that I never heard another word about the elimination of prayers in the locker rooms.

There were occasions when Gerberding could be indecisive. When we were pondering how to upgrade or replace an aging basketball facility, Edmundson Pavilion, the NBA Seattle SuperSonics were in a similar dilemma with their home venue, the Coliseum at Seattle Center. Gerberding suggested I talk with the Sonics about jointly building a new arena that would be used by both teams.

I had been pushing for a new basketball arena on the parking lot on the south side of Husky Stadium, our football facility. The talented John Skilling and his associate, Jon Magnusson, had worked up some preliminary drawings and schematics, and I was trying to sell the idea to Gerberding and Collier, the man to whom I directly reported in the UW chain of command. Skilling also had done a set of drawings to renovate Edmundson Pavilion (which was eventually done) to make it more attractive to basketball fans.

I have never liked the concept of having college and professional sports share facilities, no matter what the sport. But I did as told by my boss and broached the idea to SuperSonics executive Bob Whitsitt.

Whitsitt and Barry Ackerley, the team owner, agreed the concept was worth further discussion. When I conveyed their response to President Gerberding he said he'd changed his mind. Tell the Sonics to forget it. I got back to Whitsitt and he expressed disappointment. "Obviously, your boss wasn't too firm on his thoughts in the beginning," Whitsitt said. I couldn't disagree.

About two years passed. Seemingly out of the blue, Gerberding brought up the joint-use arena idea again and suggested we try to revive it. So I got on the phone with Whitsitt. His rejection—and I was hardly surprised—came in a few blunt words, laced with an expletive or two: the Sonics were not interested.

Nothing seemed to bother Gerberding more than the simple bonuses I handed out to our coaches, and to leaders in the athletic department staff, including myself, when our teams were successful. It's not unlike the business world when a special, super job performance is rewarded with a bonus, extra pay, incentives—you get the idea.

When a college sports program, especially football, is successful, it generates media attention, which in turn creates envy. Schools and teams that have slipped to also-ran status start coveting the magic touch of the winner. All too suddenly, coaches once deemed mere humans are branded with labels of greatness.

To keep winners in place and make outside offers less tempting, athletic directors have developed what I call honorariums for coaches and staff for superior performance: the practice was based on qualifying for bowl games, NCAA tournament appearances, or other national recognition.

This concept, as common as it is across the map, seemed like a foreign tongue to Gerberding. I started wondering if maybe Don James' teams were just too successful for our leader. Whatever, Gerberding seemed to get angry every time the subject came up, which was almost every year.

I started the bonus idea when the Husky football team earned its first Rose Bowl appearance under Don James after the 1977 season. I put together a plan and presented it to Dr. John Hogness, then the school president; Al Ulbrickson, who had been vice president for student affairs; Jim Ryan, the UW VP for business and finance; and Jim Wilson of the Attorney General's office, the school's legal adviser. They approved the policy and we moved ahead.

When Gerberding took over I advised him of the program that had been in place, and later, after I started reporting to Jim Collier, I outlined to him what our policy had been. My impression was they both had a thorough understanding of the concept and had no objection.

I clearly remember going over details of the honorariums with Collier on the return flight to Seattle following the Husky victory at the 1982 Aloha Bowl in Hawaii. I showed him the proposed salary raises and honorariums for that year, and Jim seemed to be in full agreement. I even mentioned that at most schools athletic directors receive similar bonuses and he agreed. When I asked what he thought should be the proper amount for my bonus he suggested the same number I had proposed for the football coach. So it was added to the budget.

Fast forward to the 1987 Independence Bowl. As usual, I had recommended payment of honorariums and salary increases, but the paperwork didn't get past Gerberding. I was shocked. This was the ninth straight bowl appearance for Husky football teams. I countered that I thought that our policy regarding honorariums had been made clear before, each time we went to a bowl game. Jim Ryan, the former VP of business finance, verified it; he was with me at the time I told Gerberding about it. Gerberding was not happy and insisted he had not been informed.

The issue came to a showdown while I was attending a meeting of Pac-10 athletic directors and faculty representatives in San Francisco. Gerberding, who would be attending a meeting of school presidents later in the week, telephoned me to set up a meeting when he arrived in San Francisco. Meanwhile, Gerberding called several others, including Dick Dunn, Washington's faculty representative, and Tom Hansen, the Pac-10 commissioner. Tom told me that Gerberding had been upset about bonuses for coaches and administrators and said (1) he wasn't going to approve them, and (2) other universities weren't offering similar bonuses based on performance. Hansen said he told Gerberding, as politely as he could, that he was wrong—that most schools rewarded good work.

Gerberding invited me to go across the street from the hotel where we had been meeting and have a cocktail. We spent more than an hour and he flat out told me this was wrong and that he didn't know about it. I reminded him that he had been told and that Jim Collier was involved in it and I thought everyone had signed off on the policy. From the first Rose Bowl trip, the bonus rewards were routinely reiterated in subsequent bowl seasons in 1979, 1980, 1981, 1982, 1983, 1984, 1985 and 1986 and when UW basketball teams qualified for post-season basketball tournaments in 1980, 1982, 1985 and 1986.

At the same meeting Gerberding also insisted he knew nothing about a golf club membership at Sand Point Country Club that the athletic department had provided for Collier.

Several years earlier, when I had been attending a meeting of athletic directors, Gerberding and Collier were at a women's basketball game and they saw Mike Alderson, my associate AD for business and finance. According to what Alderson told me, Gerberding asked Alderson about getting Collier a courtesy membership at Sand Point, the same as had been provided for Don James, Marv Harshman and me. Despite the efforts of Tracy King, UW director of alumni relations, and Bud Knudsen, a professor of business management, the golf club turned down the request for another honorary membership.

Then it was suggested that the athletic department pay for

Collier's golf club membership; it could be considered in lieu of a bowl honorarium as received by the coaches and me. Sure, it was a stretch for a university vice president to be rewarded for his role in a successful bowl appearance, but I wanted to keep the administration on my side. I was quite taken aback when Gerberding told me in San Francisco that he knew nothing about the Sand Point membership for Collier. In fact, he said he was angry at Collier and said he might put him on a leave of absence or even fire him.

I couldn't comprehend how Gerberding had no memory of any of this, unless I had somehow got wrong information from Mike Alderson or there was a colossal misunderstanding someplace along the line. I never found out for sure.

Meanwhile, my career at Washington was in high gear. I continued to play a prominent role in business affairs of both the NCAA and Pac-10 Conference. I got considerable exposure as president of the National Association of Collegiate Directors of Athletics (1981-'82). We brought the NCAA Final Four basketball championships to Seattle's Kingdome in 1984 and the event was a dazzling success. Gerberding's reaction prompted another note of appreciation.

"Before Seattle drowns in its self-congratulatory rhetoric, I want to tell you again how impressed I and everyone else have been by your efforts re the Final Four. You've done a wonderful job and I hope you'll take it easier for a while."

A year later a Phoenix newspaper conducted a poll to rank the country's collegiate athletic directors, and to my surprise, I finished second in the voting behind Don Canham of Michigan. I became chairman of the Pac-10 Budget Committee in 1987 and two years later took over as head of the critical conference Television Committee, the group that negotiated all of our TV contracts.

I was flattered to receive a call from a UCLA vice chancellor asking me to be a consultant in finding a new athletic director at the Los Angeles school. I was asked to go to Southern California for a meeting, which turned out to be with the selection committee. The ploy turned out to be an interview for the job. There was no offer but they seemed interested.

When I returned I met with Gerberding, and we talked at length about a wide range of issues, including expansion of Husky Stadium, tuition waivers for scholarship athletes—thus reducing one of our major budget items—my concerns about funding a wide array of new women's sports, and our need for financial help beyond what we could create on our own.

He said the intercollegiate athletic program had a high priority with him and agreed that some facilities need improvement. He was candid in saying he didn't see any significant additional revenue sources for either existing programs or the added women's sports, but he said they deserved strong support. Gerberding, a former UCLA faculty member, said I wouldn't like UCLA and urged me to stay at Washington. He told me I would be getting a new long-term contract but rejected my request to report directly to him rather than through Jim Collier.

The bottom line: I called UCLA back and said, yes, I'm interested. Before I could pursue another meeting, it was announced in Los Angeles that Peter Dalis had been named the new athletic director. With all the political overtones at UCLA, Pete was the right choice at that time. He held the job until retiring in 2002.

As my national leadership and influence was reaching its apex, I was facing an increasingly difficult time back on the University of Washington campus. It was in late 1989 when Gerberding made the decision that he was not going to agree to the addendum extending my five-year contract to June, 1992—the retirement date I thought had been spelled out when I agreed to a long-term contract in 1986. My relationship with Vice President Collier was becoming increasingly strained, despite all I had done for him.

The role that I considered the most prestigious and gave me the most pride was serving as chairman of the NCAA Football Playing Rules Committee. Few groups have so much influence in the success (or failure) of college football, and I held the gavel at those meetings from 1989 through 1991. It came shortly after I was the recipient of the James Corbett Award as the nation's Outstanding Athletic Director (1988). A year later the Final Four returned to Seattle, and I'm convinced the hospitality extended to teams and fans that made the event so successful in '84 and '89 was critical in the successful bid for the premier basketball tournament again in 1995.

Husky football teams were making regular annual trips to bowl games, and season ticket sales and Tyee Club donations were booming. After seven consecutive bowl trips, Don was anxious to keep the streak alive after his team went 8-2-1 in 1986, tied for second in the Pac-10. But when I notified Gerberding we had received a Sun Bowl invitation, he was far from enthusiastic. I had a tough sell but I kept talking. The Sunday night after our final football game, my phone was ringing every fifteen minutes with calls from the Sun Bowl Selection Committee wanting an answer.

I continued calling Gerberding while holding off the Sun Bowl, and finally he said he didn't approve but if I wanted to do it to go ahead.

And once again he voiced criticism of the honorarium program, the incentives that we used to reward the staff that had been responsible for so much success.

Still, the lure of El Paso wasn't too dazzling to Husky football fans; they seemed to be getting picky after so many bowl appearances. As the game approached it appeared we were going to fall short of the ticket guarantee we had made with Sun Bowl officials. I decided to give away a large number of tickets to military personnel stationed near the Texas city. Gerberding didn't like that, either, mainly because he didn't like the idea of accepting the bowl bid in the first place.

Likewise, Gerberding, at various times, opposed allowing the Husky men's basketball team to play in the National Invitational Tournament. He was also skeptical about keeping Washington State, Oregon, and Oregon State in the Pac-10 Conference.

In a March 1987 memo, the president said flatly: "For the record, I not only favor abolishing the NIT—pre- and post-season—but I also favor the UW not accepting an NIT bid this year. . . or any other year. I'm not going to insist on it this year, but I may in the future. The NCAA tournament stretches my conscience pretty far, coming as it does in March, during finals, etc. Not to get into the NCAA means you've had a mediocre year. I seen no reason whatsoever to extend such a season by going to an inferior post-season tournament, which also conflicts with finals."

Early in Gerberding's tenure at Washington, we were meeting in his office when he said the smaller Northwest schools probably had no business competing in the Pac-10. There had been some discussion about the disparity in the seating capacity in football stadiums and in the revenue shared by visiting teams. Some of the California schools, mainly USC and UCLA, didn't want to play road games in the smaller Northwest stadiums and had pushed through legislation mandating more seats if they were required to travel to Pullman, Eugene, and Corvallis.

I disagreed with Gerberding's concept, pointing out that these schools were long-time rivals of the University of Washington, and besides, I said with a smile, "it's nice to have corpses to beat up on." I also asked: What would we do with our other sports for scheduling? He indicated I ought to be able to work that out and changed the subject.

It's unlikely Gerberding would have predicted the reversal of fortune in the last decade by programs of Oregon, Washington State, and Oregon State, producing numerous winning teams and consistent challengers to the so-called traditional powers. As far as I know his opinion never reached fans of our Northwest rivals.

While Gerberding was always quick to condemn the action of others within the UW family that might create attention not flattering to the University of Washington, he had his own share of unfavorable media treatment.

He took a personal broadside hit in a *Seattle Times* story headlined:

"Worst boss? UW's Gerberding gets Dishonorable mention in competition"

Accompanied by a head shot of Gerberding, the article reported the university president was the third runner-up in a contest listing the nation's "downright unbelievable bosses." The contest was sponsored by a group called 9to5, the National Association of Working Women, which celebrates Professional Secretaries' Week with awards for good and bad bosses.

Gerberding supposedly failed to seek salary raises for the university's 3,000 plus office, clerical, and technical workers, something he denied. At the time it seemed like a cheap shot but looking back, I might applaud the perception of the secretaries' organization. One can only wonder about Gerberding's reaction if one of his deans or department heads had been singled out in a similar uncomplimentary manner.

In the spring of 1990, Gerberding was in the midst of what a *Seattle Weekly* writer called "one of the biggest public relations disasters of Gerberding's 12-year term." A crowd estimated at 250 protesting students gathered under the porch of the Administration Building on the UW campus. The students were singing and chanting things like "Hey hey, ho ho, racism has got to go!"

They were there to express support of a proposed ethnic studies requirement (ESR) that would mandate ten academic credits of classes dealing with race, class and gender for all undergraduate students. More so, they were calling to task the school president for a joke they felt was racist. According to *Seattle Weekly*, at a banquet two weeks earlier, "Gerberding had 'jested' that a Chicano graduate student being honored at the banquet was an illegal alien."

Not everybody seemed to think the comment was very funny. Gerberding apologized to the crowd of protesters, then answered questions, including a couple about ESR, which he managed to duck several times. Then things got ugly.

THE GERBERDING YEARS: A GOOD MARRIAGE GONE BAD ◆ 191

According to the *Weekly* story: "One woman lambastes the university's educational-opportunity program; another challenges Gerberding to define diversity. 'Diversity,' he said, 'includes all of you folks out in front of me, white, black, all in-betweens.' Shouts and catcalls greet his answer, and Gerberding turns to Ernesto Sandoval, commissioner of the Chicano student group MECHA. 'Ernesto? Have we done what we need to do?' The verbal flogging continues just as long as the president wants it to. He wraps things up with a big wave. 'OK, thanks for coming by, it's a pleasure to see you.'"

Eight months later, the University of Washington *Daily* bannered a story "ESR nears last hurdle" on its front page. Sharing the above-the-fold display on the same page was an ironic headline: "Alum revokes $1 million gift over Lude retirement." The story detailed how a wealthy UW alumnus, Will Thomas, had announced he was withdrawing a gift of one million dollars to the athletic department because of "the administration's unfair treatment of Lude, who was denied a one-year extension of his contract that would have seen him reach the mandatory retirement age of 70."

Gerberding's disdain for any deed or action that reflected badly on the institution, though, reached an even higher level at the Washington-Washington State Apple Cup football game in Husky Stadium in November 1989. That was the infamous melee that started when jubilant UW fans swarmed on the field after a 20-9 Washington victory, bent on tearing down the goal posts.

Before peace had been restored, fans had been sprayed with Mace, three students were arrested, four others were treated for minor injuries, and a campus cop received a broken wrist.

As the final seconds ticked off the scoreboard clock, about 150 fans ran onto the field and headed for the goal posts. The first student to climb the goal posts was squirted with Mace by campus police. Then a warning was broadcast by the stadium announcer than the same treatment awaited anyone who approached the posts. Some students threw chairs and beer bottles as police and staff ushers wrestled others to the ground. Soon the crowd outnumbered the security forces and the west goal posts came crashing down.

Targeted for at least some of the blame was UW *Daily* sports writer Todd San Jule. The headline of his column the day before the game read: "Tear 'em down." He predicted a Husky victory and offered this advice to UW students: "When the Huskies beat WSU and you're jumping around the stands exchanging high-fives and yelling 'Damn you Cougars,' take the celebration out on the AstroTurf. But don't stop there . . . You've always wondered what it's like to tear down the goal posts. The time is now to find out."

This proved to be bad advice for many.

Because it was a football game, much of the blame for the incident was directed by media, fans and students at the athletic department. As athletic director, I seemed to be painted with a bull's-eye, even to the point of being blamed for giving the orders to Mace the crowd. The command to use Mace did not come from me; I was not in charge of the police or of student crowd control. Vice President Ernest Morris was in charge of student control at football games and Mike Shanahan was the UW police chief.

While letting me dangle in public as the culprit in the incident, Gerberding let me off the hook, in private. In a confidential memo dated November 25, 1989, Gerberding wrote he had no interest in "allocating blame for the ugly episode." Later in the three-page, single-spaced memo he made it clear that I was not responsible. He wrote:

"By the way, it should be noted that Mike Lude—the favorite target of the students and the media—made *none* of the decisions alluded to above. He participated in the discussions in some areas, but basic decisions about the sale of tickets, seating arrangements, police practices and so forth were made by others."

I was told Gerberding did inform the Board of Regents that Mike Lude did not make the decision to use Mace, but that he—

Gerberding—was not going to make an announcement of who was responsible.

None of this ever made it to the media or general public. So to many, I carried the unfortunate designation of being the one who ordered the Mace spraying and caused those crowd control problems. The whole thing was clouded with anonymity, the usual bureaucratic approach to such matters.

My relationship with Gerberding began to deteriorate in 1987, I think, the year we finished the expansion of Husky Stadium, and continued to go sour. The busier the president got with other responsibilities the more I was left to deal with Jim Collier. As a strong believer in the chain of command I tried never to circumvent that system. Meanwhile, I kept getting reports from my people that Collier was going around my back to consult with staff members in the athletic department.

There were other issues. I had made inquiries through sources in Washington, D.C., about the possibility of acquiring part of the former Sand Point Naval Station property for UW sports fields, thus taking some of the pressure off intramural facilities. I was reprimanded and told this was none of my business.

For years I had wanted an indoor tennis center. Judy Biondi, the director of athletic development, the late Elmer Nordstrom, and I had approached Illsey Nordstrom about making a substantial gift in honor of her late husband, Lloyd. After working out details, she had agreed on a donation to finance the facility. We had hoped to have the center produce some revenue by renting court space to the public when UW demand was low. Gerberding absolutely refused to allow us to do this. I suggested to Collier that it would be no different than allowing public use of the campus golf driving range. Gerberding wouldn't budge.

We also had a tug-of-war between the athletic department and the medical school over the team physician. Dr. Steve Bramwell doubled in Sports Medicine and as our team doctor for a while and we were pleased with his work. When he decided to leave the orthopedic unit, he voiced a desire to stay on with the athletic department on an independent basis. That prompted the medical school to lobby for Bramwell's job, which I resisted. Dr. Bramwell had set up a program that handled all of our sports medical needs with a high degree of professional competence— at a reduced cost.

It was only a few weeks after the embarrassment of the goal post incident that I received a terse memo from Jim Collier saying the university was going to end my tenure as athletic director effective in August, 1991, nearly a year earlier than promised. I was sad, disappointed, embarrassed, and confused.

What a contrast to the praises heaped on me by Gerberding and Collier in June, 1988—less than two years earlier—when I was honored by my peers as the recipient of the Corbett Award, for distinguished service to collegiate athletics. It is considered by many as emblematic of Athletic Director of the Year. When Pac-10 Commissioner Tom Hansen presented me with the award at a dinner in Marco Island, Fla., he read a telegram from my UW bosses that said:

"We join this country's intercollegiate athletic community in celebrating the Corbett Award presentation to our own Mike Lude. Mike, you have brought honor to yourself, your family, your profession and your university. We know that this distinguished award honors not a single achievement, but years of hard work in, and dedicated service to, college athletics. It is richly deserved, and we salute you. With warmest regards on this special occasion."

A week later Collier had presented me with a certificate "in sincere appreciation and recognition of your years of service to the University."

But instead of retiring at the mandatory age and helping make a smooth transition to my successor, I was shoved into a downtown office away from the campus as a consultant to Collier, who had become more of an adversary than a supporter. The press release the university put out praised my accomplishments and long service during my UW career but somehow all those words seemed hollow.

At my last NCAA convention as athletic director in January, 1991, I was overwhelmed by the compliments from many of my colleagues. I was proud of the program we built and the reputation and image of the University of Washington. The reaction of my staff and so many Husky donors and boosters was bewilderment. The program that was in debt when I arrived was about $18 million on the plus side when I left.

I departed with one final thought: If I ever beat Bill Gerberding on the golf course again I wouldn't have to worry about losing my job.

# 16

## COPING WITH THE PRESIDENT'S YES-MAN

◆ ◆ ◆

Almost without exception, everyone who has ever held a job has suffered through the frustration and anxiety of working with a boss he or she couldn't stand.

In my long career in coaching and intercollegiate sports administration I was fortunate to be involved with and answer to a large number of high quality head coaches, athletic directors, and administrators. They recognized and appreciated hard work and honest effort. Rather than being envious or jealous of my success, they were supportive because it reflected well on them.

Many of these people became close personal friends.

Unfortunately, I cannot include Jim Collier in this group.

Collier was the vice president for university relations at the University of Washington during most of the fifteen-plus years I was athletic director. In my dealings with upper campus and President Bill Gerberding, I reported directly to Collier as a conduit to the president.

Sometimes I thought Collier was simply running interference for the president. He was the perfect yes-man for Gerberding. When I did meet with the president to discuss a proposal or problem involving the athletic department, Collier was usually in attendance and he quickly sided with Gerberding, putting me at a 2-1 disadvantage.

Maybe Gerberding preferred to have an intermediary between him and the UW's world of athletics, somebody he could bark orders at and who would take immediate action to remedy any potential embarrassment to the university.

There were times I was told Collier went behind my back, talking with some of my staff, invariably without my knowledge, a blatant breach of the chain of command. I am convinced Collier encouraged some of my assistants to go directly to him—Mike Alderson, whom I hired to modernize our accounting system, was a good example—and all that did was create problems of loyalty, false signals, and doubts.

Perhaps Collier liked the perks of being the administration's overseer of the athletic program. He was always well taken care of in this regard; I made sure of that, almost from the first day he arrived on the Washington campus.

Yet I feel it was Collier who stained the end of my otherwise satisfying and enjoyable stint as Washington's athletic director, one that allowed me to receive the highest honors and recognition that can come to an intercollegiate sports administrator.

During much of my career I operated on a year-to-year contract. But in 1986, after I was voted by my peers as one of the top two athletic directors in the country (the other was Don Canham of Michigan), Collier agreed that I should have a longer contract. He checked with the executive branch, and they agreed on a five-year deal. I told him I wanted to maximize my retirement income for a retirement date of June 30, 1992.

Collier agreed verbally to this. Later he insisted he did not agree.

When the lawyers returned the paperwork, the fine print said the contract was renewable for the final ten months, from September 1991 through June 1992. I said this wasn't what we had agreed. Collier said not to worry, no problem, that during the last six months I would become actively involved with choosing my successor. I said great, and that's the way we left it.

So I was surprised when Dave Cohn, a friend and member of the university's board of regents, took me aside in my hotel room in Anaheim, where the Husky football team was getting ready for the Freedom Bowl in late December 1989. He told me—and I have it on audio tape—the university would not honor the addendum to my contract that would extend my retirement date past the five years.

After months of discussion all of my proposals were ignored, and I received from Collier an ultimatum to choose between two alternatives:

1. I could bow out in accordance with the terms of the contract on August 31, 1991, or,

2. I could leave the job January, 15, 1991 and be paid through December 31, 1991, serving those final 11 months as a consultant to Collier.

I felt betrayed.

Collier had worked with Gerberding at the University of Illinois and came with him when Gerberding was named president of the University of Washington. Collier had just arrived on the Seattle campus when I got a call from Neil Stoner, the

*James Collier—not one of my favorite vice presidents*

athletic director at Illinois. He said he had socialized regularly with Collier and asked me to take good care of Jim in Seattle. At first the call looked like a routine thing on behalf of a colleague. But his request to help Collier find a place to stay, a car, and gratuitous access to private clubs seemed excessive.

Then several people whose judgment I respected, Big 10 commissioner Wayne Duke, and Walter Byers and Tom Jernstead of the NCAA, warned me to keep an eye out for Jim Collier. They suggested I chat with Ted Towe, then an assistant to Byers in the NCAA office. Towe and Collier had been involved in a small town weekly newspaper in Kansas, but when I called he declined to talk about Collier. A few years later I ran into him in the Chicago airport, and this time he agreed to talk. He was very critical of his former business associate.

I recalled what Collier said in the first meeting we had after I learned he would be my immediate superior. He came to my house, and we discussed every facet of the athletic department, a conversation I still have on tape. He said, "I want to make this clear, Mike. Remember, I am not here to interfere; I'm here to help you. You run the athletic department; you're very capable and you've had plenty of experience. I'm just lucky to be able to work with you."

In letters and notes to me Collier expressed support and praised my work. In one memo in the mid-1980s, he wrote: "I'm encouraged by the results of our frank and open discussion. Like you, I feel that among other things the two of us are back on track, personally, professionally and programatically. I stand behind you and will continue to support and admire you."

Despite those sweet words, I felt he was a meddler and second-guesser, and I was wary of his involvement.

And I remain convinced it was the differences I had with Collier that resulted in the decision by Gerberding, supported by the regents, to cut short my career.

I had tried repeatedly to get the chain of command changed so I would report directly to the president, which is the case at many universities, large and small. There's enough bureaucratic red tape involved in running a major program without having a Jim Collier lurking in the background.

Under NCAA rules the CEO of each member university is specifically designated as the overseer of institutional control over the athletic department. In my final job as athletic director at Auburn, I not only had immediate access to the president but also sat on the president's cabinet, which consisted of deans and vice presidents. It gave me standing in the scholastic realm, something that never quite happened at Washington on Gerberding's watch.

I was extremely pleased—because it jibed with my plea for

change—when Gerberding's replacement, Dr. Richard McCormick, in his first year as the UW president, gave my successor, Barbara Hedges, access to his office by having her report directly to him.

I have volumes of notes taken at meetings with Collier. These often lengthy discussions covered a wide range of matters I felt needed to be addressed in my role of athletic director. I was given the responsibility of running a large department at a major university, and I felt I had the expertise and experience to make decisions with a minimum of hand-holding from upper campus.

But the longer I remained on the job the more difficult it seemed to become to get the authority to do the job and to make things happen in a timely, efficient, and economical manner. Yes, I had the responsibility but without the necessary authority. Too much time was spent in endless meetings with large numbers of people, creating more roadblocks than progress.

President Gerberding had made it clear he wanted the department of intercollegiate athletics to be self-supporting; that is, no funds from the state or from student fees would be used to support intercollegiate sports.

This became increasingly difficult when we kept adding women's sports to follow the mandates of Title IX. As a result we increased our quest for "development" donations, some quite large, to pay the bills, especially the mounting cost of athletic scholarships.

Marilyn Dunn, vice president for university development, had coveted control of seating in Husky Stadium and pushed to merge our fund raising efforts with her department. At one point a memo from Collier indicated he was going to move Pete Liske, our associate AD for development, into Dunn's area of responsibility. I could not allow this to happen. I thought that would be bureaucratic quicksand and detract from our effort to raise funds.

I talked with our Tyee board, and it was decided that two influential members, Bruce Nordstrom and Dave Cohn, would join me to talk with Collier about the proposed merger. Nordstrom and

Cohn, both major supporters of the athletic program, cordially expressed their opposition to the idea because of its negative effect on the athletic department.

Collier tried to minimize the effect of the proposal and smooth things over. Finally, Bruce said rather bluntly that under no circumstances would the athletic development program be merged with the university program. Do you understand? Collier stammered and finally said something like, "Uh, OK, that's the way it's going to be."

Later I learned others at Washington were not exactly big fans of Collier and were unhappy to learn my contract would not be extended through the retirement date I thought had been agreed upon. One of them was Tracy King, who had retired as head of the University of Washington Alumni Association. He told me about a luncheon meeting with Gerberding when he first learned I might be retiring early. King said he had lost all respect for Collier several years earlier and told Gerberding "it would be a travesty" if Mike Lude were to be let go because of some guy on the fourth floor of the Administration Building.

After King's meeting with the president, he wrote Gerberding a letter and sent me a copy. King expressed concern that "a decent, honest, hard-working individual with peer respect" would be pushed out by Collier. Added King: "I know this more than anyone and so do many people in the university community and around the country. This would not reflect well on you or the university."

King also said that George Beckman, the university's provost, had serious questions about Collier. Beckman and I met several times. He told me that the "biggest mystery" in the Administration Building was Jim Collier and why Gerberding kept him around.

In their meeting, Gerberding had asked King for examples of Collier's misdeeds. King mentioned how Collier had convinced me to pay for Collier's membership in Sand Point Country Club with athletic department funds. This was to be in lieu of an honorarium for the success of the football team making a bowl game. King, a former Husky football player, had a hard time relating Collier's role as having the slightest effect on the team's performance. I agreed but I was willing to do anything possible to smooth the relationship of my department with upper campus.

That wasn't the first favor I did to please Collier and it wasn't the last. When he first arrived in Seattle, I put him up at the Travelodge motel near the campus and paid for it out of the athletic department budget. I did that as a result of the call from Stoner, the Illinois athletic director.

Through our courtesy car program for my staff and coaches with Seattle-area auto dealers, I arranged for Collier to get the use of a car from Jerry Kenney, a local Toyota dealer. When Collier got nervous about the ethics of that arrangement (having a free car might be questioned by deans and other leaders in the institution), I found him a token lease vehicle.

After he split with his former wife, Julie, Collier asked if I would help him find a place to live through one of our boosters. Jim Summers, a prominent developer, gave him a sweetheart deal on an apartment, described as "one of our nicest new apartments in Redmond [a Seattle suburb] for nine months at one-half the regular rent."

When Collier decided to put on a St. Patrick's Day party he asked if the supply of liquor we kept in the Hall of Fame room in Edmundson Pavilion might be available. As far as I know, we were never reimbursed for that booze, which we delivered to his party. Later, Collier and a female friend attended the annual Football Hall of Fame dinner in New York, where the athletic department provided free accommodations.

Is it any wonder I refused when, after deposing me as athletic director, Collier suggested I might get involved in fund-raising? I told one of the university's regents, Sam Stroum, that I just couldn't do that. I said, "I can't raise money for someone who said he couldn't get along with me and especially I could not seek money from those who said they wanted to withdraw their contributions because of the way I was treated." One of those was Will Thomas, a Husky booster who withdrew a pledge of one million dollars over my forced early retirement.

After I left the University of Washington some of my loyal friends still working in the department reported that anytime something went wrong I'd get blamed. They were upset and tired of my integrity being torn down. This was during the time of Desert Storm. One of the newcomers would chuckle and say: "All those Mike Lude Scud missiles are coming over the hill. I've got to shoot them down with my Patriots."

Another friend said Collier had told a Washington booster that I had received two poor performance reviews and that's why my contract had not been extended.

I wrote Collier a scathing letter: "This is a complete shock and surprise to me in as much as I do not ever recall receiving any (absolutely zero) evaluations from either you or President Gerberding. As a matter of fact, I have had commendations from you at the time when I received salary adjustments. In addition, I received correspondences from President Gerberding complimenting me that I favorably discharged my duties and responsibilities and that he and the University were fortunate to have me as the Husky athletic director."

Collier denied he ever made such a comment about performance reviews. In his response, he said, "let me state categorically that I have never told anyone that you received two poor performance reviews. As you correctly stated, you were never given such evaluations. I can assure you that I am not the source of such statements and that if I encounter them, I will be quick to correct them."

Thanks a lot, Jim.

I still don't understand why the university couldn't have extended my contract a mere 10 months as they had previously agreed, after the more than fifteen years of successful, dedicated service to a world-class athletic department. I could have left gracefully and with pride and without the repercussions from many of our supporters. It would have allowed a smooth handoff to my successor. I do understand that Collier and Gerberding did not have the professionalism or vision to see that would have been a better alternative.

After Gerberding retired and Dr. Richard McCormick became his successor in September, 1995, Collier was gone from the University in a matter of months. He became VP for university affairs at the University of Northern Colorado, but that lasted less than a year. He became VP for university advancement at San Francisco State and was still there in early 2004.

# 17
## AUBURN: TONS OF ENTHUSIASM AND TP

◆ ◆ ◆

Not long after I became athletic director at Auburn University, I was lectured by a prominent booster and a member of the school's board of trustees about the importance of football in that corner of the world.

"Coach Lude, this is not a matter of life or death," drawled Mike McCartney, a huge, rotund son of the South. "This is really important."

One of the reasons Auburn's president, Dr. William Muse, had hired me was to help him bring a touch of sanity to an athletic department that had been tiptoeing back and forth along the borderline of NCAA rules and regulations as long as most fans could remember. In no way did President Muse want to restrain the enthusiasm of Auburn's many loyal boosters; he only wanted them to express that fidelity within the confines of the rules.

Auburn University had been tainted by a series of accusations of rules violations in both its football and basketball programs. In fact, one of my first jobs would be to orchestrate an appearance before the NCAA Infractions Committee over a case involving a former football player who accused Auburn coaches and some boosters of making improper payments to him as an athlete.

I suspect at least some of those Auburn fanatics who had played loose with the rules to do whatever might be necessary to beat Alabama and the other powers of the Southeastern Conference hoped that my experience would help them elude the fine points of NCAA law.

That has never been my style, and that's not why Bill Muse brought me to the Auburn campus. As a coach and administrator I have always played by the rules. I have preached strongly to my staff about honesty, integrity, and truthfulness and playing according to the rules. I am proud of the reputation of being "Mr. Square" when it came to following the intent as well as the letter of the rules, whatever the game.

I'm appalled when I hear some of the lame excuses from coaches and athletes who get caught breaking a rule. Almost without exception these violators had full knowledge of the fine points of the law they broke. Most violations are the result of people trying to get away with something they know is wrong but thinking that they won't get caught. Those who plead ignorance of the law are contemptible.

When I was presented to the Auburn board of trustees as President Muse's choice to be the new athletic director, I was asked point-blank, "What experience do you have with any NCAA investigations?"

I held up one hand and made a zero and said, "I have no such experience. If you are looking for somebody who has been in trouble then you don't want Mike Lude."

I have always given a high priority to loyalty. I was resolutely loyal to the people I worked for and demanded the same thing from those who worked for me. That loyalty was tested during my first week at Auburn.

I got the first hint of how intense some Auburn partisans would have liked to be when it came to influencing decisions in the athletic program. I was visited in my office by an individual who came as a messenger from Bobby Lowder, a prominent banker and member of the Board of Trustees. He still is a major power player in the athletic program.

The visitor told me, "Mike, I want you to know I'm here to deliver a message. Mr. Lowder would like very much for you to call him three or four times a week and give him an update on what's happening, stay in close touch with him. And if you need help, he's the guy who can really help you. So make sure you touch base, regularly."

My response was cordial but direct. "Sir, please go back to Mr. Lowder and tell him that I am a former Marine Corps officer and the first thing I learned was the chain of command and that you don't circumvent that chain of command."

I told him I report directly to the president of this university, Dr. William Muse. If Mr. Lowder wants me to discuss something with him, he should get in touch with the president and Dr. Muse will either tell me to contact Mr. Lowder or he will contact Mr. Lowder or we both will contact Mr. Lowder. I told him I would not go behind the back of the president, who is my boss.

My rebuff made it perfectly clear that I wanted no part of Lowder's inner circle of confidants. Our relationship was strictly business. When I opened our home to a series of Friday night reception-dinners before home football games for prominent alumni and trustees, visiting school athletic department officials, community and university leaders, and media, Lowder always declined my invitation. These events made many friends for Auburn. But the next year I was told we couldn't have these parties and I learned later that Lowder, as a member of the board of trustees, had insisted they be called off.

Lowder's failure to have a direct line of communication with me as athletic director didn't prevent him from having a strong influence on the program through a network of friends, some in very high places, that he obviously had spent considerable time developing over many years. My only concern was to prevent him from doing anything that could get Auburn into any more serious trouble with the NCAA.

After all, NCAA investigators already were on campus interviewing athletes, coaches, and boosters in connection with the Eric Ramsey case. They were asking questions about possible violations, and the answers would come out at an NCAA hearing scheduled a few months after I arrived. Ramsey, a former football player, had concealed a tape recorder and used it during conversations he had with Auburn people about illegal payments.

I had never been involved in an NCAA infractions hearing before, but I knew that I had a good reputation with my colleagues in the top levels of the national organization. When Bill Muse hired me as athletic director he made it clear that he needed someone—and he apparently felt that someone was me—to help get Auburn through the process of going before the NCAA Infractions Committee and put the Ramsey case to rest with the least damage to the Auburn program and its reputation. Because of my long experience in the NCAA I had credibility and I knew all but one of the members of the Infractions Committee. That certainly didn't hurt.

I ended up at Auburn in a rather roundabout manner. While I was athletic director at Washington, I served on the Pac-10 Conference Television Committee, for a while as chairman. That group worked extensively with Raycom, the largest sports TV syndication company in the nation. I also had chaired the NCAA Post-Season Football Committee.

After Raycom won approval for a new bowl game in Fort Lauderdale, I was offered the job of executive VP of Raycom management and executive director of the Blockbuster Bowl. That was in June 1991. After a successful game, in 1992, I got a call from Frank Broyles, the Arkansas athletic director and a former coaching colleague. Our friendship of many years began when I was at Delaware and Dave Nelson sent me to Arkansas to teach Frank's coaching staff the fine points of the Wing-T offense.

Broyles had been approached by Bill Muse, the newly appointed Auburn president. He was a longtime friend who had two degrees from Arkansas, and someone Broyles regarded highly.

Muse wanted to reorganize Auburn's athletic department and needed an experienced athletic director from outside the Auburn family to take charge. Broyles said Auburn was in trouble with an NCAA investigation and needed a lot of help. Broyles had no inclination to leave Arkansas, but he recommended me for the job. I explained that I had a three-year contract with Raycom and there was no way I could change that.

Broyles said, "Well, I promised him that you would talk to him." In just a few days I received a phone call from Bill Muse, and we talked numerous times over the next two or three months. The more we talked the more I liked him. In that time I had a chance to study Auburn's sports budget, and we discussed a variety of things the athletic department needed. One of his first goals was to separate the duties of head football coach and athletic director; Pat Dye held both titles.

When Muse kept pressing me, I said again and again that Raycom simply would not let me out of my commitment to them. "OK, but what if I could get Raycom to release you from the contract?" Muse asked. With some confidence, knowing that was practically impossible, I said, "Well, that would be different."

He suggested we talk again at the coming Southeastern Conference meeting in Destin, Florida, where I would represent the Blockbuster Bowl. Auburn put on a full-court press. I was paired with Pat Dye in the golf tournament, and he invited me to his room to talk about the athletic director's job. He told me, "We need you at Auburn. I want you to come."

We talked about personnel, about the program's strengths and weaknesses, and about the athletic history and traditions, including its intense but often uphill rivalry with intrastate foe Alabama. Dye said he had offered to step down as athletic director and remain as football coach. After nearly two hours with Pat and two more hours later that night with President Muse, I was weakening. I told Muse if he could convince Raycom to break my contract, I think Auburn might be a great place to end my career.

Muse convinced Rick and Dee Ray to allow me to go to Auburn. Muse agreed to let me consult with Raycom for five days a year, but the company never asked for that time. The only condition I asked from Raycom was that they promote Brian Flajole, who had come to Florida with me from Seattle, to fill my job. Otherwise I would take Brian with me to Auburn.

Muse agreed to my salary and housing requests, two cars, and, most importantly, the authority to go with the responsibility of running the program. He responded as I had hoped: "That's what I want you for."

Rick Ray has always teased me that he should have received a tampering fee from Auburn.

The next step in the hiring process was getting formal approval from the Auburn board of trustees. The president pro-tem was Mike McCartney, who later impressed on me the importance of the football program. A former football player and highway contractor, McCartney led the interrogation of the would-be athletic director.

Leaning back in his big chair, McCartney asked, "Coach Lude, have you ever been involved in a big football game?"

I took a long pause to allow the importance of the question to settle in before responding. "Mr. McCartney, I've coached football for twenty-four years. I've been an athletic director for twenty-two years and you know what? Colorado State-Wyoming is huge out there. Washington-Washington State in the Apple Cup is about as big as you can get. The Rose Bowl is about as big as you can get; the USC-Washington rivalry is about as big as you can get."

Then I paused for nearly thirty seconds and I said, "Mr. McCartney I've been involved in a lot of big football games, but sir, I've never been involved in anything like the Auburn-Alabama game."

A broad smile came across his face, and McCartney sat up in his chair and laughed: "By gawd, that boy's all right."

Apparently that was all the trustees needed. I was hired to a two-year contract. With it I was given the full support of Dr. Muse.

"I want you to totally reorganize the program, whatever you think it needs. You do whatever you feel is right. You've got the background and the experience. Keep me informed, and we'll get this baby up and running."

My most pressing task after arriving on the Auburn campus was getting ready for the Eric Ramsey hearing. Auburn officials already had compiled a wealth of material, and I inherited an extensive file of confidential reports. It took a whole lot of reading to get up to date and have some idea of what had happened. On the advice of Thomas Samford III, the school's chief counsel, two independent lawyers, Thomas Thagard and John Scott, had been working on the case for about a year. On review, I felt they had done an excellent job.

What complicated the process were the many rumors that had circulated, and I made a concerted effort to ignore the innuendo and not rush to judgment at the expense of truth and facts. As part of my personal and professional philosophy, I felt it was important to do everything possible to get the whole truth. The names of several players who supposedly were receiving illegal payments similar to Ramsey's surfaced in gossip during the investigation. Each case was checked out by the Auburn lawyers and by the NCAA investigators, who spent extensive time and energy on the job.

When the case went to the Infractions Committee, Ramsey was the only player whose activity resulted in accusations of wrongdoing. Dr. Muse revealed later that some players refused to be interviewed by independent counsel. Those who did agree to discuss the situation denied receiving any payment.

Long after I had left the Auburn job, I heard from a reliable source about a network of prominent boosters who each contributed $5,000 to a fund for illegal payment to football players. An assistant coach supposedly kept what had been referred to as "the little black book" detailing payments.

These developments were discussed in separate interviews by Terry Bowden, the football coach we hired at Auburn, and

President Muse, after they left. These are two men I respect; I think they have a high regard for honesty, but I have no personal knowledge about the activity of which they spoke. In the report our lawyers put together for the NCAA we agreed before the hearing to disassociate two former coaches from the program and cut two football scholarships, a statement on our part that we were taking action to correct what we recognized as a problem situation.

Our delegation at the hearing in Mission, Kansas, the NCAA headquarters, included President Muse; Pat Dye, the former coach and AD; Jane Moore, the faculty athletic representative; Terry Bowden, the new football coach; Dr. David Diles, our compliance person; two lawyers, Scott and Thagard, and myself. Each of us had a chance to speak, and all things considered I thought our presentation was strong.

After we had summed up Auburn's case, the head of the NCAA's staff of investigators took the floor. What he said shocked me.

"Ladies and gentlemen, this is the sixth time that Auburn University has been before the Infractions Committee." It was a simple opening statement of fact, but it caught me unaware.

In all the reading of reports and transcripts I did not know this was the sixth time Auburn had been called on the carpet by the Infractions Committee. I should have known better, but I simply didn't have any reason to think about it. I knew about a recent problem with the basketball program, which had just been placed on probation. But I hadn't heard about the earlier problems.

So when people asked me later about the severity of the penalties we received—whether they were too severe, not severe enough or about what I expected—I can say that at that precise moment I thought they were going to put us in jail forever. Considering what the penalty might have been, we were given a light sentence.

Auburn was banned from going to a bowl game for two years and lost one year of appearing on television plus what we had already volunteered to do. The year without television was first designated not as the current year but the following year. I appealed, and the TV ban was changed to the current year.

I think it helped our cause that I was acquainted with all but one person on the committee. There were other factors, but they knew my philosophy and they respected me. And we didn't go into the hearing acting like antagonists.

In the two years I was at Auburn I experienced first-hand the importance placed on intercollegiate sports by fans in the Southeastern Conference. Because most of the schools in the South are situated where there is limited influence by professional sports, the fans put a higher priority on college football and basketball. This applies to the students, faculties, alumni, friends, and supporters. It's a very, very serious business.

I've always felt that this fiercely competitive, win-at-all-cost approach has to be tempered. Honesty, integrity, and truthfulness cannot be forgotten in the name of winning. I think for many, many years that collegiate athletics in the South was suspected of being on the edge as far as looking the other way when it came to following the rules.

I've been asked to compare Auburn and the University of Washington, where I spent more than fifteen years and it's not a fair comparison because I have so much more in my memory bank about Washington and the Pac-10 than about Auburn and the Southeastern Conference.

The enthusiasm for and support of athletics at the University of Washington in the years after Don James' first Rose Bowl victory in 1978 was second to none. Auburn's fund-raising had some catching up to do, but the experience I had at Washington helped get the program cranked up in a hurry. Auburn is raising significant support now through its athletic department development efforts. I knew the potential and put a major emphasis on this important activity. Larry Long, the athletic development director, played a significant role in our success.

Auburn's Jordan-Hare Stadium seats 84,214 and the home field has a large number of skyboxes. If Washington's Husky Stadium had skyboxes in addition to the special seating and entertainment area for major contributors—the Don James Center—there would be no end to the amount of money that could be raised at the UW. When I was there, Auburn didn't have a waiting list for season tickets as we had at Husky Stadium, which has a capacity of 72,500 after we added the north deck in the late 1980s.

In sharp contrast with Seattle, a major metropolitan city, Auburn is a small town. Yet on game day it becomes the third largest city in the state of Alabama. Most games are sellouts, especially against SEC rivals. Georgia, Florida, and Alabama are huge rival contests. Georgia Tech, a two-hour drive by freeway, is a solid rival and would be even more so except Tech plays in the Atlantic Coast Conference, not the SEC.

The Southeastern Conference arguably has no equal when it comes to strong feelings about traditional football battles. Emotions are likewise very intense about basketball and baseball. Athletics are more than an extracurricular activity in the SEC and at Auburn, generally more so than in any place I have been involved as a coach or athletic director. As Mike McCartney said, it's not life or death; it's really important.

Auburn has one tradition that almost defies description. It is called Rolling Toomer's Corners and you really have to experience it to get a sense of the mood and emotion that's involved. Toomer's Corners refers to an intersection on the edge of the Auburn campus. It is the locale of Toomer's, a drugstore that has been in the same place for more than a hundred years. Through that entire history it has been a place you could always find fresh lemonade.

According to tradition, when Auburn wins a football game, the marching band and a mob of students gather at Toomer's Corners, where they proceed to "roll" the street lights, power lines, traffic light, and trees with toilet paper. Cases and cases of the stuff. I couldn't guess how many trees are used to create the paper to "roll" the Corners after a victory, say, over Alabama.

In Terry Bowden's first season as head coach Auburn wrapped up an unbeaten season by beating Alabama. My wife, Rena, some friends, and I drove down the street at Toomer's, and I have never seen anything quite like it. The TP was three feet deep all over the street.

Unlike so many gatherings of fans cele-brating sports victories, what happens at Auburn is free of destruction of property. There are no cars rolled over, no fires. It's just good student fun. The kids and the alumni are genuinely supportive of their foot-

*Thousands of fans gather near the Auburn Campus for rolling Toomer's Corner with TP for celebration of a victory over Alabama and an unbeaten season*

ball team and let it all hang loose, but they also know how to behave. During that unbeaten season we beat Georgia and we rolled the Corners; we beat Florida and we rolled the Corners. We even rolled the Corners that year on away games. But in my two years at Auburn there were never any big problems. There was no such thing as a riot. It was great fun, a celebration of intercollegiate athletics. I loved it.

The tradition is so honored at Auburn that the huge museum in the athletic department complex includes a prominently placed tableau depicting Rolling Toomer's Corner, complete with trees and littered toilet paper.

Unlike faculty members at many schools who look down at the emphasis on the athletics program at an institution of higher learning, the professors at Auburn seemed to have a healthy appreciation of sports and what goes on in the department of ath-letics. I had been at Auburn about a week when the president of the faculty senate came to me and asked me to address that group.

I smiled and told him that in fifteen years at Washington I talked to the faculty senate just twice, and both times were to defend intercollegiate athletics.

The Auburn professor explained that at Auburn the faculty supports athletics and they like it. There may be a few who don't, but they stay in the closet and don't come out. In the first year at Auburn I also received an invitation to speak to the AAUP (American Association of University Professors). That never happened at Washington.

I felt strongly that it would take an outsider like me, working under a new president, to put the Auburn program back on track. I didn't perceive a problem coming in as an outsider; in fact, I felt it was the only way the job could be done properly and effectively. I was a hired gun, and I knew what I had come to Auburn to do. Dr. Muse asked me to reorganize, redirect, and put some substance in the athletic department.

I think my being an outsider was very beneficial for Auburn University. At that time, the school desperately needed a president and an athletic director who were not encumbered by politics, who were not influenced by friends or by old traditions or by thoughts, wishes, and dreams from the past. We did not automatically accept the old favorite line, "This is the way we have always done things at Auburn."

It wasn't a case of making certain things were done right for the sake of appearances but absolutely right as far as procedure and conduct according to the rules. Bill Muse and I had complete agreement on the scope of the job and we had discussed it at length before I agreed to accept his invitation to join him.

President Muse was great to work with. He was always accessible. I probably met with him three times a week; I would call, and if he had a full schedule he would suggest I drop by at five o'clock or come to his house on Sunday afternoon.

Bill Muse and I both heard from Auburn fans when the basketball team stumbled. The coach, Tommy Joe Eagles, came under fire after a disappointing 1992-'93 season. I felt strongly that firing Tommy Joe made no sense for Auburn and the basketball program.

I'll never forget the verbal abuse I took from one outraged critic of Eagles. It brought back memories of some of the tirades I suffered when I was in Marine Corps boot training at Parris Island. It probably didn't do any good, but I tried to reason with the telephone caller. It turned out this "expert" had seen only three home games and one road game all season. I asked him how many practices he had watched and he admitted he hadn't seen any. I said I had seen every home game and several road games and had watched Eagles at practice and had heard Eagles admonish, praise, critique, and give constructive criticism. I said I felt he was an excellent teacher and coach and that he cared about the student athletes in every way.

I said that I felt Tommy Joe was a good disciplinarian and a good representative of Auburn, but the man on the phone obviously wasn't convinced. He swore and hung up.

What I told that anti-Eagles caller was about the same thing I told President Muse. I explained I was aware of the pressure and as a result had made myself more knowledgeable about this coach than anyone else. In one conversation Muse said, "Mike, we can't save him. The pressure is too great from the board. We just can't do it."

I responded: "Bill, I don't believe you hired me to come here and always agree with you." He said he hadn't. I said firing Eagles would be a big mistake, but even if he disagreed I was ready to click my heels, do an about-face, and follow the commanding officer's orders.

The next day President Muse said, "I've made up my mind. I'm accepting your recommendations. We'll give Tommy Joe a two-year extension. But he has to have a good year [in 1993-94]."

Unfortunately, that season was more exciting than successful. We had several overtime games. One went double OT. Whatever the reason, this team consistently had problems holding a lead in the second half. When the end of the season came there was no question: Tommy Joe would not survive. I didn't hear any "I told you so" comments, but I'm sure President Muse did. It's too bad because Eagles was an honorable man of good character and a good coach.

Hiring a new basketball coach become the first order of business for David Housel, my successor as athletic director. I wasn't involved other than doing some background checks for President Muse on a couple of candidates, making sure they had followed the NCAA and conference rules in previous jobs.

Muse and Housel both liked Mike Brey, an assistant coach at Duke, and they offered him the job. After an interview and an Auburn visit he went back to Duke and told people there he decided not to take the job. So Auburn ended up hiring Cliff Ellis, who had coached earlier at South Alabama and had served on the board of a branch bank in Mobile owned by Auburn booster and trustee Bobby Lowder.

Later I heard that Lowder was not thrilled with the first choice, Brey, but instead had wanted Ellis. A member of the Auburn Board of Trustees asked me to find out why Mike Brey had rejected the job and then accepted an offer at the University of Delaware.

Brey told me that after he went back to Duke and started thinking about the Auburn situation, he decided that he didn't want to coach at a school where one member of the Board of Trustees had the university in a viselike grasp. He said he wasn't comfortable with the governance at Auburn and liked what he saw about the Delaware setup. Brey is a fine coach and a fine man and later became head coach at Notre Dame.

One facet of the Auburn Department of Intercollegiate Athletics that needed a quick overhaul in both function and identity was our women's sports program. We needed to be identified very quickly as a school with a deep commitment to gender equity and to Title IX. To do so we needed to let the world know we had a senior women's administrator, and that's why I brought in

Barbara Camp to be responsible for sports other than football and men's basketball.

I had known Barbara for more than twenty years. She was an outstanding tennis player and had spent considerable time at Southern Methodist as assistant AD before becoming associate AD at the University of California at Irvine. When we hired her in December 1992 she was UCI's acting athletic director.

The other major staff addition was Dee Glueck, whom I hired away from the University of Washington to run all of our facilities, buildings and grounds, and event management. He had done the same job previously at Louisiana State University. Dee is both architect and an engineer. If a job needed to be done, I could always count on him. He was the most valuable member of my management team.

When I got to Auburn the department was operating from two facilities, the Coliseum and the Athletic Complex. As a result, the staff was split into rival factions and created a communications gap, which resulted in a gigantic rumor mill.

Part of my reorganization was developing a complete manual of policies and procedures, including organizational charts and job descriptions for the department. It was long overdue. Buddy Davidson, assistant AD, did an excellent job of putting it all together. I held a series of one-on-one meetings with all of the staff to try to build an operation based on a team principle.

I didn't get everything done. We needed a new building for the academic support program for our athletes but we couldn't come up with the individual or corporation to donate the necessary $3.5 million. Then we looked at Sewell Hall and the Sewell Annex, the athletic residence and food service facility. By renovating the Sewell complex we could house all our counselors and advisors in one location to serve all sports.

Dr. David Diles was put in charge of the division of student athletic services, but the people involved spent so much time fighting one another and blocking progress that they couldn't get the job done. The bottom line was that those who suffered were the student athletes. Because of delays, bickering, and meddling we failed to get everything we wanted. It was a bad scene. This was not the team effort I had envisioned and I was disappointed.

I had helped launch a Hall of Fame to honor the accomplishments of teams and individual athletes at the University of Washington and wanted to create a similar setup at Auburn. We received an initial gift of about $700,000 and had an architect doing design work. I was anxious to get Phase One started before I left, but some bureaucratic roadblocks—not from President Muse—wouldn't let us get into gear. But I knew David Housel would get the job finished. And he did. The museum ranks with the best of its type in intercollegiate athletics. Bureaucracy is not unique to Auburn. At every school where I coached or served on the staff, I had faced similar situations.

I had a two-year written contract with President Muse, and we had agreed that we might consider extending it to between three and five years. But after I had been there more than eighteen months I felt strongly that Auburn needed someone who did not have a "short term" sign on his chest. Dr. Muse agreed.

David Housel, the assistant athletic director and head of our sports information program, was the likely choice, at least in my opinion. When Bill Muse asked me about Housel my response was "absolutely. He's the man for the job." President Muse agreed and named him athletic director three months before my contract expired in June 1994.

Because I had urged President Muse to pick Housel as my successor as athletic director I was less than pleased to hear from one of my Auburn friends what Bobby Lowder reportedly said about Housel.

The comment attributed to Lowder was something like this: "David Housel may not be the greatest athletic director in the country, but he's my athletic director." I only hope that David can stand tall and not compromise his principles, his honesty and integrity.

President Muse, who left Auburn in 2001, once told me of his troubles with Lowder, who was able to dominate the board of trustees. "Mike, this is the toughest job I've ever had," Muse said. "There are a lot of land mines around here. I've been able to negotiate through most of them but there's one that I just can't get around."

I said, "That's got to be Bobby Lowder." He responded, "You're right."

Thus I was not the least bit surprised to read later some of President Muse's comments indicating that Lowder had opposed the decision by Auburn trustees to hire Muse and that the president had been selected by a split vote of the board. During his Auburn tenure, Muse was quoted as saying, Lowder "seemed to look down his nose at me." Muse, who was born in Mississippi, also admitted he was overly anxious to return to the South and to a bigger school (from Akron University) and that he didn't do a good job of checking the problems he might face at Auburn.

But I feel that in the two years I spent with Dr. Muse we accomplished his major goals of putting the athletic program on an even keel. We established an organizational structure, we took steps toward upgrading the facilities, and we created a strong budgeting system at a time when we were squeezed by a $3.5 million annual debt service and loss of revenue from no bowl money and no television revenue because of the Eric Ramsey case.

I feel we addressed issues of accountability and working within the chain of command and within the rules of the NCAA and the Southeastern Conference and within the spirit of those rules.

When people would ask, "How's everything going? Are we within the rules and regulations of the NCAA and the SEC?" my response was always the same. "Yes, as far as I know. Under every rock that we have turned over I haven't found any serpents. But there are a lot more rocks that I haven't seen." Those rocks can be stepping-stones to problems no matter how careful one might be.

# 18

# AN 11-0 FOOTBALL SEASON AND SCANDAL RUMORS

◆ ◆ ◆

Terry Bowden had a head start on most football coaches. He came from one of intercollegiate football's premier coaching families. He has a law degree and studied at Oxford. He is extremely bright. He is disciplined and well organized. He is a skilled strategist.

All of those traits made Bowden a remarkably successful football coach. But when Bowden was selected as Auburn University's head coach in late 1992 he was outmaneuvered from the opening play of that hiring scenario by the soft-spoken power broker behind the scenes of Auburn athletics, Bobby Lowder.

Through a series of shrewd moves, each one perfectly executed, Lowder was able to convince Bowden that he was hired as the Auburn coach because of Lowder's influence in the selection process. Bowden credited Bobby Lowder for making him the head coach, not President Bill Muse or me, the athletic director, or the selection committee that voted unanimously for Bowden.

Only after Bowden had a falling out with Lowder, a longtime member of the Auburn board of trustees, did I learn how this promising young coach was made to feel that his first loyalty should be to Lowder. Terry told me later he had been brainwashed because he felt Bobby Lowder was his secret to success and that Lowder was really his boss.

You know what? There might have been more truth to that than fiction—at least until Bowden and Lowder parted company.

President Muse recalled how Bowden had told him repeatedly that it was Lowder who had made it possible for a young coach, one without head coaching experience in a major school, to get the Auburn job.

But let's start from the beginning. When I arrived at Auburn, Pat Dye relinquished his responsibilities as athletic director but remained as head football coach. During the 1992 season I know there were discussions and negotiations involving Dr. Muse and Dye that did not included me. Then, on Thanksgiving eve, before the final football game of the season, Dye said he was calling it quits.

I can't say his resignation caught me off guard because I knew it was in the works. But I was surprised at the timing. I thought Pat would make the announcement the week following that last game. The final decision came at a meeting involving Dye, Muse, the Athletic Committee of the board of trustees, and lawyers for both sides that started Wednesday afternoon before Thanksgiving and lasted into the night.

Dye's final season was 5-5-1, but against Southeastern Conference teams he won three and lost five games, well below what Auburn loyalists expected. Auburn officials also felt a need to try to distance themselves from the problems that eventually resulted in NCAA probation and loss of revenue and the tarnished image that goes with being banned from television and going to a bowl game.

I felt that Dye was very cooperative in the NCAA hearing before the Infractions Committee, and I consider him a personal friend. I still like him and I hope the feeling is mutual. Dye's final two seasons, 5-6 in 1991 and 5-5-1, were hardly representative of his coaching tenure with the Tigers. His career record in twelve seasons of 99-39-4 (.711) ranks among the best in school history. His teams in the 1980s were ranked consistently in the top ten of the national polls and dominated the SEC. His '83 squad was 11-1 and rated third in the country by AP. In four straight seasons ('86 through '89) Auburn teams went 10-2, 9-1-2, 10-2 and 10-2. He contributed greatly to Auburn's reputation as one of the top football schools in the nation.

With the Auburn football job vacant, President Muse and I launched the effort to find Pat's successor. Still to be settled was the Eric Ramsey case. We agreed—and that sentiment was echoed by Dr. Jane Moore, the faculty athletic representative—that the new coach must be beyond reproach in following the letter and spirit of the myriad NCAA rules. Any more significant transgressions by Auburn might even result in the "Death Penalty," the most severe punishment that could be handed out by the national governing body, which would surely cripple the entire program for years to come.

President Muse asked me to put together a list of potential head coaches. I spent most of that Thanksgiving weekend on the phone, gathering information and talking to athletic directors, seeking permission to

*Dr. William Muse (left), the Auburn president, hired Lude in his desire to return credibility to the athletic program*

talk to numerous prospects. Muse organized a search committee that included three trustees, the faculty athletic representative, a former Auburn player, the student body president, and the past president of the alumni association. In that body's first meeting I went down my preliminary list of candidates and gave the group a report on each prospective coach. I couldn't stress enough the importance of this hire; the success of every intercollegiate athletic program is reflected in the prosperity of the football team, which is the prime generator of funding for all sports.

I was already scheduled to attend the National Football Foundation Hall of Fame dinner in New York, allowing me to talk to some likely candidates for the coaching job. At that gathering I met with three well-established coaches, Mack Brown, then at North Carolina; Fisher DeBerry, the Air Force head coach, who had roots in South Carolina; and Don Nehlen, a former Bowling Green coach, who had moved on to West Virginia.

My relationship with Bobby Lowder, never exactly warm and fuzzy, didn't get any better on the New York trip. He decided to take a couple of Auburn trustees and some other Auburn people on his private plane to New York. I had agreed to keep them updated on my progress in the coaching search. But they stayed at a different hotel, refused to take my calls, and wouldn't let me know where they might be at any given time.

I arranged tickets for them to attend the black-tie affair at the Waldorf-Astoria, but they didn't show up. On the night of the dinner David Housel, later to become my successor as athletic director, and Larry Long, who headed our athletic fund-raising program, were stationed at opposite entrances to the ballroom, waiting for Lowder and his party. When they didn't show I was criticized for not staying in touch with them. Their behavior was sheer rudeness. I know now it was only an attempt to embarrass me. What they did is set me up for criticism for not taking good care of them.

One of the things coaches request when they're being considered for another job is confidentiality. If the fans at another school hear their coach mentioned for a vacancy they immediately jump to one of two conclusions: The boosters are crushed that the coach might be considering leaving their wonderful program. Secondly, if the coach is mentioned for a job but somebody else is hired, the fans conclude that their coach might not be as good as they thought when he didn't get hired by the other university.

So I agreed with every coach I talked with to keep the names of any possible candidate secret and confidential. I agreed not to talk and when the media asked I declined to say anything. Yet there were leaks from the committee. I don't know who was responsible but it upset me then and does to this day.

I kept President Muse and the screening committee informed of my progress. We eventually narrowed the list to seven names and decided to interview the candidates off campus to protect their identity. The process would take two days, and after the final interview we would make a choice. We agreed to gather in a hotel in Atlanta and informed our finalists. As we were preparing to meet, we were tipped off that an intrepid Birmingham sports writer had learned the site of our meeting so we moved to another hotel several miles away. We set up in a conference room on the third level of an atrium that gave us a view of the lobby.

At one point I looked down and saw the reporter in the lobby. He never found us but came about as close as physically possible. The candidates we considered were Dick Sheridan from North Carolina State, Larry Smith from USC, Bill Lewis from Georgia Tech, Tim Stowers from Georgia Southern, former Auburn Heisman Trophy winner Pat Sullivan and later the coach at TCU, Auburn defensive coordinator Wayne Hall, and Terry Bowden.

There was speculation that Lowder favored Hall, with whom he had close ties, but he realized Dr. Muse and I had enough clout to block Hall's appointment. So Lowder apparently decided to shift his support to Terry and make him beholden to Lowder for helping him get the job.

Terry had excellent credentials. Besides being the son of Bobby Bowden, who had transformed Florida State into a perennial national power, Terry had paid his dues as a head coach at two smaller schools. He took over a hapless program at Salem College in Salem, West Virginia, which had gone 0-9-1 and turned it around. He moved to Samford and was in the process of reviving its program.

But even Terry, who never lacked confidence, thought he was too young and lacked the big school experience to be considered seriously for the Auburn job. Lowder changed all that.

When I talked to Bowden by telephone he expressed enthusiasm about the prospect of being one of the finalists. Little did I know then that Lowder already had contacted Terry behind our backs. Bowden met at length with Lowder, Mike McCartney, and Ruel Russell at Russell's office in Birmingham to discuss the coaching job. Bowden later said he thought the session was a job interview.

Nor did we know Lowder's daughter, Katherine, had worked in the athletic department at Samford, when Bowden was the head coach. She and Bowden's wife became friends and Lowder had met Terry. When Pat Dye appeared to be on his way out, Katherine told Bowden her father liked the idea of Terry being the next Auburn coach. That led to the meeting in Birmingham that started the series of events leading to his hiring.

That wasn't the only communication between Lowder and Bowden. After the first day of interviews, the night before Bowden's session with the committee, the two talked for some time by phone, going over all the details of what might be asked and outlining a strategy of answers. Lowder, a member of the coaching search committee, had sat through the first day of interviews. That gave him a good insight to how Terry could best sell himself. Terry said it was much like an attorney preparing a client before taking the witness stand.

The next day, as one might now expect, Terry Bowden did an outstanding job. He was very well prepared. There was no question he wanted the job. He was extremely well versed on the Auburn situation and made a point of impressing the committee that he was anxious to be the Auburn coach. Terry told me after he left Auburn that the reason he was able to be so dynamic and convincing with all the right answers was that he had been briefed and prepared before the interview. He said that's why at the time he thought Lowder "was going to be my real secret to success. How naive I was."

Bowden was the final coach to be interviewed, the third one on the second day. In the discussion after the completion of the interviews, before the balloting, Lowder was the first to speak. He lauded Terry's potential, and the committee voted unanimously to offer him the job.

Before President Muse or I could contact Bowden to inform him he had been selected, Lowder called Terry immediately following the meeting and broke the news to him. I learned later that Terry and his wife spent that night in Montgomery with the Lowders, strengthening Bowden's impression that he got the job because of Lowder's clout.

That's sad because both President Muse and I supported the selection of Terry Bowden. I did considerable research on how he handled athletes, how he related to the college administration, alumni, and boosters, and how he dealt with the media—all of which are important to being a head coach.

Terry's background was especially impressive. His success in difficult prior coaching situations and the coaching bloodlines obviously enhanced his candidacy. I remember when I was coaching and recruiting at Delaware and Colorado State, I had a special feeling for recruits who were the sons of football coaches. I liked them because they knew how to work hard; they had grown up sitting on daddy's knee and watching football films. They knew the pitfalls of the job.

They also knew that if they got chewed out it didn't mean you didn't love 'em. These kids recognized that if you were getting on their case you were aware they were around. You cared. Likewise, if you didn't pay much attention to them they weren't very important to the program.

Terry Bowden's father, Bobby Bowden, is one of the top football coaches in the country. Terry grew up with coaching, and this was one of his great attributes. What he hadn't experienced as a coach he had seen as the son of a coach. Terry is a very intelligent guy; he's extremely enthusiastic and energetic, but he was never shy about asking for help if he had a coaching problem. He wouldn't hesitate to go to someone else to seek assistance, his dad included.

Even so, the members of the coaching search committee had discussed the possibility that we would likely take some flack because Terry was coming from a Division 1AA school, he was young (thirty-seven) and he hadn't coached at Auburn, arguments that were ridiculous.

Not long after the selection was announced, the heat was turned up. Bill Muse and I got letters and phone calls. People called my home and my office. They told me I had rocks in my head. They put most of the blame on me because I was an outsider and they figured I must have sold the idea to the Board of Trustees. There were even some threats, but that goes with the job.

Terry and I had one confrontation not long after he became the head coach. Looking back, it may have had something to do with his perception of the role Bobby Lowder played in his hiring. I had arranged a temporary contract and told Terry that when he got settled in we would put together his final contract.

Shortly after that he came by my office and said, "Mike, you'll be getting a call from my lawyer/agent, and he'll be working out the contract with you." That bothered me.

I got up from my desk, walked around, and went nose-to-nose with Terry. "Terry, I didn't hire a frigging agent; I didn't hire a frigging lawyer. I hired an excellent football coach. If you have an agent or a lawyer and he calls, I will not return his call. I will not talk to him. If he is a lawyer and wants to talk legal talk he can go over to Samford Hall and talk to the university attorney and do anything he wants there. But as far as a football coach—as a former football coach and as an athletic director, I did not hire an agent or a lawyer. I won't return any calls and I won't talk to him."

Terry seemed taken aback by my outburst. "Coach Lude, we can work it out, you and I." And we did.

A couple of weeks later Bobby Bowden, his father, was in town and visited my office. I told him, "Bobby, I told Terry that if he will consult with me and talk with me and listen, I can help him." Bobby turned to Terry and said, "Terry, you listen to Mike Lude. He's been there. He's done it. He's been successful and he's also been fired."

*Terry Bowden turned Auburn football around with 11-0 record in first season*

After Terry's first season—eleven wins and no losses—I got a different kind of reaction from Auburn boosters. The letters and phone calls were full of praise. It was a great feeling. Terry was and still is a talented young man and a talented coach. No Auburn coach had ever gone unbeaten in eleven games. The sad part was that the NCAA penalties handed down the previous summer prevented that team from going to a bowl game. Still, it ranked No. 4 in the final Associated Press poll of sports writers.

Terry's second year was almost as good as the first: 9-1-1. That made his two-year mark 20-1-1. He was the toast of the Southeastern Conference. Among Auburn boosters the record stirred up memories of Shug Jordan's unbeaten string of 24 games (23-0-1) in 1956-'58. The '57 Tigers went 10-0 and were voted No. 1 in the country by AP. A year later Auburn was 9-0-1 and ranked No. 4.

Although the team Terry Bowden inherited had gone 5-5-1 the season before, it was not lacking in talent. Stephen Davis, who later became a standout pro football running back with the Washington Redskins and Carolina Panthers, was a genuine talent. Pat Dye had left some other highly productive players, and Terry and his staff were able to get the program back on track.

Terry most enjoyed the offensive side of football, and his older brother, Tommy, served as his offensive coordinator before moving up to the head coaching job at Tulane. Tommy was just one of several outstanding assistant coaches with Terry, and I would recommend him highly. Tommy later moved to Clemson as head coach.

When Terry was putting together his staff I suggested it would probably be to his advantage to replace Wayne Hall, the assistant coach who had applied for the head coaching job. Hall had been a close confidant of Bobby Lowder. I told Terry he could interview everybody on the staff and keep one, two, three, or none of them. "It's up to you," I said. He decided to keep Hall, as mandated by Lowder, and retained his brother, Tommy.

It was hardly a secret that Lowder and Hall had a close relationship. One of the things I always did as an athletic director was to audit the monthly telephone charge reports. At all three schools where I was AD, the business managers routinely would put those records on my desk. I discovered Coach Hall made frequent long distance calls each week to Montgomery to the telephone number for Bobby Lowder. He wasn't the only staff member who made such calls. My only conclusion was that Hall was well connected with Lowder.

Several years later, after Bowden was well established as the Auburn coach, he did get rid of Hall, and there are those who think that probably triggered the parting of the ways between Terry and Lowder. Others think that breach also paved the way for Bowden's departure, which came midway in the 1998 season when his team fell on hard times, his first losing season. In taped conversations by Auburn faculty member and historian Dr. Wayne Flynt, President Muse fingered Lowder as the one who pushed Bowden out. Lowder and Bowden have been at odds ever since.

When the Auburn team went 11-0 in Terry's first season everybody in football, especially the South, wanted to touch his garments to see if that success rubbed off. Terry was on a high and had become something special for Auburn followers.

Considering Bowden's success—47 wins and 17 losses and one tie in five winning seasons and going to the SEC championship game in 1997, the year before he left—his departure was a bizarre twist. He had accumulated the best coaching record of any Auburn coach, a percentage of .731, just ahead of Mike Donahue, who was at Auburn for eighteen seasons from 1904 to 1922. His 99-35-5 mark was .730.

When Terry Bowden's team won just once in the first six games of the 1998 season, I think Bobby Lowder and his crew simply decided it was time to throw Terry out. President Muse, in the Auburn archives tapes, said Terry had become more and more independent because of his success. He became less reliant on Lowder and seemed to distance himself from his so-called benefactor.

"He never listened very well, almost from the beginning," Muse told Dr. Flynt. "That was one of his faults. He had enjoyed so much success and so much adulation that I couldn't get through to him . . . So it was very frustrating to try to communicate to him issues about which I might have some concern."

Paul Davis, a columnist for the *Opelika-Auburn News*, has closely followed the intrigue of the Auburn sports scene involving Terry Bowden and Bobby Lowder. In one column about eighteen months after Bowden left, Davis discussed the theory advanced by others that Bowden may have been fired because he wanted to run a clean program. Davis seemed to be on target, from what I knew about Terry.

I found a note from Terry in March 1998, that alluded to his desire to keep Auburn's program within the rules. "Thank you for the birthday card. It's nice that you remember me each and every year. I just signed a seven-year contract. Maybe I can keep this school out of trouble for a while. Time has proven you right on about every problem you recognized here and I have fought many battles to overcome the areas of concern that you recognized. Fortunately, we are now beginning to see some light at the end of the tunnel."

That was before he was ousted in the middle of the 1998 football season. That was long after I had left the Auburn scene, and I have no personal evidence of any wrongdoing while I was on the Auburn campus. But the following year, at the 1999 Pigskin Classic at Penn State, Terry told me that when he took over as head coach at Auburn, players were being paid. He talked about a little black book with a record of payments. He said he worked to put an end to the payoffs while he was coach. He told me the last "tainted" player left the program in 1995.

Subsequently, reports have surfaced about tape recordings of interviews of Terry alleging improper conduct in the Auburn program. Paul Davis interviewed Bowden at least twice. He also was tape recorded by Wayne Flynt who was accompanied by three other Auburn professors at an interview in Loachapoka. Transcripts of the tapes were made part of the archives at the Auburn library.

Terry's story was pretty much the same in all the interviews. Bowden reportedly talked about signing bonuses of $12,000 to $15,000 and salaries of $600 per month for certain players. He saw a ledger of who had been paid, who paid the money, and how much. President Bill Muse told Flynt he had heard rumors of payments to players but had no proof they existed. The only knowledge I have of any of these incidents comes from media reports long after the fact.

All of the negative publicity received by Auburn has only harmed the school. An article in the national publication of the Association of American University Professors was a blow to the image that President Muse so wanted to improve. He had been instrumental in getting Auburn removed from the AAUP's list of censured schools during the two years I was at Auburn.

The AAUP report pointed out how the Auburn Board of Trustees had been under heavy fire from a wide spectrum of campus organizations. The publication referred to accusations that Lowder runs the board and went so far as to suggest that some of the twelve appointed board members have financial ties to Lowder.

Also questioned was the pattern of the board in making quick and unanimous decisions with little discussion, leading to charges the trustees met privately before holding scheduled open meetings. Local newspapers had filed suit, charging the board with violating Alabama's open-meetings law. According to the article, Muse said the board bypassed his authority, encouraging administrators and coaches to come directly to the board with various concerns.

A unanimous vote of no confidence in the board was voted by the Auburn University Senate, made up of faculty, staff, and administrators. So did the student government senate and the alumni association's board of directors. The University Senate, the AAUP chapter at Auburn and the student newspaper called for the entire board to resign. Protests over the board's actions involved an unusually large number of constituents. At one point about two thousand students gathered to protest the appointment of two new trustees.

Auburn's credibility and its standing in the ranks of higher learning took another major hit near the end of the 2003 football season, two days before the traditional Iron Bowl game against Alabama. William Walker, the school's president, and David Housel, the athletic director, made a secret trip to Louisville to meet with the head football coach of the University of Louisville. The Alabama media later portrayed the mission as a clandestine plot to replace head coach Tommy Tuberville.

There was no mention of Bobby Lowder being in the Auburn delegation, but reporters for Birmingham newspapers identified the airplane as being the corporate jet of Colonial Bank, Lowder's business.

My first reaction: Where is the institutional control? Who is in control? Contacting the coach of another institution without prior permission is an indication the president has a hard time understanding the meaning of the term institutional control. How can anyone take seriously anything he says or does when it comes to institutional control? We all know—and they knew—that before talking to a member of another university's staff it is critical to make a courtesy phone call to ask for permission.

When I was a head football coach I had two players who got into trouble for destroying property in one of the dorms. They insisted they didn't do it. I asked if they were telling me the truth and they said, "Yes sir." So I went to the president and told him these young men are definitely telling the truth and they were not involved. Two days later without any contradiction, definite proof came out that they were absolutely the people involved. They came into the office and said, "Coach, this is the real situation. We're really telling the truth now." I asked, "How can I believe you? Last time you told me you were really telling the truth. How can I believe you now?"

Everyone who cares about the future of Auburn should be concerned. The governor of Alabama, Bob Riley, criticized Walker and Housel and the two school trustees over their rendezvous with Louisville coach Bobby Petrino. All this came as a shock to Auburn coach Tuberville, unaware of the plot to replace him after five seasons and a 37-24 record. Birmingham sports columnists had a field day over the incident, suggesting the governor should take the next step and issue an executive order to clean house at the school.

Another trustee who was unaware of the secret visit to Louisville, Jimmy Rane, called the action "shameful. I'm ashamed and embarrassed. It's just awful. There will have to be repercussions from this. There will have to be."

Perhaps the strongest words came from Ray Melick in the *Birmingham Post-Herald* who suggested that because of the incident the Auburn president had lost his ability to lead. "Not only can no head coach at Auburn University feel safe with any agreement he or she may believe is in place with the president, but can any academic dean or professor or even the student government association feel comfortable in accepting Walker's word?"

The most significant repercussion was the quick departure of Walker as Auburn's president. Later Housler retired as athletic director. Whether that will be enough for the school to regain its credibility seems unlikely.

In the aftermath of the incident, Tuberville was quoted, "Everybody has shed a lot of tears and right or wrong, everybody's learned from this."

What have we learned? I guess we have learned that nothing has changed at Auburn except that with Bill Muse gone the school's reputation has suffered another setback. Dr. Muse stood for outstanding credibility and the best of ethics. He was the best thing going for the university. He stood strongly behind following the rules. The concept of following the rules has about as much standing at Auburn as the accumulation of toilet paper at Toomer's Corner on a Saturday night following a football game.

While a storm cloud seems to hover over Auburn, Terry Bowden is doing a superb job as a football commentator for ABC. If he continues to improve in this role as he has with each year of experience, his future is limitless.

Will Terry ever return to coaching? I think that's a distinct possibility. Any university looking for a new coach should highly consider hiring Terry. He's an honest person, and that is absolutely the first thing you should look for in a coach. In addition to honesty and integrity, he is a fine teacher; he knows the game; he is familiar with the tactics and strategy that it takes to win. He's a good recruiter.

The question is whether the job he has now in television makes him unattainable. He's making substantial money. He gets speaking engagements as a result of the TV exposure. And he works only from late August through early January when the bowl games are over.

Terry is a good man and was a good coach at Auburn. He would be an even better coach now.

# 19

## SOME DOG DAYS
## FOR THE DAWGS

◆ ◆ ◆

*"And o'er the land*
*Our loyal band*
*Will sing the glory of Washington forever"*
*– From "Bow Down to Washington,"*
*fight song of the University of Washington*

There was nothing glorious about much of what happened to the University of Washington intercollegiate athletic program in calendar year 2003. What had been one of the most respected and successful programs in the country became the focal point of embarrassment and disgrace.

Caught fibbing after he gambled with neighbors in a high-stakes pool on the national collegiate basketball tournament, head football coach Rick Neuheisel was fired. Neuheisel hired a team of lawyers and sued the university, and worse, he seemed determined to do anything possible to bring down the program.

That was in June. A month later the men's basketball program was put on probation for two years and lost one scholarship because of recruiting violations by Cameron Dollar, an assistant coach, in 2002. The penalties handed down by the NCAA cited thirteen major violations and two secondary violations by an over-zealous Dollar after complaints by recruiters from rival schools.

Husky fans were still reeling from those two developments when state health department officials suspended the license of Dr. William Scheyer, the team physician for the Huskies' nationally prominent women's softball program. Scheyer was accused of writing a rash of prescriptions for improper narcotics, tranquilizers, and other drugs that were tied to the UW team. The Washington State Patrol and the U.S. Drug Enforcement Administration joined forces to launch a criminal investigation.

Even before that probe of the drug scandal had been completed, Teresa Wilson, the women's softball coach, was relieved of her coaching duties and reassigned. Wilson had amassed an impressive record, including six trips to the NCAA Women's College World Series.

By February of 2004, more trouble was brewing for the Huskies. The NCAA accused the UW of a series of misdeeds involving lack of institutional control in three specific areas: (1) Violations of NCAA rules regarding gambling on college sports, specifically the high stakes auction involvement by Neuheisel, and lesser basketball pools by others in the athletic department; (2) Illegal contact by a Husky booster with UW recruits on a boat trip from the campus to Neuheisel's waterfront home; (3) Failure of the school's compliance staff to properly monitor activities and for giving out an incorrect interpretation of NCAA rules banning gambling through basketball betting pools.

The loyal band of University of Washington followers could find nothing in any of these developments to sing about, nothing to feel warm and fuzzy about, and certainly nothing that created an aura of confidence and reassurance over the status of the program, then or in the future.

The pride of the alumni and supporters was damaged. Friends and backers of the school and the sports program—in Washington's case, the Tyee group that contributes so generously to the program—hung their heads in shame.

This is where I was saddened. The UW sports program is one I believed in and still believe in. I worked hard and long to give the very best of myself all the time to make it something above and beyond any criticism.

*It hurt when troubles hit the UW athletic program, leading to the firing of Rick Neuheisel and the retirement of Barbara Hedges*

It's unfortunate, but when a university has a problem such as Washington suffered through with Neuheisel and others involved in the athletic program, the institution itself is embarrassed. And the impact on the school and its intercollegiate athletic program can be more than emotional.

There is a serious risk of football ticket sales sliding. Contributions start to fall off. Where the football program goes can affect the total department of athletics and all of its integral parts. After all, football is the prime mover of the sports programs at most schools. It's the main engine, and when it sputters so does financial stability. There is serious risk of a repeat of the early 1990s, when a Pac-10 investigation resulted in loss of scholarships, bowl participation and television exposure.

Sadly, most of those who are responsible for the transgressions are long gone and athletes who had no part of the violations are the victims of the punishment.

Taking the brunt of criticism—much of it severe and some of it cruel and personal—has been Barbara Hedges, the school's former athletic director. In the aftershock of what happened on her watch, some unhappy fans urged her to resign; others suggested she should be fired by school officials. Sports columnists had a field day at the expense of the Washington program and Hedges.

An anonymous Internet web site (firebarbara.com) created a long list of reasons to get rid of Barbara Hedges and urged supporters to write letters to school officials as part of an organized campaign. I was disappointed and dismayed by this tactic. I thought this was terrible.

Unfortunately, in intercollegiate athletics, that sort of thing also seems to go with the territory. I do not condone it, I do not support it, and I have a great deal of sympathy and empathy for Barbara. But I don't blame Hedges; I would put the onus on the former Washington administrators, president William Gerberding and vice president James Collier. Ignoring the recommendation of their own search committee, Gerberding and Collier picked Hedges as my replacement. They should have known better.

When Barbara was hired in 1991 I was pleased for her but surprised at the choice. I had observed her in Pac-10 meetings when she was an associate athletic director at the University of Southern California, working with AD Dick Perry and his successor, Mike McGee. I always liked her.

I was somewhat taken aback because I had been told by Dr. Dick Dunn, the chairman of the screening committee for a new AD, that his group's recommendation to be my successor was Don Purvis, then the athletic director at Ball State.

Like Kent State, where I first served as an athletic director, Ball State is a great place for on-the-job training, developing management and leadership skills right in the eye of the storm. You don't have a huge budget. You learn to do more with less. You become very, very assiduous in managing funds; you know the cash flow, and you know about personnel management because staff turnover—losing good people to larger schools—is almost unavoidable. Barbara had yet to earn her stripes as an AD.

I thought Purvis was a good choice. I knew him well. He had done a fine job at Ball State and had a great reputation among his peers. When Dr. Dunn went to Ball State to check out Purvis' credentials he returned with a glowing report about his skills as an administrator. He felt Don was a good leader. Purvis had been a successful coach and knew how to work with coaches; he got along well with alumni and fund-raising groups.

I agreed that Purvis would have been a good fit at the University of Washington. But when Dunn took the recommendation of his committee to the UW administration, the powers that be didn't agree. Gerberding seemed determined to make a statement that the institution was open and progressive about hiring women in athletic administration. His choice was Hedges.

There was no way that Barbara could get comparable experience as an associate AD at a big school like USC. I certainly wasn't surprised when Barbara told a Pac-10 official not long after she had been on the job in Seattle that she had no idea of the magnitude of what was involved. That's understandable. Considering the enormity and complexities of the job she handled some of the areas extremely well.

I think she made the right decision in firing Neuheisel. Absolutely. There is no question that with the many transgressions Coach Neuheisel put in his professional bank that his account should have been closed. It's that simple. At Colorado, where he was head football coach for four seasons before coming to Washington, he was the subject of an NCAA investigation that went on for three years. The NCAA found fifty-one recruiting violations, which resulted in the Buffaloes being put on probation for two years.

Earlier, Neuheisel was censured and put on probation for one year by the American Football Coaches Association for his "lack of remorse" over those infractions. He was in more hot water when he was caught in a mistruth when he insisted he hadn't been interviewed by the 49ers for the San Francisco NFL job in February 2003.

I am certain if Barbara Hedges could relive the Rick Neuheisel segment of history she would have checked his background at Colorado even more thoroughly. I heard from some of my old friends in Boulder that Neuheisel was happy to leave the University of Colorado and they were happy to see him go.

Indirectly, they warned the University of Washington, and as a result that warning was very prophetic of what would happen during Neuheisel's coaching tenure in Seattle.

Would I have hired Rick Neuheisel if I were an athletic director? I was not in that role when he was hired so the question is strictly a hypothetical one. But the answer is no; from all of the things I knew about the many things that happened in Boulder, I would not have hired him.

I must say I like Rick Neuheisel. He is a charming guy and a very fun person to be around. He has been very complimentary about me and my administration of the Husky program. Rick is a likeable guy. But would I hire him? There are a lot of my friends I like a lot whom I wouldn't hire.

Considering his problems at both Colorado and Washington, I think it will probably be difficult for him to get a head coaching job at a major school. In most reputable institutions his track record will be a considerable obstacle to hiring him. That's not to say somebody won't. Some institution might say, well, here's a coach with great visibility who has put quite a number of wins together; we need somebody who is high profile, can speak well, has intelligence and charm, and can resurrect our program. It is very possible that could happen.

I can't immediately think of any athletic directors who are friends of mine who would hire him, but that doesn't mean someone wouldn't. An even bigger question would be whether the president of a university would approve such a hiring. With the pressure Neuheisel put on the University of Washington and the legal complications involved in his departure, I would assume that a president or chancellor with a sense of high integrity and outstanding attention to detail regarding rules and regulations would tell the athletic director this is not the direction we would like to go.

Don't confuse my comments about Neuheisel with the fact that I recommended Gary Pinkel, a former Don James assistant, for the

Washington coaching vacancy. Pinkel had been a big success as a head coach at the University of Toledo and was ready to take the next step. I don't know precisely what went on when the search committee interviewed the finalists—Pinkel, Chris Tormey, John Mackovic, and Neuheisel—but I understand Rick mesmerized the group. Hedges wasn't the only one he impressed. Since then Pinkel has moved to the head coaching job at Missouri and turned that team into a Big 12 contender despite the presence of national powers such as Oklahoma, Texas, and Nebraska. Mackovic was fired midway in the 2003 season at Arizona, and Tormey's Nevada-Reno team, despite an upset win over Washington, faltered and he was let go at the end of the season.

Hedges' culpability in the University of Washington's Dog Days of 2003-04 will focus on "institutional control," something that invariably comes under close scrutiny whenever a school is being investigated for breaking an NCAA rule. Almost without exception, when a coach, staff member, or athlete has a problem the investigators try to assess the responsibility of the institution in the alleged infraction. Were those in command aware of the violation? Did they take proper action beforehand? Did they know or suspect something wrong was going on but looked the other way? What was done to prevent a repeat performance?

Some NCAA rules may seem to be contradictory and subject to interpretation, but they are quite specific in making the college president or chancellor (the CEO) of each institution the "ultimate responsibility and final authority" for institutional control.

For expediency, though, the school president invariably delegates to the director of intercollegiate athletics total responsibility for making sure institutional control happens. I don't consider that passing the buck. It's delegating the responsibility to the person he or she knows must make it happen.

That also means the athletic director must take extreme precautions to make certain every coach and staff member knows and understands the rules. Early in my career as an athletic director, I made a point of personally meeting with each coach and team to explain the importance of following the rules and the consequences to the athlete and the school of an infraction. To be on the safe side, I required every staff member and coach to sign a statement annually—when the latest copies of the NCAA manual and the Pac-10 handbook arrived—verifying they had read and fully understood the rules and would follow those regulations.

If there was a chauvinistic reaction over the selection of Hedges—and this is hardly surprising in a world once totally dominated by men—Barbara hushed some of her critics by what she accomplished at the University of Washington. For example, she did a magnificent job with fund-raising. On her watch, new facilities were built and old ones in need of refurbishing were remodeled or completely rebuilt. She upgraded many of the non-revenue sports.

Arguably the most significant project was the $43 million renovation of Edmundson Pavilion, increasing its permanent seating capacity to 10,000 and putting the men's basketball program in a position to be a positive revenue producer, given a competitive team. The old facility was built in 1927 and was seriously in need of an overhaul.

The other major athletic projects on campus were the new Dempsey Indoor Practice Facility, built at a cost of $28 million with space for a football field and a six-lane indoor track, and the $18 million renovation of Conibear Shellhouse, with a completion date in 2004. In addition to supporting the Huskies' nationally ranked men's and women's crew programs, Conibear was designed to house the athletic department's academic services program for the more than 650 varsity athletes in 23 sports.

Another $3 million went to a new women's softball stadium. Side-by-side soccer and baseball fields were built north of the shellhouse. Long-range plans called for permanent facilities between the two playing fields to be shared by the two sports: grandstands, locker rooms, press box, and concession facilities. The estimated cost is $12 million.

To make all this happen, Hedges was able to raise more than $100 million in donations through a major fund drive and surcharges on Husky season tickets ($50 per ticket on football, $25 on basketball, and $40 for faculty and staff members). The surcharges have produced about $2.5 million per year for the athletic budget.

As disappointed as I am over the problems and transgressions that have plagued the UW program in 2003-04. I have a great deal of compassion for Barbara Hedges. I understand what it's like when things go badly. I will never forget my first year as head football coach at Colorado State University. I had accepted the responsibility of coaching a football program that had lost sixteen games in succession and I piled ten more losses on top of that in my first season on the job.

I know how it feels when it seems like everything is going wrong and the world is collapsing around you and you can only wonder what can possibly go wrong next.

Complicating matters during the troubled times at Washington in 2003 was the absence of a permanent university president. Dr. Richard McCormick had resigned, and his duties were being carried out by an interim replacement.

I feel the presence of a strong CEO, like Dr. Bill Muse at Auburn, has a critical role in supporting the efforts of every athletic director. I was impressed when Dr. McCormick, in his first year at Washington (1995-'96) changed the chain of command in his relationship with the athletic director by having Mrs. Hedges report directly to him, rather than to a vice president, as was the case when I held the job. I had asked repeatedly for this relationship with Dr. Gerberding, but was always turned down.

Despite the pressure Barbara Hedges faced because of the problems near the end of her career, I can understand her reluctance to retire. I grew up being an athlete, then a coach and an athletic administrator. That was my whole life. I had never done anything else. I felt I was successful and I enjoyed my job, even the times of stress and strain. I thought I had the respect of my peers and the majority of the coaches and staff.

One thing I took a lot of pride in was problem solving. I liked to find a solution immediately and not put them off; it's often easier to delay, hoping a problem will solve itself. But indecision invariably allows something simple to become a full-blown crisis.

When the problems began piling up, critics questioned Hedges' leadership ability to deal with them; she became the focus of attention rather than the department's programs and the athletes.

When Hedges retired in mid-January of 2004 she said she wanted to shift the focus of attention away from herself and the problems she had to deal with the preceding six months. She made the right decision for herself and for the University of Washington.

I'm sure Barbara had a wealth of satisfaction and gratification in working with the student athletes, alumni, faculty, staff, and support groups and didn't feel ready to step down at that point of her career. However, under the circumstances I understand why she decided it would be best for the program if she left.

While her critics will not forget the myriad problems of the Husky program that remained as part of her legacy, Barbara's achievements over twelve years resonate the success of her career. She should be proud of Washington's non-revenue sports and the things she did to improve the facilities. She had a wonderful ride; her career was extremely significant in intercollegiate athletics as one of the very first female athletic directors at a major institution.

I could be critical of those who were remiss in following the NCAA rules and brought dishonor to the Washington program and, as a result, were disloyal to Barbara. But there is no intent to second guess or express sour grapes with my successor. She did a good job in many facets of the job and deserves much credit for what she accomplished. But at the time, she was the wrong choice for the wrong reason.

Don Purvis of Ball State wasn't the only person disappointed over not being hired as Washington's athletic director. Chuck Armstrong, the interim athletic director after I left, told me he had been promised the job and was justifiably furious with Gerberding when he changed his mind. Mike Alderson, who had become close to Jim Collier, the UW's vice president of university relations, also thought he had a chance to be the new AD.

Armstrong, who had come to Seattle from California to oversee the Mariners for absentee owner George Argyros, was looking for a job after Argyros sold the team to Jeff Smulyan. So Chuck was available and wanted to turn the interim role into something permanent. We had several meetings to discuss the status of the UW program and I was candid. I said, "Chuck, if you think working for George [Argyros] was frustrating, let me tell you about the bureaucracy of a state university and some of the things that happened to me." I said that I had been told repeatedly that I was doing an excellent job. I was never informed what I was doing wrong, if I was doing anything wrong, and I had never received a poor performance evaluation.

At one point Gerberding was pushing for an answer from Armstrong about the interim job and Chuck asked me, "Do you think I should take the job?" I told him, "I can't tell you that. I think that's up to you." But I said if the situation were reversed I would tell them to "stick it."

When he was having problems with Argyros, Chuck would meet with me and spill his troubles. I was a good listener. I called him. I saw him. I counseled him. When he did take the interim position he said he knew I was going through some deep hurt and he was sorry if I felt that he had betrayed me.

Not long after Armstrong was passed over for the permanent job, the Mariners changed owners again and Chuck returned to the baseball team's front office. Now he's president of one of the most successful teams in baseball.

# 20
## SHORT TAKES: WHAT I THINK ABOUT...

◆ ◆ ◆

### The NCAA Arms Race

Want to know the most shameful and disgraceful trend of intercollegiate athletics in the last decade or so? It's the so-called arms race.

I call it immoral.

That's the most precise word I can think of to describe the mammoth salaries that are being paid to head coaches by universities and colleges across America.

A recent survey indicated at least thirty football coaches were receiving a base pay of $1 million or more per year. The way things are going with the arms race soaring out of control, both numbers could double in a very few years.

There are other nuances of the arms race that make me wonder if sanity has totally escaped the powers that be in intercollegiate sports. For example:

In addition to the inflated guaranteed base pay, the head coaches of almost every major college program now have a wide range of bonus incentives written into their contracts.

Athletic directors, anxious to wrap up the services of a successful coach, are extending the length of contracts beyond reason, sometimes for ten or twelve years, resulting in commitments of millions of dollars.

Power coaches, supported by agents and lawyers to represent them, have made greed a major part of the picture. They have multi-endorsements for multi-dollars; they get paid for television and radio shows. Some even get paid to speak to alumni groups. It seems to me that's part of the coach's responsibility, to represent the institution to its constituents.

Please don't misunderstand this criticism. I am a strong believer in coaches and athletic directors being fairly compensated. I have no problem with them getting paid what they are really worth and what is reasonable. And that's the key word: reasonable. I think when coaches win championships and go to bowl games or post-season tournaments they should receive bonuses for being successful. That's reasonable. I think a five-year contract is reasonable. But I have a major problem with what are almost lifetime contracts.

I don't think that speaks well to the concept that athletics are part of the educational process and the university system.

According to a survey by the American Association of University Professors, the average salary of a full professor with a PhD at a U.S. public university is just under $93,000 per year. Many, many head football coaches have the potential of making double that amount *in bonuses alone.*

Consider the income potential of Bob Stoops, the head coach at the University of Oklahoma. On top of his $2.2 million salary, Stoops had the potential of collecting a whopping $257,000 in year-end bonuses in 2003. That's almost as much as the $285,304 salary of the school president, David Boren.

Perhaps the ultimate bonus clause was part of the 2003 contract of Louisiana State coach Nick Saban. It required LSU to renegotiate Saban's contract and make him the highest-paid coach in the country, by at least $1, as a result of LSU's victory over Oklahoma in the BCS national championship game. That moved Saban ahead of Stoops at the top of the list of coaches making the most money.

Besides sending a horrible message to the faculty and staff of an institution, this alarming trend puts a terrible strain on the budget of any athletic department. I don't think it's right and I don't believe in it.

How can athletics be part of the educational system when a coach is getting paid $2 million a year and at the same time the athletic budget is operating in the red? I agree with William Friday, co-chair of the Knight Foundation Commission on Intercollegiate Athletics and a critic of the over rewarding of college coaches.

Friday said bonuses for coaches are unnecessary because they reward coaches for doing expressly what they were hired and being paid extremely well to accomplish. He pointed out that no history professor would expect a bonus for helping to develop a Rhodes scholar.

How did it all start? I would say the perceived value of a head football coach started to skyrocket in the mid-1990s. More and more coaches began using agents to negotiate contracts. Some athletic directors dug in their heels, but others, anxious to keep up with the Joneses in a competitive world, jumped into the arms race. Unfortunately, the University of Washington, where I had served as AD, followed the trend. Rick Neuheisel wasn't the first coach to hit the million-dollar salary level but his doing so got a lot of attention and was a wakeup call for fans in the Northwest.

Budgets are already strained. The non-revenue sports are at risk. Gender-equity sports, which are starting to thrive and expand the opportunities for women athletes at the collegiate level, may suffer. Something will have to give because there's only so much money to go around.

This merry-go-round simply can't keep going as it is. The university presidents and boards of regents, the governing bodies of universities, simply have to realize that the arms race has to be slowed down and that it's time to get off.

I strongly disagree with those in intercollegiate sports that insist these shameful compensation packages are justifiable because of the large amounts of money generated by a successful football or basketball program. Yes, I realize more than most how important this revenue is to support the other teams who don't pay their own way.

But I also know there are a lot of really good coaches at all levels of intercollegiate athletics who would simply be elated to coach at one of the larger institutions for considerably less money than those million-dollar salaries and huge incentive bonuses.

How can the arms race be slowed down? Unfortunately, we may have to see programs go bankrupt and boards of regents and trustees conclude that some sports programs are not an absolute necessity for the existence of higher education. And that would be sad.

If that domino effect starts, it would certainly get some attention. So far we have not seen this at the major school level. Not yet. There are college presidents who are concerned and want to take remedial action, but they also say, "I can't do this unilaterally."

And they are right. You can't even do it by getting all the schools in one conference to agree. The Big 10 tried it with a so-called sanity code in the 1950s but it failed after a few years.

I think if the half-dozen or so major conferences got together and agreed to stop the arms race—put a salary cap on head coaches and athletic directors—then a return to sanity might be possible. That would be the best thing that could happen in intercollegiate athletics. It would have a great appeal to the faculty people who have distanced themselves from the athletic program at so many schools.

Considering their respective contributions to society, it's hard to justify a football coach earning three or four times more than a researcher finding a vaccine to end a dreaded disease or a noted expert in space exploration.

An offshoot of the arms race is the competition for new facilities. Certainly, it's great to have an indoor practice facility. But there are times when intercollegiate athletics appear to be following a pattern from the fashion industry. In women's fashions, the hemlines go up and down. Something that's in one year is out the next.

This one-upsmanship over offices and locker rooms occurs within individual programs. An athletic director recently told me about getting a call from his secretary telling him the senior women's administrator and the volleyball coach had been in the men's baseball locker room measuring the square footage, the size of the lockers, and the shower room. Next they were heading for the women's softball facilities to do the same thing.

I have no desire to go back to the "old days." I'm not one to live in the past. But if we build a huge, classy weight room and conditioning facility, then someone else has to build a larger one with more gimmicks. Not long ago, a team in the Sun Belt built a huge indoor practice facility. That makes about as much sense as trying to take a prize bull and enter him in the Kentucky Derby.

When it comes to pushing aside the distractions and unrealistic aspects of intercollegiate sports, no single organization has had a more positive effect or done a better job than the National Association of Collegiate Directors of Athletics (NACDA). Under the strong guidance of Mike Cleary, one of the organization's founders close to 40 years ago, the group has been a beacon of leadership.

During my term as the NACDA's president, I had a close-up look at Cleary's vision, a product of years of experience in collegiate sports. Mike's efforts have given the national group a high level of credibility with its members and our bosses, the college presidents. He combines a deep understanding of the goals of college athletics with a down-to-earth practical approach in helping reach those objectives.

The NACDA institute and the instructional programs it offers have been significant in helping many athletic directors do a better job. One of the proudest moments of my career was receiving in

1988 the James J. Corbett Award, an honor presented annually by NACDA for service to college athletics. I have remained active in the organization since retiring.

## National College Football Playoffs

Despite all the problems with the Bowl Championship Series (BCS) and previous attempts to determine a Division 1A football champion, I'm against a playoff format. I don't care how much revenue it might produce.

I like the bowl system the way it used to be, when being invited to a bowl game gave a football team respect and credibility. As things stand now, there are far too many bowls, and too many teams are playing that have no right to be competing beyond the regular season. Why should a 6-5 team deserve a bowl invitation, other than to make it appear the season was a success and save a coach's job? What amazes me is that people will pay money to watch two mediocre teams compete in the name of "bowling" it.

Let's say there are 117 1-A football programs in the country and 28 bowl games. That means 56 of the teams, or nearly half, will compete in post-season games. I can only wonder how many of those 56 coaches received a bonus for making it to a bowl game. And how many really deserved a bonus?

When I was chairman of the NCAA Post-Season Bowl Committee we tried to put a cap on the number of bowl games. We tried to avoid the proliferation of bowls, so many of which are meaningless, and at one time we suggested that sixteen would be plenty. At least that was the consensus of the committee, right or wrong.

When we had a meeting to discuss that concept the NCAA attorney at the time, George Gangwear, joined us. He said, "You can't do that. You can't arbitrarily control it. If sponsors want to have a bowl game and meet the criteria, then they ought to be able to do it."

I responded, "George, you're the NCAA attorney and you are

here to advise us." He agreed. I said, "Then it seems to me that your job is to tell us how we can do it, not how we can't do it." He didn't care for that at all. Our strategy was to make the requirements so strict that the bowl hopefuls would not be able to meet the criteria. The existing bowl games, of course, supported the plan.

When I went to the NCAA council meeting to explain the proposal I looked around the table and saw representatives from about thirty different universities and noted that not a single one of them had any experience in a major bowl game. So I knew the plan was doomed and they voted it down.

## Pay for College Athletes

Because of the huge amounts of money being generated by college sports, mainly football and the NCAA basketball tournament, more and more people think the competitors should get a piece of the action. Pay the athletes. They attract the big crowds; they deserve some of the box office take.

I totally disagree.

One reason this issue is getting any attention goes directly back to the arms race problem of huge coaching salaries. The athletes are saying, "Look at what my head coach is making and what the assistant coaches are getting. I want mine."

Certainly, college football generates a lot of revenue. But student athletes now are being well taken care of. A full scholarship, including tuition, fees, room and board, and books, isn't something to be sneezed at. Athletes are going to college and reaping all the benefits of a college education at no expense because of their skills and expertise in sports. But I don't believe in paying athletes additional money other than scholarships.

For student athletes who have serious financial problems there are a variety of programs that respond to special needs. There are Pell grants to supplement the scholarships of those with the utmost needs. The NCAA has set up a student fund for disadvantaged athletes. If an athlete is really destitute, the fund is available to pay for a trip home for a family emergency, to attend a funeral or visit a parent in the hospital.

The NCAA points out that it allocated about $750 million to three funds over a period of eleven years starting in 1991. The number of athletes who received help jumped from fewer than 4,500 in 1991-'92 to more than 25,000 in 2002-03. That's in addition to the athletic scholarships awarded by each school, valued at as much as $40,000 per year.

But if colleges were to pay athletes a stipend—whatever the amount—it would not be long before somebody said, "you know, I just can't afford my Lincoln Navigator on that amount of money. I need more. And I'm playing better than Joe Dokes, who's getting the same amount that I am and he doesn't even get into the lineup."

Another dilemma for every athletic department would be finding a source of revenue to pay for salaries for individual athletes. Only two of five athletic departments of the NCAA's 117 Division 1-A football-playing schools operated in the black in 2001, the most recent year for which statistics are available. But without subsidies from the school and state, only 6 percent of those 117 schools made money. Chances are the sports that would take the biggest hit would be the non-revenue sports.

If college athletes were to receive pay for play, the money likely would go to those in all sports, not just the major revenue producers, football and men's basketball. That would avoid a legal challenge. But do the math. If each of the estimated 150,000 Division 1-A athletes received $2,000 a year—the number mentioned in a recent article on the subject by NCAA president Myles Brand—the total cost would be $300 million, and that would be only the start.

As a college athlete I had to work at a series of campus jobs in lieu of a scholarship. I got an undergraduate degree; I got a masters degree. I was hired at jobs that required me to have a college degree. I was paid more that my high school classmates who didn't go to college. If I had not gone to college my net worth today would be a lot less than it is. I was a beneficiary of a system that provided me the opportunity to go to college. I was paid for life, and most of us are fortunate when it comes to a lifestyle. And we often end up meeting a special kind of lady in the process.

Because football makes a lot of money doesn't mean every player is a shareholder and should be getting part of the revenue. You are going to college. What is the mission of a college or university? Let's remember that every university and the concept of providing an education existed before there was an athletic program.

In many countries, athletic programs have no part in higher education; I would hate to see that happen in America. But if we don't watch out, someday we may not have athletics at the intercollegiate level. We always will have colleges and universities.

A college education is not a four-year experience that ends when an athlete's eligibility is over. Go research the value: What does a four-year degree mean in a person's lifetime income compared to that of a person with a high school diploma? A college degree is an insurance policy for life.

If you are feeling bad over the plight of the collegiate athlete, go to any college at three o'clock in the afternoon and check all the nice cars and sports utility vehicles in the parking lot near the building that houses the athletic department locker rooms.

Then perhaps you won't feel so guilty about players not getting a monthly stipend.

## Farm Teams for Pro Sports

There are some otherwise extremely bright people who look on college athletics as no more than a stepping stone to the professional ranks. They try to categorize college teams as farm teams for the major pro leagues. I take strong exception to that idea. I don't ever want colleges and universities to be classified as minor leagues for the pro teams, even indirectly. After all, less than one percent of the men and women who compete at the college level move on to the professional ranks.

Intercollegiate sports competition has a long and storied history of its own. The intensity of the rivalries in the college game, in a wide range of sports, is unmatched at any level. This applies not just to the high exposure sports, football and basketball, but to everything from crew racing to women's soccer.

The college game is teeming with tradition and excitement. The loyalties go far beyond the geographic regional ties that are typical for followers of most professional teams. The pageantry, the emotions, the involvement of alumni and their allegiance to alma mater create a stadium ambiance totally different from the pro game. The cheerleaders and band members are students, not hired dancers or hired musicians.

So it's demeaning to the college game to be classified as a farm program for the pros.

I realize the courts have ruled that it is legal for promising young athletes to turn professional before completing their college eligibility. Too many see their hopes shattered by the fierce competition and wake up to the reality of a future without a professional career or college degree.

As with the separation of church and state, I suggest there should be a separation of professional and collegiate sport.

I don't mean they should be adversaries. They should be able to work together in their communities. In Seattle, the University of Washington had a great relationship with the Seattle Seahawks of the NFL. I enjoyed working with John Thompson, the Seahawks' first general manager. We avoided the situation in some cities where collegiate and pro teams ended up being adversarial.

And I would be the last person to discourage any youngster from aspiring to a career in big league sports. It's a big jump going from the high school ranks to playing college sports, and only a small percentage of college players make it to the professional level.

But there's nothing wrong with having lofty goals and a willingness to work hard to reach those goals. I believe in that. I strongly feel that you should have goals that make you stretch so far they are virtually unattainable. There's nothing wrong with shooting for the moon and working hard to get there, climbing as many rungs on the ladder to success as possible. And there's nothing wrong with having intermediate goals on the way to seemingly unreachable heights.

While on the subject of professional sports, I also think the salaries are hopelessly out of control, thanks to overwhelming greed on the part of both owners and players. To pay a baseball player more than $10 million a year for five or ten years is just as immoral as what some college football coaches are receiving. Guys who are hitting .220 are getting millions of dollars, and the salaries are guaranteed. No wonder so many teams are losing so much money.

**Role Models, Like it or Not**

I totally believe those involved in the leadership of intercollegiate athletics are held to a higher standard. They should be held to a higher standard and conduct themselves with the knowledge of that standard.

In my view, anybody who says he or she shouldn't be or doesn't want to be a role model shouldn't be a teacher.

When I was athletic director at Kent State, Washington and Auburn, I made a point of meeting personally with each squad and their coaches in every sport once a year and talked about this responsibility. I made it an absolute must to go over the rules and regulations and the forms the student athletes had to sign for the NCAA. I would read the rules and emphasize my philosophy and beliefs. I emphasized that each of them would be identified as an athlete the rest of their lives. I told them, "Good or bad, you will carry that label."

Right now I may be retired, but if I go out and misbehave—

whatever way—the media will refer to me as "former athletic director at the University of Washington." When coaches and athletes said they didn't want to be considered role models and protested, "I'm on my own time," I had a standard response: "You are until you get into trouble."

## Throwing Out the NCAA Rulebook

Sure, I've heard a lot of criticism of the NCAA and suggestions that the entire rule book should be rewritten. As Pogo of the comics once said: "We have met the enemy and he is us."

The rules of the National Collegiate Athletic Association were made over many years and approved by the members in an effort to give all schools a level playing field. Many of the rules were made because some of the members were doing things considered improper.

The unfortunate part is that the NCAA hierarchy has grown so large that if you were to call the NCAA about a particular rule or an interpretation of a rule you might get somewhat different answers, depending on which staff member responded to your question. That's a matter of coordination, getting everyone on the same page.

I disagree with the idea there are too many rules and I don't know how you could rewrite the rule book. It's much like the government makes new laws to handle different situations, when people are not able to live and work harmoniously together. The NCAA makes new rules because some schools or athletic administrators are not able to interact successfully.

And I know when a school president or an athletic director or a coach criticizes the NCAA they are really criticizing themselves because NCAA rules are made by the members of the association.

I hope there will always be a governing body for intercollegiate teams and athletes, and that they wouldn't be turned loose like a bunch of cannibals.

**Random thoughts of an athletic director on:**

**Handling coaches—** I never felt being an athletic director was an impossible job because I had been an assistant coach and a head coach. I'd been in positions where I had been very successful and in one role where I experienced trauma and defeat and had been fired as a head football coach. No one could come into my office and say, "Mike, you just don't know what it's like out there." Certainly, it's an advantage for an athletic director to have been in the trenches. Sure, a lot of coaches have tremendous egos. It's the nature of the game to have confidence. I don't find it difficult to work with people with large egos. To a certain extent it's very helpful.

**Coexisting with the academic world—**The athletic director needs to impress the CEO that the AD should sit on the president's cabinet and be invited to meetings of the regents or trustees. He or she should speak to faculty groups such as the faculty senate. The AD should display a broad interest in all areas of the campus—drama and music productions, commencements, and other faculty affairs. Don't expect the faculty to come to you. Making the rounds of deans and vice presidents and inviting them to events also lets them know your interest goes beyond the football stadium. I have always stressed that as the CEO of the athletic department the AD should stand for honesty and truth. I demanded that others in the department operate within the rules—and the spirit of the rules—of the NCAA and of the conference in which the school was a member. The university comes first; it was there before any athletic program.

**Dealing with the media—**It's an important part of the job, but it has never frightened me. It never posed what I considered a problem. There have been, of course, times when I've been asked very unusual questions, but I always tried to deal with the media truthfully. If there was something I could not share, I would simply say that I couldn't talk about it at that time. I tried to be straightforward and honest. I always believed in returning phone calls as promptly as possible, even those I felt would be difficult. I think in dealing with the media you must recognize they have a difficult job but that they realize that works both ways. I wanted to help make their job easier by being accessible and telling them the truth. I tried to make friends with them. At football games I would make a point of shaking hands and chatting with them in the press box. I would never hide from the media. When going into a new job I liked to make the rounds, visiting the newspapers, radio and television stations, calling on them to get acquainted. Sure, it takes time and effort, but it's the right thing to do, and it pays off in the long run.

**Working with alumni, boosters**—The most effective way to handle these supporters is the way you handle any constituent group. You're honest with them, you require them to live within the rules, and if somebody is circumventing the rules you disassociate them from the program. Keep them in the loop. Be sure to keep them informed through a variety of communication devices: newsletters, meetings, radio, and television. It's important they understand that you, as athletic director, are responsible for the ethical conduct and institutional control of that area of the university.

**Traits of a successful AD**—I learned a lot from my Marine Corps experience about dealing with people. I feel you should be straightforward and tell it like it is. I strongly believe in being honest and truthful. Agree or not, I respected the opinion of others as a matter of dignity and respect. I always was willing to work hard and put in long hours on the job. Other qualities that are important include being fiscally responsible, having an ability to communicate, and knowing the territory, like the song from *The Music*

*Man.* To know the territory, I believe, you have to have had the experience of involvement. That's why I think some of the better athletic directors are former head football or basketball coaches who have experience relating to student athletes, faculty, and alumni. Other traits include strong leadership skills, intelligence, and an ability to respect others. You should be a good manager; you need to be a people person. You can't pretend to know all the answers, but you should know where to find the answers. You have to be a decision maker. You can't be afraid to make a decision. Don James would say I didn't always give him the answer he had wanted or hoped for, but I always gave him an answer. The biggest trap is trying to please everybody; that's often impossible. You have to do what is right, what is ethical, what is honest, and what works, and learn from your mistakes.

**The future of intercollegiate sports**—The NCAA has so many pressures on it, and the management is so frightened because of legal problems. I know in my heart that the NCAA will survive but may be changed seriously. Its role may end up being nothing more than simply running championships. However, intercollegiate athletics has stood the test of time with considerable resiliency. The standards and values remain, including some intangibles. At more than one institution where I worked, I was asked to lecture by the school of business on the team principle and the value of competition. Throughout business, science, and industry there are references to teams: the sales team, the surgical team, the space team. But as one professor explained to me, "We don't have any place in all of this university outside the practice fields and gymnasiums where the team principle is being taught." In athletics you teach by explaining, demonstrating, doing, and then examining. The examination is the intercollegiate contest. As I've said many times, intercollegiate athletics must be an integral part of the total educational process.

**On my Christian faith and ethics**—I am very sincere about my religious faith. I don't wear it on my sleeve and pretend to be evangelical and push my faith on others. But it's been important in my marriage to Rena and the way we raised our three wonderful daughters. I'm not ashamed to say I pray about decisions, and I benefited so much from the Fellowship of Christian Athletes and from the pastors at churches I attended wherever I worked. I remember talking with an assistant pastor when I was coaching at Delaware. He was a graduate of Wheaton College and Princeton Theological Seminary. I told him I wasn't sure I was a true Christian because I'd heard others talk about having a mountaintop experience with cymbals or drums or something like that, and I hadn't. He told me that not everybody has to—and he hadn't, either.

**Rating the college presidents**—Dr. William Muse, who hired me to restructure the athletic department and bring credibility to Auburn University, ranks No. 1 of the 10 presidents of institutions where I was either a coach or athletic director. I was Dr. Muse's hired gun, and he made it clear I had the responsibility and authority and reported directly to him. The second best job, for the first thirteen years, was at the University of Washington although it deteriorated at the end. The man at the bottom of the list is Glenn Olds, who took over at Kent State after I was hired there. My ranking:

Bill Muse, Auburn

Bob White, who hired me at Kent State University

Harvey Turner, Hillsdale College where I was a student and assistant

John Perkins, University of Delaware

Bill Morgan, when I was hired at Colorado State University

John Hogness, who hired me at the University of Washington

Arthur Hauck, University of Maine

William Gerberding, University of Washington

Ray Chamberlain, Colorado State University
Glenn Olds, Kent State University

**The Cream of the crop**—Naming the outstanding athletic directors I had the pleasure of working with is a hazardous task because I know I will leave someone out who should be included. So let's say the ADs on this list are among the best. The list includes directors I introduced when they received the Corbett Award as the outstanding athletic director of the year of the National Association of Collegiate Directors of Athletics. They are Gary Cunningham, University of California-Santa Barbara; Jack Lengyel, U.S. Naval Academy; Betty Kruczek, Fitchburg State University; Homer Rice, Georgia Tech; George King, Purdue; John Toner, University of Connecticut; and Carl Maddox, Mississippi State. Others are Frank Broyles, Arkansas; Cedric Dempsey, Arizona; Doug Weaver, Michigan State; Jim Jones, Ohio State; Don Canham, Michigan;

Pac-10 Commissioner Tom Hansen presents the Corbett Award as athletic director of the year in 1988

Bump Elliott, Iowa; Dave Nelson, Delaware; Bob Woodruff, Tennessee; Dick Tamburo, Missouri, Arizona State and Texas Tech; Cecil Coleman, Illinois; Bill Flynn, Boston College; Bill Byrne, Oregon, Nebraska and Texas A&M; J. D. Morgan, UCLA; Bill Orwig, Indiana; Bill Rohr, Ohio University; Fred Miller, Arizona State and San Diego State; John Swofford, North Carolina; Joe Castiglione, Oklahoma; Gene DeFilippo, Boston College; Kevin White, Notre Dame; Mike McGee, South Carolina; Dave Maggard, California-Berkeley, Miami-Florida and Houston, Jim Livengood, University of Arizona and

Washington State; Vince Dooley, Georgia; David Hart Jr., Florida State University, and Gene Smith, Arizona State, Iowa State and Eastern Michigan and many others.

**Being on the job at dawn**—It never was hard for me to be in my office at work early in the morning, usually about six a.m., before most others arrived, and I recommend it to anyone in such a complex position. It gave me an opportunity to think alone, to plan my day with a things-to-be-done list, and to make phone calls to the Eastern and Central time zones. The other early bird when I was at the University of Washington was Don James, the head football coach. Often we shared a ride.

**Some special individuals**—Earlier I discussed in separate chapters or mentioned many of the outstanding coaches I worked with during my career. Who were the best? I'd have to rank Dave Nelson and Don James at the top of that list. Nelson was my coaching mentor for years; he was a great organizer, and his understanding of football and its place in the overall scheme of a university, his character and ethics were superb. James was an excellent teacher, highly organized, extremely ethical, intelligent, and hard working. Several others should be mentioned in the elite category: Marv Harshman, the Washington basketball coach, was an outstanding teacher and strategist and never made demands, a great team player. The same goes for Tommy Joe Eagles, the Auburn basketball coach. Bob MacDonald, the UW baseball coach was a dedicated hard worker who was totally loyal. There were three swimming coaches in my career, and each was a superb coach, a team player, and totally loyal: David Marsh at Auburn, Todd Boyle at Kent State and Earl Ellis at Washington. In Washington rowing, Bob Ernst and Jan Harville won a shell load of national honors and were great teachers. Kent State track coach Doug Raymond was a fiery individual who lived an exemplary life and was a dedicated teacher. I've met a lot of nice guys, but no one rates higher in my book in that department than Al Lavan, who played for me at Colorado State and went on to coach with several pro teams and a half-dozen college programs.

**One last thought**—After this book went to the printer, but before the press rolled, the University of Washington named a longtime friend and colleague Todd Turner as its 15th Athletic Director. Time limitations and space requirements only allow me to say I believe he is a proven and able athletic administrator, and I wish him and the University of Washington the best of luck as they enter a new era.

**Having a great day, every day**—In my personal and professional life I have adopted an approach most eloquently expressed by Norman Vincent Peale in his book, *Have a Great Day Every Day*: "A sure way to a great day is to have enthusiasm. It contains a tremendous power to produce vitality, vigor, joyousness. So great is enthusiasm as a positive motivational force that it surmounts adversity and difficulty and, moreover, if cultivated, does not run down. It keeps one going strong, even when the going is tough. It may even slow down the aging process for, as Henry Thoreau said, 'None are so old as those who have outlived enthusiasm.'"

I've lived a full and wonderful life. I still have a lot of enthusiasm. I've had the privilege of experiencing a world of intercollegiate sports that many can only read about or participate in as spectators. I've been blessed in so many ways, the best of which is Rena, my beautiful wife and three beautiful daughters. The many friends I've made along the way have made it a rich experience. If I've been able to give back a small portion of the abundance I have received then I have accomplished more than anything I could have hoped for when I left that family farm in rural Michigan.

# EPILOGUE

◆ ◆ ◆

For a working journalist, playing the role of ghost writer rarely produces much satisfaction. Stringing together words and sentences that appear in print under someone else's byline never quite triggers the creative juices endemic to the writing process.

Nevertheless, in my 40-plus years in journalism I have had occasion to play ghost for some reasonably well known sports personalities. I did a magazine piece with National Football League Hall of Fame star Steve Largent on how to play wide receiver. I ghosted the basketball expertise of television commentator Al Maguire in a series of newspaper articles when Seattle played host to the Final Four of college basketball and repeated the exercise with Billy Packer a few years later.

As a sports editor of the *Seattle Post-Intelligencer* I convinced pro football coach Chuck Knox (Los Angeles Rams, Buffalo Bills and Seattle Seahawks) to play expert before and during a Super bowl, offering his insight on the game; then I handled the logistics of getting his message to the readers in a week-long series. I reluctantly took on the assignment of helping Olympic sailing gold medalist Bill Buchan explain in detail his race course tactics for an article in a boating magazine.

In each instance, I probed the author-to-be with a lengthy string of questions, tape recording the answers. After transcribing the tapes, I sorted through the text for the most relevant and provocative answers and created a first-person narrative that, hopefully, was authoritative and convincing. The articles usually were less than 2,000 words, relatively short compared to a book.

I read books, lots of them; but I had never written one. I wasn't even sure how many words were involved in the average book, but I knew it was much more than 2,000. So when I was approached about the possibility of helping Mike Lude in his project I was skeptical. Most of my experience was with the daily deadlines of the newspaper routine. Besides, as I asked Mike in our first meeting, why do you want to do this, and why me?

I put Lude off a couple of months. He sensed I was weakening and persisted. In a second session we met for three days, and he captivated me with his enthusiasm; he fascinated me with story after story about the hardships of his youth, his survival in college, then his emergence as a football coach and, eventually, an athletic director. When we started outlining the book, chapter by chapter, I realized I was hooked.

After nearly 85,000 words and a gestation period of about eighteen months, this is the result. The book was dictated in Tucson, Arizona; those tapes were transcribed in Bellevue, Washington. Mike's modesty got in the way, at first. He seemed almost embarrassed to talk about the details of his many accomplishments for fear of having it sound like he was bragging. I e-mailed him hundreds of follow-up questions to get him to open up and talk in detail about his exploits, how he felt at the time and how others reacted. He went to work and sent more tapes.

Chapter by chapter, it came together—written, revised, corrected, reworked and, finally, edited in New York by Anne Greenberg. Her expertise greatly enhanced the final manuscript and her encouragement was confirmation of my decision to take on the project.

And, by the way, it was an enjoyable and satisfying experience, far more so than my prior ghost writing escapades—thanks to Mike Lude. When I knew him professionally I respected Mike's success as an athletic director. But like so many people in Seattle I had only a hint of how widely respected he was across the country.

Being around him and getting to know him closely over the last couple of years I have been touched by his kindness and thoughtfulness as much as I have been impressed with his enthusiastic determination to finish the task, and the Marine-style organization of his effort. I was constantly amazed at his recall of events more than 50 years earlier, much of it supported by his endless files of notes, memos and documents. I appreciated his warm sense of humor and his attention to accuracy.

As troubled as Mike was about more recent problems in the athletic department at the University of Washington, he was reluctant to comment. He didn't want anything he said to sound like sour grapes over his successor as UW athletic director, Barbara Hedges. He didn't want to be accused of second guessing Hedges or appear to be against women athletic directors. To keep his credibility with

*Bill Knight*

many supporters, he credits Hedges with significant accomplishments but blames the melt down on former UW administrators for picking someone not ready to handle all the nuances of the job.

Make no mistake this book is Mike Lude's story. If it were a hockey game he would be credited with the goal and all of those he touched along the way would get an assist. Consider my role as that of a recorder.

I understand now why dozens of friends and admirers—some of the biggest names in coaching, athletic administration, and the sports media in the country—were so willing to sing the praises of Mike Lude in the section at the front of this volume titled "Endorsements." Most of those comments are excerpts from far longer tributes.

Finally, I thank my wife, Dorothy Graham, who was a patient, supportive onlooker and a painstaking copy reader. Her suggestions made the book a better read.

– Bill Knight

# Index

◆ ◆ ◆

* Endorsements

* Endorsements

* Endorsements

* Endorsements

"A book of terrific personal and professional insight and a must read for anyone who bleeds purple and gold. Mike takes us behind the often closed doors of big time college athletics."

– **Tom Glasgow,** Veteran Seattle Sportscaster, Sports Director KOMO 1000 News.

"At the age of 29 I became an Athletics Director at Eastern Michigan University. As one of only a few African American AD's of a D1-A program, I looked for a mentor I felt comfortable with. Mike Lude was awesome. He is a great man, I owe so much to him for his guidance."

– **Gene Smith,** Athletics Director Arizona State University.

"Mike always was up front with everything. When he told you it would be a certain way, that's the way it was. Sometimes we didn't like it, but we knew it was going to be that way. He gave the coaches the rules and saw that they were followed to a 'T.' I worked for three wonderful athletics directors, all different, but all excellent. The University was much better for having Mike as the athletics director."

– **Marv Harshman,** Retired Head Men's Basketball Coach, University of Washington, Washington State University and Pacific Lutheran University.

"It comes as no surprise to me that Mike Lude achieved such great success as a college coach and athletics director. There is nothing phony about this man, and yes, he will (and does) tell you exactly what he thinks."

– **R.R. "Ruly" Carpenter,** former owner Philadelphia Phillies Baseball Club, Member of the University of Delaware Board of Trustees.

"Mike's enthusiasm and passion for college athletics was and is immediately evident and contagious. His competitive drive and leadership enabled us to experience unbelievable growth and success at both Kent State and the University of Washington. Mike gives you an inside look from his perspective at the challenges, complexities, highs and lows of college athletics. Anyone aspiring to be in college athletics should read this book."

– **Bob Stull,** Athletics Director University of Texas El Paso, and Former University of Washington Assistant Football Coach.

"This book can only give the reader a glimpse of the huge success Mike Lude enjoyed in getting Auburn University's athletic 'ox out of the ditch' during his short tenure as Athletics Director. Mike met all the goals assigned to him by restoring Auburn to credibility with the NCAA and hired a coach who produced an 11-0 season. While Mike's success at Auburn is only part of his remarkable story, it is certainly one of the most outstanding achievements of any athletics director in the history of college sports"

**– John Denson,** Former Trustee Auburn University.

"As a kid who also grew up in a rural area of the Midwest, I can truly relate to the experiences that Mike Lude encountered as he pursued his goals of coaching big-time football and later emerged into the world of college athletic administration. He climbed the mountain with vigor, maintained his lofty position with great character and retired from it all with pride and dignity."

**– Don DeVoe,** Retired Head Men's Basketball Coach U.S. Naval Academy.

"I've known Mike for 57 years. We've been friends since he was the captain of the first football team my husband (Dave Nelson) coached. Following Mike's career as a student, coach, administrator, it is no surprise to me that he has been able to rise above his disappointments and succeed. His many achievements are the reward for his dedication to what is best for college sports."

**– Shirley Nelson,** wife of the late Dave Nelson who gave Mike his first coaching job at Hillsdale College and later the University of Delaware.

"Mike Lude has experienced it all when it comes to athletics. Now he has decided to share his numerous experiences with all. This book shares his trials as well as his triumphs. It is great reading for those of us who have been in the business, but also compelling reading for those entering the profession, as well as the avid sports fan. It has something for everyone."

**– Judy Rose,** Athletics Director University of North Carolina, Charlotte, President of the National Association of Collegiate Directors of Athletics.

"I often reflect on how lucky I was to have you visit the Rullo home on one of your recruiting visits for the University of Delaware. After enjoying the Lenten Hot Cross pastries that you brought, my mother was not letting me play football/baseball anywhere but Delaware. I have been blessed with a ton of good fortune in my life since that night in 1958, but it all started with that great decision. Thanks."

**– Fred P. Rullo,** Former Vice President ARCO Oil Company and Former Football Player University of Delaware.

"Very few have witnessed the development of college athletics from the perspective Mike has, and I'm sure the reader of this book will gain new insights into the field of sports. A highly recommended reading!"

— **Ced Dempsey,** Former Athletics Director University of Arizona, University of Houston and Executive Director of the NCAA.

"I've just finished Mike Lude's wonderful story about his career as a leader in college athletics and it is a great read. For those of us who love the college game, here is a wonderful story told from the viewpoint of one of the giants of the field. The insight of dealing with coaches, conferences and the university administration make this book a fascinating and educational treatise for sports fans that care about the industry. You learn first hand the strategies that go into running a modern day athletic program that offers great wisdom to those of us inside as well as outside of the athletic business. Great job Mike!"

— **Bill Byrne,** Athletics Director Texas A&M, Former Athletics Director University of Nebraska and University of Oregon.

"I have always been captivated by Mike's enthusiasm, by his grasp of the subject matter, and by his unique ability to instruct an enraptured audience of peers. We became friends, and over the years, I have followed his progress as a coach and as an athletic administrator with great interest and satisfaction. Mike Lude is respected, admired, and truly liked by all of us who have shared this profession with him. His words continue to be inspiring and worthy of careful study."

— **Marv Levy,** Head Football Coach University of New Mexico, University of California, Berkley, Montreal, Kansas City Chiefs and the Buffalo Bills. Currently analyst for NFL radio and television.

"When you judge a man's career you have to look at what he accomplished and how he accomplished it. With Mike Lude this is easy, 'A Lot and the Right Way!'"

— **Art Modell,** Owner Baltimore Ravens, Former Owner Cleveland Browns.

"Mike Lude had a great impact on my career as a coach and as a person. He is an innovator, and a great teacher of coaching football techniques. He was very responsible for the development of the Wing-T formation and was instrumental in my getting the Head Coaching position with the Seattle Seahawks by recommending me for the job to Jim Nordstrom, who was one of·the owners."

— **Chuck Knox,** Former Head Coach Seattle Seahawks, Los Angeles Rams, Buffalo Bills.

"Today when I hear the name Mike Lude, two things come to mind. One is Mike's faith in people. The second is his character. This book does a wonderful job capturing his faith and character."

    – **Earlie Thomas,** Defensive Back Colorado State University,
        New York Jets, Denver Broncos and Current Director
        CSU Environmental Health Services.

"Mike Lude is, we are proud to say, a graduate of our little college. We have always been a stubborn place, ready to fight for freedom, ready to stand up for principle whenever it is challenged. Often they have been manifested on the battlefield. Often they have been manifested on the athletic field too. Mike has gone on from his education and work here to be one of the makers of modern intercollegiate athletics. He has seen both its troubles and its glories. He believes that college athletics should be for students, and that the classroom comes first. He has fought for this through a long career. He tells a most interesting story about that battle."

    – **Dr. Larry Arnn,** President Hillsdale College.

"Mike Lude's life has been truly remarkable, and he has always been a class act, a Christian gentleman and a role model to all of those who served with him and under him. He rose to the top of his ultimate profession as a university athletics director from the most humble beginnings. There is a moral to his story, and he explains it well."

    – **Paul Cressman, Sr., Esq.,** recognized as a "Super Lawyer" for the
        past three years by "Law & Politics" magazine. He is the only
        Washington lawyer who is a Fellow in both the American College of
        Trial Lawyers and the American College of Trust and Estate Counsel.
        Past President of the University of Washington President's Club.

"I first met Mike in June, 1965, on a cold night at Estes Park, Colorado at my first F.C.A. Conference. His thoughtful sharing of his faith with me was instrumental in my accepting Jesus Christ as my Savior a week later. Coach Lude is a rare person. He was a football player, coach, athletics director and a pillar in the team of NCAA and BCS leaders that will determine the direction of college football. His insight and his life will be an adventure to behold in this book. I wholeheartedly recommend Coach Mike Lude."

    – **Ken Hatfield,** Head Football Coach Rice University.

"I have known Mike Lude for approximately 25 years and know of no one who has more passion for the college game and particularly for the student-athlete. I have never seen him without a smile on his face or heard him without a good word for his fellow man. This book is significant in that it puts in a very candid format and a proper format what needs to be said about a number of issues regarding college athletics. One of the key issues, in my judgment, is the hypocrisy of college presidents. Those who hide behind academia and claim foul when something happens regarding athletics and the student-athlete. I truly believe that the whole future of college athletics is at stake with the current position of how college athletics has changed and particularly the emphasis through various institutions. Mike Lude points out these issues in a very, very well written book."

    – **Jim Host**, Chairman of the Board Host Communications,
      State of Kentucky Secretary of Commerce.

"Energy, honesty, and professionalism describe the tenure of Mike Lude as Director of Intercollegiate Athletics at the University of Washington. Mike, who had the foresight to hire Don James at Kent State, had the drive to expand Washington's football stadium, making it one of the great venues in America. As the first radio play-by-play announcer of Washington Husky Women's Basketball, I applaud Mike Lude for demanding equal media coverage for women's sports. He developed Washington into a model sports program for the West Coast. Mike Lude's enthusiasm, and genuine concern for the student-athlete come through clearly in his book. If you want to know the inner-workings and politics of big-time college sports, it's a must read. There are life lessons we can all share from Mike's story."

    – **Bill Swartz**, Former Basketball Voice of the Washington Husky
      Women, and Football Sideline Announcer, Current Sports Anchor at
      710 KIRO Radio in Seattle.

"No one that I know is in a better position nor is better prepared to write a book about the Fast Lane of Intercollegiate Sports than Mike Lude. Mike has had a distinguished career as a football player, coach and athletics director at several of America's distinguished universities. Furthermore, he has been a leader at the national level in shaping intercollegiate sports policy. He was a very successful athletics director at the University of Washington while I was president of Washington State University. The competitive sports programs were very successful during his tenure. In fact, since the Cougars of WSU and the Huskies of UW are chief rivals, I would have been happier if Mike had not been so successful. Despite the rivalry of our schools, I value my friendship with Mike immensely."

    – **Glenn Terrell**, Retired President Washington State University.

"Mike always would fight for what he believed in. Yet, he was always fair. His drive and determination is why he was so successful, and why so much was accomplished under his leadership."

– **Kyle Kallander,** Commissioner Big South Conference.

"Life as a college sports administrator has its ups and downs. But Mike Lude didn't appreciate the extreme limits of 'down' until the day he glanced out his office window to admire the progress on a $17 million expansion project. Before his eyes, Husky Stadium became the Hula Bowl. The 130-foot steel structure for the stadium's new second deck swayed this way, leaned that way and collapsed. Fortunately, there were a lot more 'ups' than 'downs' in the remarkable career of the man who brought championship programs and unrelenting integrity to the University of Washington, Auburn University and beyond. Mike's fascinating life story should be required reading for anyone contemplating a career in sports administration."

– **John Owen,** Retired Sports Editor Seattle Post-Intelligencer.

"In 1959 as a post graduate student at Bordentown Military Institute in Bordentown, NJ, I met a gentleman named Mike Lude. He had come to BMI to recruit me and several other players for the University of Delaware. I knew the minute I met Mike that he was an honest, straightforward, no nonsense type person. The seeds of friendship were sown at that time, and it is an honor to call him friend."

– **Jim Quirk,** NFL official.

"Fifty years would seem to be a sufficient time to learn and judge the mettle of a man. In 1952, when I was 17 years old, Mike came to my high school and asked me to play football at the University of Delaware. I had never met a man like him. Mike Lude was the most enthusiastic, overwhelming man I had ever met. Now, 50 years later, he is still the same, Mr. Enthusiasm."

– **Jim Shelton,** Brigadier General, United States Army (Retired).

"Mike Lude resides in Tucson, but his influence and inspiration can be found all over this country. His long list of achievements has deservedly earned him a great deal of respect. His legacy, however, may be best defined by what he has returned to the profession in leadership, insight, education and mentoring. Simply put, he has helped make intercollegiate athletics better for all those seeking the same opportunity he had—a chance to lead his own program."

– **Joseph R. Castiglione,** Director of Athletics University of Oklahoma.

"Mike Lude prepared me well for the turbulent, exciting, drama-filled world of intercollegiate athletics. This book captures that world better than a reality television show could. Mike is Mr. Enthusiasm and his passion for college sports comes across loud and clear. One of the reasons we got along well together the 13 years we both worked for the University of Washington is because there is no deception with Mike; what you see is what you get. While Mike and I did not always agree on every issue (and the reader might not either) we respected each other because we shared a mutual concern about doing what was best for the student-athletes, the sports they played and the University."

**– Elsa Kircher-Cole,** Former Assistant Attorney General for the University of Washington, now General Council for the NCAA.

"Every fan of college sports should read this book. Its impact will be to make the reader much more knowledgeable about the world of collegiate athletics because it is written by one who has been part of that world at every level. The book…entices the reader to follow Lude's story because of his candor about events that have been widely reported elsewhere. It gives the reader a glimpse into the real world of collegiate athletics."

**– Frank Broyles,** Athletics Director University of Arkansas.

"During the formative years of an athletic administrator role models are absolutely critical, if not essential. To that end, Mike Lude was one of the elite, strong and determined sub-sector leaders that warranted every understudy's emulation. Quite frankly, he transitioned in stellar fashion from his well-documented coaching background to become one of the eminent athletics director in our country."

**– Kevin White,** Athletics Director Notre Dame.

"This book and its subject, Mike Lude, is testimony to all that is good in college athletics. Coach Lude's passion, integrity, genius and loyalty have been the cornerstones of his successful career as both coach and athletics director. If there ever was a choice between taking a path that drifted away from the 'rules' of the game and the right way, you could bet that Mike would select the ethical and correct path."

**– Dr. Dan Tripodi,** Former Football Player, University of Delaware.

"There are three things that distinguish the successful, modern Division 1-A athletics director. He gets to run his very own crisis clinic, he has to be knowledgeable enough to hire the best people possible, and he has the pleasure of working with coaches and athletes in the wildly competitive world of collegiate competition all while making sure the athletes are also students making progress toward their degrees. It's a tall order. If you follow Mike Lude's saga from his humble beginnings to his exceptional career in intercollegiate athletics you will come to know a fascinating man whose love of the game drove him to success he had never dreamed of as a boy. I have known Mike for over 30 years. These are the characteristics that mark him. He has boundless energy, is highly motivated, is very competitive, has great integrity, is loyal and has demonstrated outstanding leadership and professionalism during his challenging and diverse career. Mike and I have a couple of things in common. Each of us served as athletic directors at the University of Washington, Mike hired Don James at Kent State and I hired Don at Washington. Each of us received our profession's highest honor, the Corbett Award, and, finally, we were each blessed with understanding and helpful helpmates throughout our careers. Enjoy the book. Mike has earned his reputation as one of the nation's top leaders in intercollegiate athletics."

   – **Dr. Joe Kearney,** Former WAC commissioner, Former Athletic
      Director  University of Washington, Michigan State and Arizona and
      Former USOC Board Member.

"While serving as a young programmer for the then-new ESPN in 1984, I was fortunate to get heavily involved in the collegiate game, and not only did I see a lot of great games, but I met many terrific people who remain friends to this day—including the coach-turned athletic director-turned author, Mike Lude.

   With Mike you always get a smile, a hearty handshake, good humor and kind words. Whether you see him once in several months or on several occasions in a short period of time, it's always a pleasure. I suffered a heart attack about ten years ago and went through quadruple bypass surgery. I was fortunate to hear from a lot of people during my convalescence—but none more frequently than Mike. You remember and appreciate things like that. That's Mike Lude.

   That college football's living legend Keith Jackson is writing the forward is testimony to high esteem in which Mike is held. I have read some excepts from his book and it is Mike through and through. An honest and entertaining account of a true gentleman who honored his profession every day and continues to honor it even in retirement.

   – **Loren E. Matthews,** Senior Vice President, Programming ABC Sports